"Melding the savory insights of experts from Augustine to Switchfoot in this elegantly structured book, David Naugle also displays his own distinctively variegated pursuit of happiness. This is a book about what matters to us most. Spend a little time alongside this remarkable pilgrim, and find yourself encouraged on the journey."

— Esther Lightcap Meek
author of *Longing to Know: The Philosophy of Knowledge for Ordinary People*

"I regard David Naugle as one of the most gifted professors in America. Perennially his students learn to think and care about the most important things — remarkably so, in fact. *Reordered Love, Reordered Lives* allows all of us the grace of learning over his shoulder and through his heart, listening in on the unusual pedagogy that is uniquely his. Amazingly wise, incredibly well-read, he is always attentive to what matters most, and his book should find its way into hearts and minds, courses and colleges, far and wide."

— Steven Garber
author of *The Fabric of Faithfulness*
director of The Washington Institute
for Faith, Vocation, and Culture

"In the Middle Ages priests were urged by their bishops to preach about the seven deadly sins four times a year 'in the vulgar tongue without any fantastical imagination or any manner of subtlety or curiosity.' Today frank talk about sin is couched in a pop psychology that dilutes its moral seriousness. Hollywood screenwriters have done more honest analysis than most evangelical pastors. David Naugle has picked up the ancient challenge once more. Here in plain language copiously illustrated, he explains the price of loving the wrong things in the wrong way. More importantly, he shows us how to live lives of well-ordered love. The church fathers were right; this is a topic we neglect at great cost. *Reordered Love, Reordered Lives* is a book to be read again and again."

— JOHN SEEL
Donegality Productions LLC


"David Naugle writes as a philosopher, master teacher, and child of God. He draws on a wide range of classic Christian texts and crystallizes this countercultural wisdom about a virtuous and happy life for students of all ages. His candid discussion of the disordered human condition is particularly crucial for explaining just how dramatic and transformative the gospel really is."

— JOHN D. WITVLIET
Calvin College and
Calvin Theological Seminary

# Reordered Love, Reordered Lives

## LEARNING THE DEEP MEANING
## OF HAPPINESS

David K. Naugle

WILLIAM B. EERDMANS PUBLISHING COMPANY
GRAND RAPIDS, MICHIGAN / CAMBRIDGE, U.K.

Published 2008 by
Wm. B. Eerdmans Publishing Co.
2140 Oak Industrial Drive N.E., Grand Rapids, Michigan 49505 /
P.O. Box 163, Cambridge CB3 9PU U.K.
www.eerdmans.com

Printed in the United States of America

14  13  12  11  10  09  08      7  6  5  4  3  2  1

**Library of Congress Cataloging-in-Publication Data**

Naugle, David K.
Reordered love, reordered lives: learning the deep meaning of happiness /
David K. Naugle.
p.     cm.
Includes bibliographical references and index.
ISBN 978-0-8028-2817-0 (pbk.: alk. paper)
1. Happiness — Religious aspects — Christianity.     I. Title.

BV4647.J68N38     2008
248.4 — dc22

2008013158

Dedicated to
Deemie, Courtney, and Mark

And in memory of my parents,
Dave and Beverly Naugle

# Contents

# Acknowledgements

*"Thanking God over and over for you is not only a pleasure;
it's a must."*

2 Thessalonians 1: 3, *The Message*

I have the immense pleasure of recognizing and thanking those who have played a significant role in helping this book become a reality. I thank former students Ryan Swindle, Leigh Hickman, and Lauren Hickman-King (the latter two twins extraordinaire) for ideas, research and resources, but most of all for their friendship and encouragement. Along with these are many other students, present and past, who have offered explicit or implicit support for my work: Erick "Theophan" Alvarez, Amos and Alisha Barker, Steve and Alyssan Barnes, Benny Barrett, Rob and Crystal Barrett, Rachel Barsness, Joylyn and Todd Blake, Mark Boone, Joe Brewer, Dayspring Brock, Josh and Jennifer Combs, Joanna and Ben Crawford, Grant Daves, Tim and Sara Davis, Daniel and Allison Haynes, Russ and Christi Hemati, Britt Herrington, Shelly Hobbs, Andrew and Melissa Holm, Brice King, Julie Linn, Joy McCalla, Steve and Kristen Michaelis, David Miller, Sara and Jason Morris, Kevin Neece, Bethany Obert, Mark and Kendra Petras, Matt Slay, Natalie Stilwell, Michael and Julie Stone, Amber Swindle, Artyom and Lydia Tonoyan, Chris Vitatoe, Erika Wiegand, Cole and Erin Wilkins, Aften Wilson, Lily Wu, Leonardo Zuno, and many others.

I am also grateful to colleagues and friends at Dallas Baptist University for their ongoing support of this project: Gary Cook, Gail and Dennis

Linam, Blair Blackburn, Craig Dunn, Blake Killingsworth, Deborah McCollister, Philip Mitchell, Chris Nkhoma, Harold Norris, Todd Von Helms, Mike Williams, and finally John Jaeger, who has the research librarian's Midas touch!

I am also thankful for a larger community of friends and co-workers elsewhere who share with me a comprehensive vision of the kingdom of God and have encouraged me over the years personally and through their service to our university community. I am also grateful to special friends Annie Wang Day, Rob Moore, Mike Francis, and Fred and Luann Wilkinson for their personal encouragement and support in many significant ways. My appreciation also goes to Jon Foreman and the band "Switchfoot" for the intellectual and spiritual stimulation through their musical imagination and gifts of song. They have served me well!

I am certainly indebted to many good people at William B. Eerdmans Publishing Company who have contributed significantly to this work. I especially thank Vice-President and Editor-in-Chief Jon Pott, who waited patiently for this tardy manuscript. I am indebted to David Bratt, a more than capable editor, and to freelance editor Andrew Hoogheem for securing the permissions for this book. I am also sincerely appreciative to the rest of the Eerdmans staff who worked on this project in various ways with consummate professionalism.

Of course, the last are first. My deep gratitude goes to my wife Deemie for her love and encouragement throughout this project (she happily and patiently listened to my reading through the rough drafts of multiple chapters after many evening meals), to our daughter Courtney for her genuine enthusiasm for the publication of this book, and to my brother Mark for his abiding love and friendship and also for inspiring a central point in the first chapter of this volume. Finally, how could I forget our dog Kuyper, who has as much energy as his namesake!

*Soli Deo gloria.*

# Preface

*"Such is each one as is his love."*

St. Augustine, *Homilies on the First Epistle of John*[1]

*What* do you love? *How* do you love the things that you love? What do you *expect* to receive from the things you love? There aren't too many questions more important than these. Why? Because as we love in our hearts, so are we. We reap what we love. Indeed, wherever we go and whatever we do, it is our loves that move us and take us there,[2] especially in our pursuit of happiness. Consciously or not, in our brokenness and pain, we attach our loves, affections, and desires to people, places, or things with the hope that we will finally find the felicity we have been searching for all our lives. Our quest for happiness based on our loves is what our lives — and this book — are all about.

Happiness, however, is not an easy topic to write or talk about. Indeed, once we get beneath such surface-level wishes as "Happy Birthday" or "Happy New Year," it is so easy to sound silly or succumb to clichés when addressing happiness. In fact, *unhappiness* is a much easier and trendier theme to discuss, probably because it is our more common lot. Thus, I

---

1. St. Augustine, *Homilies on the First Epistle of John*, trans. H. Browne, rev. and ed. Joseph H. Myers, *The Nicene and Post-Nicene Fathers*, vol. 7, ed. Philip Schaff (Peabody, MA: Hendrickson Publishers, Inc., 1994), p. 475 (Homily 2).

2. Augustine, *Confessions* 13.9.

begin chapter one by acknowledging our heartaches, only to realize that there is something resilient about human nature that compels us to try to improve our circumstances. While some may think of the pursuit of happiness as particularly American, it is of course a universal objective. Indeed, a main point of the first chapter is to show that the happiness of human beings as embodied creatures living in this world was originally God's idea, seen clearly in the biblical account of creation. This original and constant divine purpose has been well encapsulated in the beautiful Hebrew term *shalom* — peace, soundness, wholeness, and well-being. Sadly, rebellion against God at the time of humanity's fall into sin meant that we forfeited this divine intention of a generous human flourishing. We lost happiness when we sinned, but we did not lose our love and longing for it, as St. Augustine has helpfully pointed out.[3] In fact, in a sinful world we pursue it with even greater enthusiasm, with even higher hopes. Yet we do so in profound ignorance. We attach our loves to various things for happiness' sake in horribly disordered ways.

In chapter two we examine the theological and cultural reasons why we are so mystified about what happiness really is and how to get it. Diverse worldviews with their diverse perspectives and the bogus messages of contemporary culture play their parts, and we end up confusing the true meaning of happiness with its many counterfeits. In a state of great need and deception, we foolishly leave God out of the picture and proceed to love the objects of our desire without reference to the one who made them all. Consequently, we love things foolishly, excessively, and unrealistically without ever finding what we are looking for. The results push us toward cynicism and despair.

How, then, do our disordered loves disorder our lives? In chapter three, I answer this question by pointing to idolatry, the seven deadly sins, habits and addictions, and even crime and warfare as the chief culprits. In idolatry, we love and serve some aspect of the creation independently of the creator. We end up adoring some desirable entity, since we human beings cannot *not* worship. Hardly anything in all creation has not been serviceable to us in taking God's place.[4] Normally we idolize ourselves,

---

3. Augustine, *The City of God*, 22.30.

4. Blaise Pascal, *Pensées*, trans. W. F. Trotter, *Great Books of the Western World*, ed. Robert Maynard Hutchins, vol. 33 (Chicago: William Benton, Publisher, Encyclopedia Britannica Inc., 1952), p. 244 (Section 7, #425).

wealth, food, or sex, as the seven deadly sins specify. If the things we pursue fail to satisfy us, we will continue at them harder and harder, full-throttle, to the point of excessive, unhealthy dependence. Hence our bad habits and addictions. We will resort to crime and violence, or even warfare if we can wage it, if this is what we think it takes to get what we want. Disordered love, then, not only explains the disorder in our lives, but also the tragic character of human history, all motivated by the need to satisfy the cavernous hungers of our hearts. What, if anything, can save us from our desperate, desolate, and disconsolate state, from this hell on earth?

The Christian gospel offers us a way out. My discussion in chapter four of the good news about Jesus Christ forms the heart and hinge of this book. It acknowledges our problems and offers the remedy. Since Christ is always controversial, I affirm his classic identity as God in the flesh, and review his revolutionary life and claims as a prelude to clarifying the meaning of his work of salvation through his kingdom and cross. In Jesus' words and deeds, God's kingdom graciously breaks into history and defeats the powers of evil that had frustrated God's purposes of peace. St. Paul employs images from the temple (propitiation), the marketplace (redemption), personal relationships (reconciliation), and the courtroom (justification) to convey the significance of Christ's achievement on our behalf. Because Christ has averted God's anger, set us free from slavery to sin, Satan, and death, and made friendship with God and the gift of righteousness possible, we can be saved by grace through faith in him. We express this faith publicly in baptism, and become involved in the church as we seek to live a life worthy of the gospel.

To be sure, Jesus "saves" us and promises us a place with God eternally in heaven when we die.[5] But this is only the icing on the cake. As believers, we can presently experience the fullness of life *after birth* and *before death*. In chapter five, therefore, I claim that one of the primary purposes of the gospel is the reordering of our deepest loves and affections. It gives us new purposes and desires for our lives in this world, here and now. Our disordered loves are displaced by reordered loves, as we learn to love God with all our heart, soul, mind, and strength in obedience to the first and greatest commandment. In making God our top priority, we also learn how to love ourselves, our neighbors, and indeed the whole creation and all it

---

5. More accurately, our eternal destination with God will be as resurrected persons living in a new heaven and a new earth (1 Corinthians 15; Revelation 21–22).

contains in the right way, as the second greatest commandment requires. Reordered love implanted in a transformed heart is the distinctive mark of the Christian.

Reordered love cannot help but reorder our lives in significant ways. As I discuss in chapter six, various idolatries give way to the genuine worship of God in our personal lives, in public settings, and in church. Intellectual, moral, and physical virtues begin to replace multiple vices. The power of God's renovating love breaks the chains of our habits and addictions and also undermines inclinations toward crime, violence, and warfare, since God is now the source of our fulfillment and we turn to him to secure what we need. The reordered loves that reorder our lives become the source of the deep meaning of happiness rooted in God, who enables us to esteem and enjoy all things well.

Of course, the happiness we experience here and now through the gospel is significant, but it is not yet complete. As I clarify in the final chapter, at this point in God's narrative plan for history, we live in between the times of Christ's first and second comings, and much remains to be done. Presently, we have work to do, callings to fulfill, and service to render. Our God-given tasks will entail sacrifice and suffering for Christ's glory and others' good. We are called to a cruciform life, which is not incompatible with a life of *bona fide* happiness in God. We rejoice always, and in all things give thanks. In light of these challenges we experience along the way, we must enroll in the school of Christ for the ongoing mending of our hearts. We are his student-learners in an educational program where the knowledge and practice of the spiritual disciplines are at the heart of the curriculum that we might love well and be found faithful over the long haul.

From this overview of the book to come, three additional points are worth making. First, my discussion of the deep meaning of happiness in this book follows the unfolding narrative of a biblical worldview in terms of creation, fall, and redemption:

- The deep meaning of happiness as God intended at creation rooted in *rightly* ordered loves and lives;
- Happiness lost in the fall of humanity into sin and replaced with devastating ignorance and *disordered* loves and lives;
- The deep meaning of happiness already redeemed and one day fully restored in Jesus Christ who graciously *reorders* our loves and lives through the gospel in this present life.

This grand narrative disclosed in Scripture is enormously helpful in elucidating the deep meaning of happiness — what it ought to be, what it has become, and what it can and will be.[6]

Second, the view of happiness I have presented here is significantly countercultural. Contrary to popular opinion, happiness is not person-relative or an intense hedonistic pursuit. Rather, it is the condition of genuine human fulfillment and flourishing rooted in a relationship with God, whose mercy and grace demonstrated in Jesus Christ reorders our loves and lives in righteous and virtuous ways so that we are able to enjoy — indeed, to relish — all aspects of life and creation appropriately in him. This view of happiness is grounded in *revealed and knowable* truth in Scripture about God, the creation, human nature, sin and evil, the need for redemption, and the nature of happiness itself in connection with God and the things we love. Personal alignment with these "permanent things" is the real way to discover and experience the fullness of life and peace that God offers to us in Jesus Christ.

Third, the content of this book is a contemporary expression of the grand tradition of Christian (not secular) humanism. Christianity is *true* humanism, since it provides the only adequate basis for affirming the value and dignity of human beings who are *made and remade* as the image and likeness of God. Indeed, God created us as whole persons of both body and soul, and has saved us, "not as souls but as wholes."[7] At its best, Christianity unflinchingly addresses *all* of our human needs and desires spiritually and physically, including our longing for a real and lasting happiness. Despite the stereotypes, the Christian faith is life-affirming rather than life-denying. It encourages believing people to discover what it means to be fully and truly human, to live exuberantly and fruitfully as God's creatures abiding in God's creation that was, and still is, very good. St. Irenaeus summed it up: "The glory of God is a person fully alive!"[8]

In Philippians 1:9-11, St. Paul offers a prayer that appropriately concludes this preface and commences this book. In it the apostle asks God that our love might flourish in wise and intelligent ways through Christ so

---

6. My thanks to Mike Metzger of The Clapham Institute for this fresh way of translating the language of creation, fall, redemption.

7. N. T. Wright, *Surprised by Hope: Rethinking Heaven, the Resurrection, and the Mission of the Church* (New York: Harper One, 2008), 199.

8. Irenaeus, *Against Heresies*, 20.7.

that we might live exemplary lives and that God will be exalted. This is also my prayer for you, the reader of this book, an answer to which will surely change lives and help bring about a revolutionary culture of charity or "civilization of love"[9] as the true hope of the whole world.

> And this I pray, that your love may abound still more and more in real knowledge and all discernment, so that you may approve the things that are excellent, in order to be sincere and blameless until the day of Christ; having been filled with the fruit of righteousness which comes through Jesus Christ, to the glory and praise of God.

David K. Naugle
*Eighth Week after Pentecost*
*July 9, 2008*
*Dallas, Texas*

Reordered Love, Reordered Lives online.
Contact the author, find additional discussion questions, bibliography,
and other information at the author's website: www.reorderedlove.com

9. Carl Anderson, *A Civilization of Love: What Every Catholic Can Do to Transform the World* (New York: Harper One, 2008). This book is inspired by the seminal thought of Pope John Paul II and his successor, Pope Benedict XVI, and their shared vision to build up a "civilization of love" through the Holy Spirit.

## CHAPTER ONE

# A Broken Heart and the Pursuit of Happiness

*"And yet — happiness, happiness — where is it? Who can say of himself that he is happy?"*

Dostoevsky, *The Brothers Karamazov*[1]

## Introduction

I begin this book with the assumption of a broken heart.[2] If my assumption is premature in your case, it's just a matter of time before the inevitable occurs. The world fractures everyone's heart sometime, somehow, some way, to one degree or another. No one is exempt. In the midst of our difficult circumstances, we feel the weight of our woes and long for some semblance of a happy life once again. Hope springs eternal in the human breast.

In the acclaimed Nasher Sculpture Center in the Dallas arts district, there is a beautiful bronze statue of a woman who seems to embody this inevitable condition of brokenness and pain. The work is by the noted French sculptor Aristide Maillol (1861-1944) and is provocatively titled "Night" *(La Nuit)*. The female figure is folded in upon herself in an upright

1. Fyodor Dostoevsky, *The Brothers Karamazov,* trans. Constance Garnett, The Great Books of the Western World, ed. Robert M. Hutchins, vol. 52 (Chicago: William Benton, Publisher, Encyclopedia Britannica, Inc., 1952), p. 26.

2. I owe this thought to Jon Foreman.

fetal position with her feet together and her knees pulled up tightly towards her chest. Her bowed head is buried in her crossed arms as they rest
atop her knees in an apparent state of weariness and introspection.

What is she thinking about and feeling as she sits there in the dark all
alone? Has she simply endured a difficult day? Is she mentally or physically exhausted? Maybe the ordinary challenges of life have just caught up
with her and she is in a focused state of self-examination or prayer. Perhaps she is muttering to herself "I am a little weary of my life . . . I am
weary of weariness and strife,"[3] to borrow a wintry sentiment from
George MacDonald. Whatever the causes of this woman's "dark night of
the soul," we can be pretty sure that her overall happiness or sense of well-
being is at stake and under negotiation.

Her crestfallen condition is not uncommon. We too may feel emotionally fragile and depleted; we too may consider our troubles as vast as
the sea, as great as a galaxy. Maybe she's asking questions we sometimes
ask: Who am I, and what is it I have become? How did my life wind up like
this? Will it ever change? Whatever happened to my hope for a happy life?
How am I supposed to be happy? What is happiness, anyway? Is the search
for it fruitless? The woman represented in the Maillol sculpture, should
she come to life, could probably empathize with Leo Tolstoy's conflicted
character Anna Karenina, who on one occasion said, "I'm simply unhappy. If anyone is unhappy, I am."[4]

Our lives are often miserable. Is there any sorrow like my sorrow? Is
there any pain like my pain?[5] Maybe those who once observed birthdays
with tears and celebrated funerals with joy knew what they were doing!
Given the injustices and sufferings that seem to rule in the world, perhaps
those who believed it was best to expire quickly, or even better, to have
never been born, showed remarkably good judgment. How unfortunate
we were to be born! How lucky should we die soon![6]

3. George MacDonald, *Diary of an Old Soul: 366 Writings for Devotional Reflection* (Minneapolis: Augsburg Fortress, 1994, Augsburg Publishing House, 1975), p. 120.

4. Leo Tolstoy, *Anna Karenina*, trans. Constance Garnett, intro. Henry Troyat (New
York: The Modern Library, Random House, 1950), p. 749.

5. See Lamentations 1:12 in both the New American Standard and English Standard
Versions.

6. John Calvin, *Institutes of the Christian Religion*, ed. John T. McNeill, trans. Ford Lewis
Battles, The Library of Christian Classics, vol. 20 (Philadelphia: The Westminster Press,
1960), p. 715 (§3.9.4).

Then I looked again at all the acts of oppression which were being done under the sun. And behold I saw the tears of the oppressed and that they had no one to comfort them; and on the side of their oppressors was power, but they had no one to comfort them. So I congratulated the dead who are already dead more than the living who are still living. But better off than both of them is the one who has never existed, who has never seen the evil activity that is done under the sun. (Eccles. 4:1-3)

Still, human beings are remarkably resilient. Despite the odds, the hope for a better and even happy life, whatever we think it is, endures in most of us.

## Happiness and Human Nature

*"Life is just a bowl of cherries."*

Anonymous

*"Life is a bowl of pits."*

Rodney Dangerfield[7]

Intense interest in happiness — especially our own — is constant in human history, and it is a constant in human history because it is a constant of human nature. As persons comprised of body and soul, we earnestly desire and seek whatever we think it takes to fulfill these combined aspects of our nature. We all aspire to felicity, both mentally and physically, whether we are willing to admit it or not. The components of our nature are fixed, and our compelling needs are unyielding. They scream for attention and demand a satisfying response. This is the unalterable human condition. As C. S. Lewis once noted, "nothing about us except our neediness is, in this life, permanent."[8] Contemporary poet David Hopes agrees:

we are of one ambition and one lineage:
*Want.* Want not in proportion to any need,

---

7. Quoted in Robert C. Solomon, *The Big Questions: A Short Introduction to Philosophy*, 6th ed. (Fort Worth: Harcourt College Publishers, 2002), p. 57.

8. C. S. Lewis, *The Four Loves* (San Diego: Harcourt, Inc., A Harvest Book, 1960, 1988), p. 17.

*want* unreasonable and overflowing,
our days and nights overshadowed with *desire.* . . .[9]

If we pay attention to our own lives and observe the lives of others, we will soon discern that a desire for happiness of one kind or another is the conscious, subconscious, or unconscious motivation for just about everything we do. Most of our daily lives and activities are aimed at the goal of experiencing and enhancing some measure of well-being and delight, even if such intentions are in the unacknowledged background of our minds.

What besides our own welfare could possibly lie silently behind our feverish educational, vocational, or economic pursuits? Why else would we seek knowledge, career success, or basic material provision, if our own good wasn't somehow at stake? What else other than a sense of joy and fulfillment motivates us in our family relationships, in our friendships, in our recreations, and in our faith? Food and drink, clothing and shelter, while necessary for survival, are also things we desire and seek to enjoy. Why do I do what I do? Why do you do what you do? Here is the answer: we want to live happily, both now and ever after! "In every real man the will for life is also the will for joy," writes theologian Karl Barth. "It is hypocrisy," he says, "to hide this from oneself."[10] Perhaps this is why we tend to think that real gusto is just the next relationship, the next purchase, or the next achievement away.

Like Karl Barth, just about all the great religions, philosophies, and worldviews past to present have confirmed what our intuitions and experiences in life indicate about the universality of the quest for delight in life. Though their teachings and methods differ, Islam, Buddhism, Taoism, and Hinduism all acknowledge some form of personal well-being and the well-being of others to be at the forefront of their respective religious traditions, whether in this life or the next, or in both somehow. The Judeo-Christian scriptures affirm the reality of a holy bliss for God's people and the fulfillment of our desires in God. In the Old Testament, for example, we read,

9. David Brendon Hopes, "The Invalid of Park Street," in *Upholding Mystery: An Anthology of Contemporary Christian Poetry,* ed. David Impastato (New York: Oxford, 1997), pp. 205-6 (emphasis added).

10. Karl Barth, *Church Dogmatics,* vol. 3, *The Doctrine of Creation,* part 4, ed. G. W. Bromiley and T. F. Torrance, trans. G. W. Bromiley and R. J. Ehrlich (Edinburgh: T & T Clark, 1960), p. 374.

In Your presence is fullness of joy;
In Your right hand there are pleasures forever. (Ps. 16:11)

Delight yourself in the Lord;
And He will give you the desires of your heart. (Ps. 37:4)

Likewise, Jesus taught that the blessing of beatitude — "true happiness" in John Calvin's estimation — was discovered in his kingdom (Matt. 5:1-11).[11] He also said that he came to earth so that his followers might have "life" and have it "abundantly" (John 10:10b). He taught his disciples that his joy might be in them and that their joy would be made full (John 15:11).

Paul in Philippians 4:4 encouraged Christian believers to "rejoice in the Lord always." John wrote his first epistle "so that our joy may be made complete" (1 John 1:4). Peter asserted that though many Christians in his day hadn't seen Christ personally, they believed in him anyway, and "greatly rejoice with joy inexpressible and full of glory" (1 Pet. 1:8). Beatitude, bountiful life, and joy, indeed, a deep and meaningful notion of the happy life, is at the heart of biblical religion.

Plato (427/8-347 B.C.) believed that every desire we have is for good things or happiness, and that happiness is equated with the things we love most dearly and sometimes recklessly. Aristotle (384-322 B.C.) affirmed that happiness was "the end of the things pursued in action"[12] and was the product of moral and intellectual virtue, sustained by a sufficient supply of external goods such as food, clothing, shelter, work, friends, and so on. Both of these giants of the Western intellectual tradition recognized happiness as the end of a well-ordered life through reason and virtue.

In the Christian tradition, the early church father Augustine (A.D. 354-430) once wrote, "It is the decided opinion of all who use their brains, that all people desire to be happy."[13] Medieval Christian philosopher Thomas Aquinas (A.D. 1225-1274) believed that happiness was the ultimate end of human life both naturally and supernaturally, culminating in the "beatific vision"

---

11. John Calvin, *Commentary on a Harmony of the Evangelists: Matthew, Mark and Luke*, trans. William Pringle, vol. 1 (Grand Rapids: Baker Books, reprint 2003), p. 259.

12. Aristotle, *Nichomachean Ethics*, trans. Terence Irwin (Indianapolis: Hackett Publishing Company, 1985), p. 15 (§1097b).

13. Augustine, *The City of God*, The Nicene and Post-Nicene Fathers, ed. Philip Schaff, trans. Marcus Dods, vol. 2 (Peabody, Mass.: Hendrickson Publishers, Inc., 1994), p. 180 (§10.1). In this citation, I substituted the word "people" for "men."

when we will see God face to face for all eternity. The French theologian Blaise Pascal (1623-1662) asserted that "All people are in search of happiness. There is no exception to this whatever different methods are employed."[14] American theologian Jonathan Edwards (1703-1758) declared that "saints and sinners, and all alike, love happiness, and have the same unalterable and instinctive inclination to desire and seek it."[15] C. S. Lewis (1989-1963) maintained that "It is a Christian duty . . . for everyone to be as happy as he can."[16]

Though there is significant disagreement on what happiness is and how to get it, there is substantial agreement in recognizing it as the bull's eye on the target at which we aim our lives. As Aristotle said, people agree that the highest of all goods pursued in life is happiness, but they "disagree about what happiness is, and the many do not give the same answer as the wise."[17] Certainly, then, since this hope for happiness is a non-negotiable ingredient built in to our very nature — regardless of the what, where, and how — the desire and quest for happiness will remain with us as long as our race shall last.

## The Pursuit of Happiness, American Style

*"The truly revolutionary promise of our nation's founding document is the freedom to pursue happiness-with-a-capital-H. . . ."*

Dan Savage, *Skipping Towards Gomorrah:*
*The Seven Deadly Sins and the Pursuit*
*of Happiness in America*[18]

While happiness is undoubtedly a universal human quest, its pursuit seems closely associated with the American experience. Whatever Mr. Jef-

14. Blaise Pascal, *Pensées*, trans. Honor Levi, intro. and notes Anthony Levi, The World's Classics (New York: Oxford University Press, 1995), p. 51 (#181). In this citation, I substituted the word "people" for "men."

15. Jonathan Edwards, *Christian Love and Its Fruits* (Grand Rapids: Sovereign Grace Publishers, 1971), p. 79.

16. Sheldon Vanauken, *A Severe Mercy* (New York: Harper & Row, 1977), p. 189.

17. Aristotle, *Nicomachean Ethics*, p. 5 (§1095a).

18. Dan Savage, *Skipping Towards Gomorrah: The Seven Deadly Sins and the Pursuit of Happiness in America* (New York: Plume, The Penguin Group 2002), p. 1. This book is an irreverent attack on the "virtuecrats" who hypocritically impose their moral values on others.

ferson and other Founders may have meant by "the pursuit of happiness," this theme has effectively worked its way into the vocabulary, consciousness, and lifestyles of most Americans. Currently, one of the most popular courses at Harvard University is on the psychology of happiness taught by Daniel Gilbert and based on his book, *Stumbling on Happiness* — "a book that describes what science has to tell us about how and how well the human brain can imagine its own future, and about how and how well it can predict which of those futures it will most enjoy."[19] The quest for the happy life seems to be the one thing most Americans can agree on. Though serious divisions of religion, race, class, gender, and politics plague our society, the pursuit of happiness seems to be the social glue that makes us one out of many. "We are . . . bound together by a gospel of psychological happiness," asserts Eva Moskowitz in her discussion of America's obsession with self-fulfillment and its consummate trust in psychotherapy to get us there.[20]

Since the concept of happiness is so socially important, how are Americans doing? In a recent study, the U.S. came in number twenty-three on a list of the world's happiest countries. Denmark was number one.[21] According to a Pew Research Center Publication, about one-third of American adults rank themselves as "very happy," fifty percent say they are "pretty happy," and about fifteen percent have the doldrums.[22]

19. Daniel Gilbert, *Stumbling on Happiness* (New York: Knopf Publishing Group, 2006), from the Foreword. Gilbert's official website, with information about this book, is available at http://www.randomhouse.com/kvpa/gilbert/ (accessed July 8, 2007). Courses on positive psychology are taught on about 200 other campuses across the nation. For a discussion of the course at Harvard and the movement of "positive psychology" as a whole, see *Harvard Magazine*, July/August 2007, available at http://www.harvardmagazine.com/2007/01/the-science-of-happiness.html (accessed July 8, 2007). The growing happiness movement in America was also featured in *The New York Times Magazine*, January 7, 2007.

20. Eva S. Moskowitz, *In Therapy We Trust: America's Obsession with Self-Fulfillment* (Baltimore: The Johns Hopkins University Press, 2001), p. 1.

21. According to analytic social psychologist Adrian White at the University of Leicester, which has produced the first "world map of happiness." See http://www2.le.ac.uk/ebulletin/news/press-releases/2000-2009/2006/07/nparticle.2006-07-28.2448323827 (accessed March 27, 2007).

22. "Are We Happy Yet?" The Pew Research Center Publications. Study available at: http://pewresearch.org/pubs/301/are-we-happy-yet (accessed June 13, 2007).

## The Happiness Business

*"How do you define happiness? What are the best ways to get there? Who is happy . . . happier . . . happiest? What doesn't lead to happiness (that we mistakenly think will)? Has the definition of happiness changed significantly over the last few decades?"*

John Reich and Ed Diener, "The Road to Happiness"[23]

Given this fixation on felicity, happiness gurus abound to tell us how this ever-present longing can be suitably satisfied. It is impossible to keep up with the flood of books, seminars, and websites devoted to helping us find our bliss. Popular periodicals provide updates on the state of this science or art regularly. Some of the advice on offer smacks of common sense and is somewhat helpful. A lot of it, on the other hand, is plain silly and ultimately empty. Regardless, the happiness business is flourishing.[24]

Needless to say, it's hard to talk about happiness in a meaningful way "without sounding like a child, or a cynic, or more likely a purveyor of tired and shallow truisms," as Wilfred McClay tells us, adding,

> The problem is that while happiness is a subject of central importance to our existence, and a matter of irrepressibly consuming interest, many of the most reliable truths about it may easily come across disappointingly flat and trite and commonplace. Surely, we think to ourselves, this elusive thing we all pant after can't have been captured by a

23. John Reich and Ed Diener, "The Road to Happiness," *Psychology Today* 27, no. 4 (July/August 1994): 33.

24. "It's All About You," *Reader's Digest*, August 2005, p. 97. For an update on recent thinking about happiness, see Claudia Wallis, "The New Science of Happiness," *Time* 165, no. 3 (January 17, 2005). Other resources on this topic include Jonathan Haidt, *The Happiness Hypothesis: Finding Modern Truth in Ancient Wisdom* (New York: Basic Books, 2005); Anna Quindlen, *A Short Guide to a Happy Life* (New York: Random House, 2000); Dan Baker and Cameron Stauth, *What Happy People Know: How the New Science of Happiness Can Change Your Life for the Better* (New York: St. Martin's Griffin, 2003); Robert Ellsberg, *The Saints' Guide to Happiness: Everyday Wisdom from the Lives of the Saints* (New York: North Point Press, 2003); Desmond Morris, *The Nature of Happiness* (London: Little Books by Big Names, 2004). Prominent happiness websites include the following: www.thehappyguy.com; www.eur.nl/fsw/research/happiness; www.authentichappiness.org; www.happiness.com; www.reflectivehappiness.com. See also the major study on happiness at http://news.bbc.co.uk/2/hi/programmes/happiness_formula/4886848.stm (accessed May 3, 2007).

sugary Hallmark card inscription or the maudlin lyrics of a country-and-western song.[25]

One of the main problems, of course, is coming up with a suitable definition of the term. In surveying the chaos surrounding the notion in his day, the ancient Roman philosopher Seneca (c. 5 B.C.–A.D. 65) reminded us:

> There is not any thing in this world, perhaps, that is more talked of, and less understood, than the business of a *happy life*. It is every person's wish and design; and yet not one of a thousand . . . knows wherein that happiness consists. We live, however, in a blind and eager pursuit of it; and the more haste we make in a wrong way, the further we are from our journey's end.[26]

Many purport to offer help and direction for our energetic but often indiscriminate pursuit. Scientific, economic, and cultural forces have produced a paradigm shift in the way most people understand happiness. It has morphed in the minds of many Americans into a promise of sustained pleasure and painlessness. More than a few conceive of the concept in sensualistic, materialistic, and egotistical terms. Food and sex, wealth and possessions, achievement and power are the goals that goad so many of us into action. We are in search of the everlasting ideal in education, finances, work, technology, marriage, parenting, friendship, travel, adventure, health, entertainment, recreation, religion, food, drink, sex, and self. Not only is this pursuit exhausting; it also trivializes a once-noble concept, as we have moved from a concern with being and doing good to a fixation on feeling good. Philip Rieff calls it the triumph of the therapeutic: "That a sense of well-being has become the end, rather than a by-product of striving after some superior communal end, announces a fundamental change of focus in the entire cast of our culture."[27] Draining the notion of happiness of its deeper meaning has made its pursuit both more frantic and less fulfilling.

---

25. Wilfred M. McClay, "A Short History of Happiness," *Implications: Reflections and Provocations on Faith and Life* (December 2006). Available at: www.ttf.org/index/journal/detail/paradox-of-happiness (accessed March 27, 2007).

26. Seneca, *Seneca's Morals of a Happy Life, Benefits, Anger and Clemency*, trans. Sir Roger L'Estrange (Chicago: Cornelius H. Shaver, 1882), p. 125 (italics original). I have substituted the word "person's" for "man's" in this quote.

27. Philip Rieff, *The Triumph of the Therapeutic: Uses of Faith After Freud* (New York: Harper & Row, Harper Torchbooks, 1966), p. 261.

## "Happy Is a Yuppie Word"

*"Don't worry — be happy"*

Bobby McFerrin, "Don't Worry, Be Happy"[28]

Those who have studied the history of the idea of happiness in a Western context have observed how it migrated from its original home in religion and philosophy to the political sphere and, most recently, into the domain of individual experience. Classically, among the great Western philosophers and theologians, happiness denoted the state of the genuine fulfillment of human nature that resulted from being properly related as a person to the truth of reality. Educating the soul to conform it to reality, rather than conforming reality to the dictates of the individual soul, was the secret to the happy life. But those days of defining happiness and the good life, and what it means to be truly human, are long gone.[29]

When serious doubts arose about knowing the truth about human nature and reality in the modern period, governments — especially of the democratic variety — became the guarantors of freedom for people to pursue happiness as they saw fit. In some cases, the government took it upon itself to be a partial source of its provision, at least in a material way. As we have seen, America led the way in this regard; it fought the Revolutionary War in part to provide freedom for felicity's sake. During the modern period, happiness fell increasingly within the jurisdiction of politics.

Nowadays, happiness is still protected by cherished political ideals and institutions, but under the massive influence of a capitalistic and technological society centered in the sovereign self, the term has been thoroughly subjectivized and relativized. Happiness is now a person-relative concept, often associated with individual choice, agreeable circumstances, and pleasure-giving experiences. Happiness is often focused on the trivial and the ephemeral, catering to feelings and the flesh, even if such a basic pattern of life is punctuated by an occasional generous or selfless act.[30]

---

28. Bobby McFerrin, "Don't Worry, Be Happy," EMI Special Products, 1988.

29. C. S. Lewis, *The Abolition of Man* (New York: Simon and Schuster, A Touchstone Book, 1996), pp. 83-84.

30. John H. Schaar, ". . . And The Pursuit of Happiness," The *Virginia Quarterly Review* 46 (Winter 1970): 25. See also V. J. McGill, *The Idea of Happiness*, Concepts in Western Thought Series, Mortimer J. Adler, gen. ed. (New York: Frederick A. Praeger, 1967); Darrin M. McMahon, *Happiness: A History*, reprint edition (New York: Grove Press, 2006).

Because of its increasingly materialistic, superficial orientation, some have denigrated the very idea of happiness. Bob Dylan is a case in point. When *Rolling Stone* interviewed the American music icon on the occasion of his fiftieth birthday, the interviewer asked him whether or not he was a happy man. Finding the question a bit jarring, he fell silent for a few moments as he stared at his folded hands. Then drawing on his experience of faith, he offered a trademark response: "You know," he said, "these are yuppie words, happiness and unhappiness. It's not happiness or unhappiness, it's either blessed or unblessed."[31]

Dylan's words struck a chord, literally, with the band "Switchfoot." In their CD *Nothing Is Sound,* "Happy is a yuppie word" is the steady refrain of its title song based on Dylan's comments:

> Happy is a yuppie word
> Nothing in the world could fail me now
> It's empty as an argument
> I'm running down a life that won't cash out[32]

Both Dylan and Switchfoot have tapped into something important in highlighting puny conceptions of happiness in our day and age as materialistic, temporary, smiley-faced, feel-good, and ultimately sappy.

## Happiness and the Church

> "... Priests in black gowns were walking their rounds,
> And binding with briars my joys & desires."
>
>                         William Blake, "The Garden of Love"[33]

Many in the Christian community would heartily agree with Dylan and Switchfoot about the yuppie-ness of happiness. Both leaders and laity in

---

31. Mikal Gilmore, "Bob Dylan at Fifty," *Rolling Stone,* May 30, 1991, p. 60. Some are, in fact, anti-happiness. See Eric G. Wilson, *Against Happiness: In Praise of Melancholy* (New York: Sarah Crichton Books/Farrar, Straus & Giroux, 2008).

32. Jonathan Foreman, "Happy Is Yuppie Word," © 2005 Meadowgreen Music Company / Sugar Pete Songs. All rights reserved. Used by permission.

33. William Blake, "The Garden of Love," in *The Norton Anthology of English Literature,* rev. ed., M. H. Abrams, gen. ed., vol. 2 (New York: W. W. Norton & Company, Inc., 1962, 1968), p. 58.

the church tend to throw a wet blanket on the idea of a happy life as a legit-imate spiritual concern. Ask a group of veteran Christians if they want to be happy, and many of them are reluctant to answer positively out of fear of appearing unspiritual, even if they secretly desire it.

There is a reason for this. The standard rhetoric proclaimed from the pulpit and other teaching venues in the church goes something like this. Happiness depends on happenings, but God is the source of lasting joy. It's the spiritual life and the soul, not the physical life and the body, that really count. God isn't concerned about happiness, but rather about holiness. To God, your character matters, not your comfort or convenience. Christian-ity is a spiritually serious and morally rigorous religion, and we should not be distracted by worldly preoccupations with happiness that distract us from important spiritual principles and purposes. End of story.

To be sure, this kind of language convicts us with a piercing, even if momentary, guilt complex. We feel trapped in what looks like an irresolvable conflict between Christian teaching and our natural human aspirations. As a result, the church's denigration of happiness has gar-nered it a rather melancholy reputation. Christianity, many think, is a dehumanizing and life-denying, rather than re-humanizing and life-affirming, religion. Believers are straight-laced, sober, and sad. Some are cold; a few are frozen. Bitter Christian critics like H. L. Mencken seem jus-tified in asserting that people in the church sometimes seem haunted by a "fear that someone, somewhere, may be happy."[34]

## Happiness as a Christian Concept

*"The saints love their own happiness."*

Jonathan Edwards, *Christian Love and Its Fruits*[35]

Let's think again about this concept of happiness a little more carefully. Undoubtedly, happy is a "yuppie" word if we define it *hedonistically*. If it's a physical or emotional pleasure principle *only*, then it would run contrary to Christian spirituality. Self-indulgent interpretations of happiness have

---

34. H. L. Mencken on the Puritans is quoted in Leland Ryken, *Worldly Saints: The Puritans as They Really Were* (Grand Rapids: Academie Books, Zondervan Publishing House, 1986), p. 1.

35. Edwards, *Christian Love and Its Fruits*, p. 78.

serious consequences, and we can understand why the church and many well-intentioned Christians reject it as such forthrightly.

Still, if there is something meaningful to this notion of the happy life, if it is an indispensable requirement of human nature, as the Scriptures, our own experience, and the sages of the ages have indicated, then we can't just toss it out all together along with its dirty bath water. We find ourselves in a quandary, since neither its yuppie embrace nor its churchly rejection will do. It seems to me, therefore, that what we need is a view of happiness and the happy life that does justice to our undeniable human aspirations and simultaneously avoids its reigning "don't worry, be happy" superficiality. How might we to do this in Christian terms?

We use our minds regularly to figure out as many things as we can, and we have been notably successful in our various scientific, technological, economic, social and cultural pursuits. At the same time, our minds eventually reach a limit, especially when we encounter life's deep mysteries and face the big questions, such as the question about happiness. So we need some help on this. As Augustine says, "But when we come to divine things, this faculty [of reason] turns away; it cannot behold; it pants, it gasps, and burns with desire; it falls back from the light of truth, and turns again to its wonted [customary] obscurity, not from choice, but from exhaustion." In light of our fatigue and failure to offer a credible conception of happiness, we need God's help if we are to sketch an adequate portrait. Let us, then, as Augustine recommends, "hear the oracles, and submit our weak inferences to the announcements of Heaven."[36] God's oracles and heavenly announcements are found in Scripture, so what we need is a biblically informed conception of the happy life.

## Edenistic, not Hedonistic Happiness

*"For everything created by God is good, and nothing is to be rejected if it is received with gratitude; for it is sanctified by means of the word of God and prayer."*

1 Timothy 4:4-5

36. Augustine, "Of the Morals of the Catholic Church," trans. Richard Stothert, *Nicene and Post-Nicene Fathers*, ed. Philip Schaff, First Series, vol. 4 (Peabody, Mass.: Hendrickson Publishers, Inc., 1994), p. 44 (§7.11-12).

In turning to the Scriptures, my main point is that instead of defining the happy life *hedonistically* in pleasure-seeking terms as the world does, we ought to grasp the concept of the happy life *edenistically* as the Bible does on the basis of the narrative of creation in Genesis 1–2.[37] The opening story of the Scriptures presents the divine paradigm for the happy life, and we need to survey its contents to understand how God originally planned for human beings to thrive in his very good world.

However you work out the details scientifically, Genesis 1–2 is clear *that God created the heavens and the earth.* The chief characteristic of the cosmos is that it is *created.* Specifically, God prepared the earth to be a delightful habitation or home for us where we could live and flourish. The account opens with the majestic declaration in Genesis 1:1 that "In the beginning, God created the heavens and the earth." In verse 2, our attention is rifled immediately to our planet. At this early stage, our future home was formless, empty, and dark. God's Spirit was hovering over the surface of the waters in anticipation of shaping the chaos into a well-ordered cosmos. That is exactly what happened in the six days of creation detailed in verses 3-31.

On the first three days of creation (vv. 3-13), God formed that which was formless by creating light, the skies, the seas, the dry land, vegetation, plants and fruit trees, declaring each successive thing to be good. On God's second three creative days (vv. 14-25), he filled that which was empty by making the sun, moon and stars, fish and birds, cattle, creeping things, and the beasts of the earth. First God made the realms, then he filled them with their rulers and he affirmed the goodness of each individual thing that he made along the way.

Then at the summit of God's creative work, God made us — both male and female — as the image and likeness of God (a notion that includes the body as well as the soul). God blessed us as embodied human beings. That blessing consisted of three things: (1) a loving relationship with God himself, (2) the institutions of marriage and family life, and (3) the mandate to rule and subdue the earth and its creatures. These divinely ordained purposes for our lives — spiritual, social, and cultural, respectively — are delineated in the "creation decree" of Genesis 1:26-28.

Then God said, "Let Us make man in our image, according to our likeness; and let them rule over the fish of the sea and over the birds of the

37. I owe this central point to my brother, Mark Naugle.

sky and over the cattle and over all the earth, and over every creeping thing that creeps on the earth." And God created man in His own image, in the image of God He created him; male and female He created them. And God blessed them; and God said to them, "Be fruitful and multiply, and fill the earth, and subdue it; and rule over the fish of the sea and over the birds of the sky, and over every living thing that moves on the earth."

Following this succinct statement of the human project, God provided abundant food in the form of a vegetarian diet of green plants and fruit-bearing trees for people and animals (vv. 29-30). At the conclusion of this sixth day, God observed his handiwork and declared it all to be "very good" (v. 31). Each part of this world was "good" independently. As a whole, however, it was truly excellent and utterly beautiful in its sheer being. Everything God created was and is unspeakably good (see 1 Tim. 4:1-5).

This assertion of the original goodness of all things is important for understanding how God designed the world with our well-being in mind. To be sure, it exists for God's glory first and foremost. According to Isaiah the prophet, the angels cry out before God saying, "Holy, Holy, Holy, is the Lord of hosts, *the fullness of the whole earth is His glory*" (Isa. 6:3).[38]

While the world exists for God's glory, God also created it as the place of blessing for us. As Dietrich Bonhoeffer reminds us, "This blessing — *be fruitful and multiply, and fill the earth and subdue it* — affirms man totally in the world of the living in which he is placed. It is his total empirical existence that is blessed here, his creatureliness, his worldliness, and his earthliness."[39]

The first part of the creation account is wrapped up in Genesis 2:1-3 with a word about the special character of the seventh day. By then, God had completed his creative work and rested, not because he was tired, but because he was finished. God sanctified the seventh day as a day of rest, because on it he ceased from his labors and began to enjoy what he had made.

The rest of Genesis 2 focuses specifically on the origin of humans, the Garden of Eden, and the institution of marriage. After a brief word of introduction about the early condition of the earth (vv. 4-6), we learn how

38. According to the marginal reading of the New American Standard Bible, this is the literal Hebrew rendering of Isaiah 6:3.

39. Dietrich Bonhoeffer, *Creation and Fall, Temptation: Two Biblical Studies*, trans. John C. Fletcher (New York: Macmillan Publishing Company, Inc., 1959), p. 41.

God created the first man from the ground itself and breathed into his nostrils the breath of life. This first man became a living being, a composite of body and soul, both physical and spiritual in nature (v. 7). God also planted a beautiful garden eastward in Eden where there were beautiful and fruitful trees and a bountiful river of water. He placed the man there whom he had created to cultivate it and keep it (vv. 8-15). To sustain him in his life and work as a gardener, the man was to eat freely from the trees of the garden. There was one exception, however: he was not to eat from the fruit of the tree of the knowledge of good and evil. This prohibition served as a test of the man's obedience to God (vv. 16-17).

Despite the abundance of the man's surroundings, the only thing that wasn't good was the man's solitude (v. 18). After creating the animals and disclosing their social insufficiency, God made a woman from the man's side for the sake of companionship. Like the father of a bride, God presented the woman to the man that she might be his wife and that he might be her husband (vv. 19-22). This initial encounter inspired the man to wax poetic for the very first time:

> This is now bone of my bones,
> And flesh of my flesh;
> She shall be called Woman,
> Because she was taken out of Man. (Gen. 2:23)

This episode concludes with a declaration of God's intent for marriage. It was to be a total life union between man and woman in an exclusive and permanent covenantal relationship of faithfulness and love (vv. 23-24). The first human couple enjoyed unhindered communication and acceptance of one another in the absence of any impediment. They both were naked and not ashamed (v. 25).

Eden overall, as the name in Hebrew literally suggests, was a garden of delight. It is called paradise for a purpose. A trace of it in the most glorious of spring days reminded the poet Gerard Manley Hopkins of the original creation:

> What is all this juice and all this joy?
> A strain of the earth's sweet being in the beginning
> In Eden garden.[40]

40. Gerard Manley Hopkins, "Spring," in *A Hopkins Reader*, ed. and intro. John Pick, rev.

The universe and our world in particular, then, were no cosmic accidents. The creation was the result of God's purposeful design. God intended us to live in the fullness of community with himself, others, and the world around us. This blessed estate established the setting for the truly happy life, six components of which are evident in the creation account:

1. Spiritually, we were made to enjoy intimate union with God the creator in obedience to his will, rooted in our identity as God's image and likeness.

2. Vocationally, we were made to undertake fulfilling work based on the commandment to rule the earth and to cultivate and keep the creation.

3. Socially, we were made for human companionship especially as man and woman in the context of marriage and family life.

4. Nutritionally, we were made to partake freely of food and drink, as seen in the generous provision of plants, fruitful trees, and water in the garden of Eden.

5. Sabbatically, we were made to rest and play in the enjoyment of the world, based upon the blessing and sanctification of the seventh day.

6. Habitationally, we were made to take pleasure in our surroundings, in the nature of the locations and places where we live, since God set us in the delightfulness of Eden and in the context of the creation's astounding wonder and beauty.[41]

These are the six ingredients in God's recipe for the happy life. It is, we might say, "a state made perfect by the aggregation [combination] of all good things."[42] God intended us to live fully in the largess of indescribable blessing mediated through multifaceted aspects of God's marvelous world in a complete and satisfying way. It's not a hedonistic but an edenistic happiness that roots the fullness of human life in God and his creation.

---

and enlarged edition (Garden City, N.Y.: Image Books, A Division of Doubleday & Company, Inc., 1966), p. 49.

41. On the importance of habitat to happiness, see Alain de Botton, *The Architecture of Happiness* (New York: Pantheon, 2006).

42. Boethius, *Consolation of Philosophy* 4.2, quoted in Thomas Aquinas, *Summa Theologica*, trans. Fathers of the English Dominican Province, rev. Daniel J. Sullivan, *Great Books of the Western World*, ed. Robert Maynard Hutchins, vol. 19 (Chicago: William Benton, Publisher, Encyclopedia Britannica, Inc., 1952), p. 150 (§1.1.Q26).

## Happiness and Shalom

*"Christianity is almost the only one of the great religions which
thoroughly approves of the body — which believes that matter is
good, that God Himself once took on a human body. . . ."*

C. S. Lewis, *Mere Christianity*[43]

The word *shalom* is used in the Scriptures to refer to the totality of beatitude that God intended for all creation, including ourselves. Though *shalom* is commonly translated "peace," we should not limit its definition to serenity or absence of conflict. It includes these things, but it also signifies soundness, wholeness, security, and the fullness of life. As one scholar explains, shalom "indicates the well-being of daily existence, the state of the man who lives in harmony with nature, with himself, with God. Concretely, it is blessing, rest, glory, riches, salvation, life."[44] Shalom is human flourishing with God the Creator and Redeemer at the center of our embodied existence, living heartily as complete persons of soul and body in right relationship to God's good creation and its blessings.

Celtic Christianity was firmly established upon the cornerstone of shalom as the basis of its revolutionary spiritual vision. Irish believers have been noted for their enthusiastic embrace of creation under the blessing of God in the broad range of human experiences. Their love for God the trinity as Creator and Redeemer of all things, their recognition of God's presence in the world, their passion for nature and its creatures, their love of art, poetry, and storytelling, their respect for the life of the mind and learning, their emphasis on Christ's incarnation and its humanizing implications, their enthusiasm for the church and the richness of its historic liturgy, their focus on family, friendship, and hospitality, all together reveal a radical understanding of the goodness of embodied human life in rightly ordered relationships of love with God, self, others, and all things. Perhaps these traits help to explain why the Irish have been duly credited with saving Western civilization at a low point in its history. Celtic Christians would resonate enthusiastically with this realistic vision of living in the fullness of our humanity unto God: "To be holy is not to be

43. C. S. Lewis, *Mere Christianity* (New York: The Macmillan Company, 1958), p. 77.
44. *Dictionary of Biblical Theology*, ed. Xavier Léon-Dufour, 2nd ed. (New York: Seabury Press, 1973), s.v. "Peace."

heavenly but to know God in one's earthiness and in one's flesh," as Stephen Verney has put it.[45]

Shalom wasn't just the luck of the Irish, so to speak, but also the providential legacy of a Frenchman. No less a figure than the allegedly austere Protestant reformer John Calvin (1509-64) recognized that God not only created the world for our necessary use, but also for our robust enjoyment and delight. "Now if we ponder to what end God created food," Calvin once mused, "we shall find that he meant not only to provide for necessity but also for delight and good cheer. Thus the purpose of clothing, apart from necessity, was comeliness [charm] and decency. In grasses, trees, and fruit, apart from their various uses, there is beauty of appearance and pleasantness of odor."

Calvin could hardly contain his excitement over God's goodness manifested to us in physical ways in his world. Here he wraps up praise for the bountiful role of nature in our lives with a rhetorical flourish:

> Has the Lord clothed the flowers with the great beauty that greets our eyes, the sweetness of smell that is wafted on our nostrils, and yet will it be unlawful for our eyes to be affected by that beauty, or our sense of smell by the sweetness of that odor? What? Did he not so distinguish colors as to make some more lovely than others? What? Did he not endow gold and silver, ivory and marble, with a loveliness that renders them more precious than other metals or stones? Did he not, in short, render many things attractive to us, apart from their necessary use?

Indeed, God did, and we thank him for it! With Calvin, then, we must reject teachings, often promoted by sincere but misinformed saints, that legalistically reduce God's creation to its usefulness and forbid us to enjoy its bounty as human beings. "Away, then," Calvin declared, "with that inhuman philosophy which, while conceding only a necessary use of creatures [things in the world], not only malignantly deprives us of the lawful fruit of God's beneficence but cannot be practiced unless it robs a man of all his senses and degrades him to a block."[46] Anybody reading this want to be robbed of his or her senses and be reduced to a "block"? Unlikely!

---

45. Stephen Verney, *Water into Wine* (Fount, 1958), p. 180, quoted in Margaret Magdalen, *Jesus: Man of Prayer — Expanding Your Horizons in Prayer*, foreword Michael Green (Guildford, Surrey, England: Eagle of Inter Publishing Service, 1987), p. 38.

46. Calvin, *Institutes of the Christian Religion*, pp. 720-21 (§3.10.2).

Under Calvin's influence, William Cowper (1731-1800) was a shalom-drenched English poet in the Christian tradition who also celebrated the enjoyment of creation's bounty in God, as these lines from his greatest blank verse poem *The Task* indicate:

> Hath God indeed giv'n appetites to man,
> And stored the earth so plenteously with means
> To gratify the hunger of his wish,
> And doth he reprobate and will he damn
> The use of his own bounty? Making first
> So frail a kind [humans], and then enacting laws
> So strict, that less than perfect must despair?
> Falsehood! Which whoso but suspects of truth,
> Dishonors God, and makes a slave of man.[47]

There is, then, in the Christian tradition, as the Celts, Calvin, and Cowper show, an important tradition of shalom that contributes significantly to our understanding of the happy life. Surprisingly, Christianity as a religion advocates a kind of "holy materialism" that neither venerates nor repudiates God's creation, but recognizes its important role when it is loved and enjoyed appropriately.

While it is true that man does not live by bread alone, but also by God, it is also true that man does not live by God alone, but also by bread. We see the importance of both God and bread at the beginning and middle of the Lord's Prayer: "Our Father who art in heaven, hallowed be thy name . . . give us this day our daily bread." Deprive us of either God or bread and we will die, spiritually or physically or both. We enjoy our bread in God and God in our bread. If either is missing or mis-loved, our well-being is diminished. When we recognize this, we begin to learn about the deep meaning of happiness in a Christian perspective.

---

47. William Cowper, "The Winter Morning Walk," book 5 of *The Task*, in *Cowper: Poetical Works*, ed. H. S. Milford, 4th ed., corrections and additions Norma Russell (London: Oxford University Press, 1967), pp. 213-14 (lines 635-43).

## The Deep Meaning of Happiness

*"I serve You and worship You that I may be happy in You, to whom I owe that I am a being capable of happiness."*

Augustine, *Confessions*[48]

To be sure, things in the created world can fulfill many of our needs. Yet we also have a most significant need that only God can satisfy. If there is both a Creator and a creation, then the mistake of all mistakes is to think that created things on their own can replace and satisfy the need we have for the Creator. The creation can't do it; it is simply not designed to do so. Only God can fulfill the role that God is supposed to fulfill in our lives. That's why the greatest commandment demands that we love him with everything we are, everything we have, and in everything we do — with all our heart, soul, mind, and strength (see Deut. 6:5; Matt. 22:37). A relationship of supreme love with God is the only thing that can satisfy the longing for the infinite that is so deeply rooted in our hearts; nothing else will do. Hear Pascal again:

> What is it, then, that this desire and this inability proclaim to us, but that there was once in man a true happiness of which there now remain to him only the mark and empty trace, which he in vain tries to fill from all his surroundings, seeking from things absent the help he does not obtain in things present? But these are all inadequate, because the infinite abyss can only be filled by an infinite and immutable object, that is to say, only by God Himself.[49]

The genius of the Christian faith, however, is that it does not call upon us to eliminate our love for things on earth out of our love for God in heaven. It's not either God or the world, but both God and the world in a proper relationship. When he is at the top of our list of loves, we are able to love and enjoy all things in the context of our relationship with him.

That's why Jesus said that the second greatest commandment, to love

---

48. Augustine, *Confessions*, trans. F. J. Sheed, intro. Peter Brown (Indianapolis: Hackett Publishing Company, 1992), p. 259 (§13.1).

49. Blaise Pascal, *Pensées*, trans. W. F. Trotter, *Great Books of the Western World*, ed. Robert Maynard Hutchins, vol. 33 (Chicago: William Benton, Publisher, Encyclopedia Britannica, Inc., 1952), p. 244 (#425).

our neighbors as we love ourselves, is like the first (Lev. 19:18; Matt. 22:39). The two greatest commandments are integrally connected. In loving our neighbor, who is a creature made in God's image and likeness, we love God. In loving God, who is the Creator, we love our neighbor, whom he created. Thus, love for God and neighbor — that is, love for the Creator and his creation, people and other things too — are inseparable.

The happy life, then, consists of learning how to love both God supremely and the world in the right way at the very same time. In fact, the world and its resources exist to point us to God and his glory, that we might recognize God in, and love him for, his gifts. As Alexander Schmemann explains,

> It is *this world* (and not any "other world"), it is *this life* (and not any "other life") that were given to man to be a sacrament of the divine presence, given as communion with God, and it is only through this world, this life, by "transforming" them into communion with God that man *was to be.*[50]

In another place, Schmemann adds these thoughts to help us understand this sacramental viewpoint and how we are to know and experience God through the world he has made and the gifts he has given to us in it:

> All that exists is God's gift to man, and it all exists to make God known to man, to make man's life communion with God. It is divine love made food, made life for man. God *blesses* everything He creates, and, in biblical language, this means that He makes all creation the sign and means of His presence and wisdom, love and revelation: "O taste and see that the Lord is good."[51]

In Christianity, the happy life is a sacramental life, in which we see and love God supremely in relationship to all things, and in which we see and love all things properly in relationship to God, whom we love the most. In Augustine's apt phrase, we "learn in the creature to love the Creator; and in the work Him who made it."[52]

---

50. Alexander Schmemann, *For the Life of the World: Sacraments and Orthodoxy* (Crestwood, N.Y.: St. Vladimir's Seminary Press, 1973), p. 100 (emphasis in original).

51. Schmemann, *For the Life of the World*, p. 14.

52. Augustine, *Expositions on the Book of Psalms*, Nicene and Post-Nicene Fathers, ed. Philip Schaff, vol. 8 (Peabody, Mass.: Hendrickson Publishers, Inc., 1994), p. 122 (§40.8).

Thus, if we refer all our human activities and experiences to God in love — work, marriage, sexuality, children, family, friendship, food, rest, recreation, place, and anything else you can think of — then we discover contentment, satisfaction, fulfillment, joy, and happiness in life, all summed up in the word *shalom*. If God is the proper reference point for all aspects and things in life, then God gives them their true meaning and puts them in the proper order in our lives. This grand union of God, ourselves, and the whole cosmos in a sacred synthesis of rightly ordered love constitutes the deep meaning of happiness.

## Countercultural Happiness

This viewpoint is quite contrary to our culture's hedonistic view of happiness. It is also contrary to the misguidedly pious view of happiness that omits creation. The worldly mistake is to focus on the physical creation, forfeiting the soul for the body, sacrificing the transcendent for the immanent, and eliminating the sacred from the secular. The mistake the church sometimes makes is to focus on the heavenly Creator, forfeiting the body for the soul, sacrificing the immanent for the transcendent, and eliminating the secular from the sacred. At the root of both errors is a common but malicious dualism that separates or eliminates one indispensable realm of reality from the other. As a result of this split, the favored portion receives excessive, if not distorted, attention, and the unfavored portion suffers inappropriate, if not slanderous, neglect.

The truth is that the two domains of Creator and creation are so closely intertwined that we can't live happily if one or the other is negated or excluded. Trying to live in the creation without the Creator, or trying to live with the Creator without creation is incomplete and ultimately harmful. If we are to discover the happy life, we must embrace a holistic vision that unites God and humanity, connects the Creator with the creation, joins the spiritual and the physical, binds the transcendent and the immanent, and fuses the sacred and the secular into an integrated whole in which all aspects of reality are correctly understood and rightly loved. If either part of the whole is missing — Creator or creation — then something has gone wrong, and happiness is proportionately diminished. The story of Job illustrates this well.

## Grief in the Land of Uz

*"Let the day perish on which I was to be born,*
*And the night which said, 'A boy is conceived.'"*

Job 3:3

This sacred union of God and goods rightly ordered as the formula for the happy life is necessary to make sense of the reactions of Job and Jesus to significant human needs and losses. Both of them demonstrate that something catastrophic happened to God's original plan that has thwarted our welfare. We will see how Jesus responded to the tragedies of the human condition in chapter four. Here we will focus on Job's reaction in his loss of shalom and edenistic happiness.

When a series of tragedies befell the righteous man from Uz and deprived him of his wealth, family, and health, he experienced great pain and suffered tremendous grief. Though he never abandoned his faith in God even when he was encouraged to do so, his losses shook him to the core. Things were not well with his soul.

My spirit is broken, my days are extinguished,
The grave is ready for me. (Job 17:1; see also Job 16:12-17; 29:1-6; 30:16-23)

Obviously, Job was no stoic in his response to the loss of his substance and strength. Job wept (Job 16:20). The things he lost were *not* matters of indifference; they had made significant contributions to his sense of self and welfare in life. His story suggests that God placed us among people, in places, and with things to play important roles in our lives, and he made no mistake in doing so.[53] Job's bereavement when he lost all these elements of his life and his joy at their eventual restoration reveals as much (cf. Job 42:10-17). Any other response would have been, well, inhuman.

Job's sufferings demonstrate that something catastrophic happened to God's original plan, and it has resulted in considerable evil and pain. Our misery and that of our loved ones and friends, plus past and present reports of manifold disasters and hardships, testify to the pervasive brokenness of the world. The Maillol sculpture of the woman mentioned at the beginning of this chapter seems to know such sorrow well.

53. Gina Bria, "A Theology of Things," *Mars Hill Review: Essays, Studies, Reminders of God,* no. 10 (Winter/Spring 1998): 10.

## The Loss of Happiness and Shalom

*"Of Man's first disobedience, and the fruit*
*Of that forbidden tree, whose mortal taste*
*Brought death into the world, and all our woe. . . ."*

John Milton, *Paradise Lost*[54]

What robbed us of the blessing and peace that God originally intended? To answer this question, we must return again to the beginning of the Bible, this time to Genesis 3. In this chapter, we read the story of the fall of humanity into sin. In traditional Jewish and Christian understanding, this narrative explains the origin of evil and suffering in the world, and accounts for the tragic character of the human condition. The world is now flooded with abnormalities so prevalent that they seem all too normal: idolatry, immorality, falsehood, warfare, disease, famine, earthquakes, poverty, injustice, greed, and so on. Life and the world are no longer the way they are supposed to be. Shalom has been vandalized. The peace has been drastically disturbed.[55] Though modern assumptions lead many to brush this narrative aside as an inconsequential myth, we must take its message seriously. As Peter Kreeft states, "What happened in Eden may be hard to understand, but it makes everything else understandable."[56]

What this story helps us to understand is our devastating brokenness, about which Bob Dylan sings mournfully in one of his classic songs:

Broken bottles, broken plates,
Broken switches, broken gates,
Broken dishes, broken parts,
Streets are filled with broken hearts.
Broken words never meant to be spoken,
Everything is broken.[57]

54. John Milton, *Paradise Lost*, in *The Portable Milton*, ed. and intro. Douglas Bush (New York: Viking Penguin, Inc., 1977), p. 232 (Book 1, lines 1-3).

55. Cornelius Plantinga Jr., *Not the Way It's Supposed to Be: A Breviary of Sin* (Grand Rapids: Eerdmans, 1995), chapter 1.

56. Peter J. Kreeft, "C. S. Lewis's Argument from Desire," in *G. K. Chesterton and C. S. Lewis: The Riddle of Joy*, ed. Michael H. Macdonald and Andrew A. Tadie, foreword Janet Blumberg Knedlik (Grand Rapids: Eerdmans, 1989), p. 260.

57. Bob Dylan, "Everything is Broken," Copyright 1989 Special Rider Music. All rights reserved. International copyright secured. Used by permission.

Why is everything broken? The false promise of a happiness greater than the one God provided prompted the primeval revolt.[58] As Genesis 3 informs us, we errantly sought autonomy, if not self-deification, by an act of insubordination against God and his divine authority. This pursuit of unchecked freedom and independence was achieved by the willful violation of the divine commandment that prohibited the consumption of forbidden fruit.

This rebellious act turned out to be a deadly mistake, just as the first human couple had been forewarned. Death resulted, and the world became a universal cemetery. It disrupted our covenant relationship with God and brought real guilt and great grief into all our lives. We were separated from God spiritually, alienated from ourselves psychologically, and estranged from one another socially. The entire earth and the whole human race fell under the curse and judgment of God. We were exiled tragically from the splendor of Eden and escorted into a wilderness-like world, choked with brambles, and besmeared with blood, sweat, and tears.

> Cursed is the ground because of you;
> In toil you shall eat of it
> All the days of your life.
> Both thorns and thistles it shall grow for you;
> And you will eat the plants of the field;
> By the sweat of your face
> You shall eat bread,
> Till you return to the ground,
> Because from it you were taken;
> For you are dust,
> And to dust you shall return. (Gen. 3:17b-19)

As a result of our rebellion and God's judgment, we have forgotten that the world is God's creation. No longer do we seek to love God in all things and to love all things in God, in a sacramental life of genuine happiness. Instead, we now live non-sacred lives in a non-sacred world in which we fail to see God in his own creation and give him thanks for his gifts. Schmemann can see just how benighted this state of affairs has become:

---

58. See Milton, *Paradise Lost*, p. 546 (Book 12, line 587).

Man has loved the world, but as an end in itself and not as transparent to God. He has done it so consistently that it has become something that is "in the air." It seems natural for man to experience the world as opaque, and not shot through with the presence of God. It seems natural not to live a life of thanksgiving for God's gift of a world. It seems natural not to be eucharistic.[59]

Still, we have a residual memory of paradise in our minds. We intuitively know of our previous state and the way things are supposed to be. We are acutely aware of what is now absent. We long for some kind of recovery of happiness with all our hearts. Despite this major alteration in our consciousness and circumstances, our interest in the happy life has remained intact. As Augustine writes in *The City of God*, "For certainly by sinning, we lost both piety and happiness; but when we lost happiness, we did not lose the love of it."[60]

In fact, our love and longing for happiness deepened, because what we once enjoyed is gone, and so much misery has replaced it. Now we resolve even more intensely to find enduring delights and consolations that make our lives bearable, if not enjoyable, once again. In our confusion, though, we make many mistakes along the way, multiplying our pain. "We commit sin," says Augustine, "to promote our welfare, and it results instead in our misfortune; or we sin to increase our welfare, and the result is rather to increase our misfortune."[61] Undeterred by our calamities, our search for satisfaction continues. As one bumper sticker puts it, we remain "In Search of the Eternal Buzz."

## An Inconsolable Longing

*"Yibin was a very atmospheric town, even in the middle of the Cultural Revolution. The waving rivers and serene hills, and the*

59. Schmemann, *For the Life of the World*, p. 16.

60. Augustine, *The City of God*, trans. Marcus Dods, Great Books of the Western World, ed. Robert Maynard Hutchins, vol. 18 (Chicago: William Benton, Publisher, Encyclopedia Britannica, Inc., 1952), p. 617 (§22. 30).

61. Augustine, *The City of God*, trans. Henry Bettenson, intro. John O'Meara (New York: Penguin Books, 1972, 1984), p. 553 (§14.4).

*hazy horizon beyond, produced a* sense of eternity *in me, and*
*soothed me temporarily. . . ."*

Jung Chang, Wild Swans — Three Daughters of China[62]

The German term *Sehnsucht* describes this obstinate aspiration for something that satisfies even though we seem perpetually estranged from it.
Amidst the storms and stresses of daily life, this "inconsolable longing"
gets triggered unexpectedly and stabs us in mind and heart with a "pang"
in most unexpected ways and times.[63] Whether it's elicited by a blue sky, a
beautiful face, the melancholy of a requiem, the lure of romance, the
crashing waves of the sea, the scintillations of sex, the profundity of a film,
an illuminating line of poetry, a beautiful song, or an unobstructed view
of the Milky Way, we occasionally experience a mysterious and tremendous feeling that attracts and baffles us simultaneously. We need "it" and
want "it," whatever "it" is. We are convinced it is what we have been
searching for all our lives.

The late newspaper columnist Paul Crume experienced this feeling unexpectedly on at least two occasions. He documented both of them in an
editorial that appeared on Christmas day 1967 in *The Dallas Morning News.*

> I remember a time in my final days in college when the chinaberry trees
> were abloom and the air was sweet with spring blossoms and I stood
> still on the street, suddenly struck with the feeling of something that
> was an enormous promise and yet was no tangible promise at all.
>
> And there was another night in a small boat when the moon was
> full and the distant headlands were dark but beautiful and we were
> lonely. The pull of a nameless emotion was so strong that it filled the at-
> mosphere. The small boy within me cried.[64]

Most of us have had experiences like these sometime, somewhere
along the way. How, when, and where has it ever happened to you? For

---

62. Jung Chang, *Wild Swans — Three Daughters of China* (New York: Touchstone/Simon
Schuster, 2003; Globalflair Ltd., 1991), p. 390 (emphasis added).

63. C. S. Lewis, *Surprised by Joy: The Shape of My Early Life* (New York: Harcourt, Brace &
Company, 1956), p. 72.

64. Paul Crume, "Angels Among Us," "Big D" column, first published on Christmas
morning in 1967 in *The Dallas Morning News.* Reprinted *The Dallas Morning News*, December
24, 2005, p. 23A. Available at http://www.dallasnews.com/s/dws/spe/2002/angels_2002/
angels.html (accessed July 23, 2007).

C. S. Lewis, *Sehnsucht* as the search for and experience of joy was the "central story" of his life. He wrote about it in his autobiography *Surprised by Joy*. He also reflected on this theme extensively in many of his writings.[65] For example, in *The Weight of Glory*, Lewis calls this pursuit "the secret we cannot hide and cannot tell, though we desire to do both."

To be sure, Lewis says we give this experience of longing some interesting names, like beauty, for example, and we often mistake the thing itself we are longing for with its means, the shadow for the substance. The things through which the longing reaches us are good things, to be sure, yet at the same time they are potential idols, should we worship them. Lewis explains the proper perspective: For they are not the thing itself; they are only the scent of a flower we have not found, the echo of a tune we have not heard, news from a country we have never yet visited.[66]

For Lewis, this longing, even apart from its fulfillment, is sweeter than the actual fulfillment of any other human desire — "this poverty better than all other wealth."[67] It is a highly individual experience, so much so that it is difficult if not impossible for one person to communicate it to another. As Lewis indicates, however, the problem we have is that we tend to confuse the medium of the experience with what it communicates. We idolize the people, places, or things that point us to their greater divine cause, failing to realize they are just signals of what satisfies ultimately. Thus we have enormous problems. Because of our sin, our profound ignorance and disordered loves have frustrated our persistent efforts to discover the deep meaning of happiness — and the fulfillment of that inconsolable longing for we know not what — right up to the present time.

---

65. Lewis, *Surprised by Joy*, pp. 17, 238. Lewis also reflects on this theme in *The Pilgrim's Regress: Allegorical Apology for Christianity Reason and Romanticism* (Grand Rapids: Eerdmans, 1958; reprint, 1977), pp. 7-10. For a book-length treatment of this theme in Lewis, see Corbin Scott Carnell, *Bright Shadow of Reality: Spiritual Longing in C. S. Lewis* (Grand Rapids: Eerdmans, 1974, 1999).

66. C. S. Lewis, *The Weight of Glory and Other Addresses* (Grand Rapids: Eerdmans, 1965), pp. 4-5.

67. Lewis, *The Pilgrim's Regress*, p. 7.

## CHAPTER TWO

# Disordered Love:
# Everything I Love Is Killing Me

*"Look what a mess we've made of love."*

Switchfoot, "Ammunition"[1]

## Introduction

Ignorance and disordered love are two of the primary consequences of humanity's fall into sin, and St. Augustine's story illustrates them both. One of the most important figures in Western civilization, Augustine was an early church father who lived from A.D. 354-430. He was a full-blown sinner before he was an exemplary saint. He was deeply unhappy without God, but he found happiness when he began to love God and love the creation in him.

1. Jonathan Foreman, "Ammunition," © 2003 Meadowgreen Music Company / Sugar Pete Songs. All rights reserved. Used by permission.

## Augustine's Story

*"The life of Saint Augustine has a special appeal because he was a*
*great sinner who became a great saint."*

R. S. Pine-Coffin, Introduction to *Confessions*[2]

In infancy, Augustine was a handful. As he grew up and learned to speak, it was obvious that he was a precocious child. Other than that, he was like most boys his own age. He did not like going to school. His teachers punished him often and harshly for his academic laziness. Instead, he loved to play — and especially to win at play. As a "Type-A" personality, he was very competitive. He also enjoyed games and shows and going to the theater. For the most part, his young life revolved around having fun. His active childhood, however, was nearly cut short because of a severe stomach ailment. Fortunately, he re-covered. But later on, when Augustine was a teenager, one of his closest friends did die of a fever, and this loss caused Augustine great grief.

Augustine's mother was deeply religious and quite concerned about her boy's spiritual development. His father, on the other hand, had no real interest in such matters. He was focused primarily on his son's worldly suc-cess. Though many of his young friends made church commitments early on, Augustine didn't. He lived recklessly throughout his adolescent years, and with the onset of puberty and its blast of hormones, he did not resist the urges that accompanied a maturing body. Also, he and a gang of his friends got into trouble all too often for various misdeeds, including some petty thievery, particularly in a case of some stolen pears. He was motivated to participate in such mischief by the thrill of it all, not to mention some con-siderable pressure from his peers. Only later did he feel any remorse.

In due course, Augustine went away to school to study, but his real in-terests were fame, fortune, and females. The liberty of his unchaperoned educational environment was more conducive to sexual escapades and theatrical amusements than it was to diligent study. As a matter of fact, his self-indulgent patterns of behavior and the bad habits he acquired during these bawdy years garnered him several mistresses over time. Eventually he fathered an illegitimate son, whose name was Adeodatus. He never dis-closed the name of the mother.

---

2. R. S. Pine-Coffin, "Introduction" to Augustine, *Confessions*, trans. R. S. Pine-Coffin (New York: Penguin, 1961), p. 11.

Then something happened quite unexpectedly, an event that shook the young Augustine to the core. In the course of his studies, he read a book by the noted Roman orator Cicero that contained an exhortation to philosophy and the discovery of the happy life. A fire was lit in his soul. This book produced a change in the way he lived and what he wanted, in his fundamental purposes and desires. It even sparked a new religious interest within him. Augustine thought he was on the right path. Then again, maybe he wasn't. He became quite agitated and uncertain. Question after question plagued his formerly happy-go-lucky mind. In this perplexing period, he began to search his heart and ask some serious questions: Did he have *any clue* about this life, and what was he doing here? Were the things he loved and cared about really all that important?

His ignorance and the disorder of his loves were beginning to dawn on him. Much of what Augustine thought he knew now seemed false. The things he once cherished now struck him as silly and vain. His search for truth and happiness — indeed, for the happiness of truth — had begun.

The pathway Augustine was on, however, was anything but smooth or straight. He reconsidered Christianity briefly, but it seemed primitive to his cosmopolitan mind. Then he got involved in a rather bizarre religious cult. At first it seemed intellectually impressive, but the deeper he probed, the more suspect it became. It turned out he knew more than its highly respected leaders did. After a lengthy affiliation, he abandoned it completely, disillusioned once again. He had a short-lived interest in astrology, but his rational mind told him this outlook was nonsense. His cynicism was growing. For a short time, he sided with the skeptics who had given up on the possibility of truth altogether. They argued that nothing ultimate or meaningful could be known by anyone. He believed them, at least temporarily, until he recognized the inconsistency of the certainty of their uncertainty.

By now Augustine was well into his twenties, and his career was beginning to flourish. He was living with his mistress and his son, and they moved from town to town, searching for a better life. Incidentally, his tenacious mother, inspired by her faith, followed them just about everywhere they went, out of concern for her son's spiritual well-being. (His father had already passed away by this time.)

Nonetheless, cohabitation was a growing occupational and social liability, and Augustine sent his live-in lover away, though his son remained with him. Meanwhile, he picked up an interim partner while he was waiting to marry a younger woman who would be more advantageous to his personal and professional life. He seemed like a borderline sex addict. His personal confusion increased. His troubles deepened. He was trapped in a chasm of despair.

Finally a word of hope reached Augustine's mind and heart. With the assistance of a concerned clergyman and others, he turned to Christ and became a Christian. Picking up and reading Romans 13:13-14 was the catalyst to his conversion: "Let us behave properly as in the day, not in carousing and drunkenness, not in sexual promiscuity and sensuality, not in strife and jealousy. But put on the Lord Jesus Christ, and make no provision for the flesh in regard to its lusts." At long last, his mother's diligent prayers for her son's salvation were answered. She had labored harder for his spiritual birth than she had for his physical one. Though Augustine's ignorance and his bad habits had held him in check, he abandoned these hindrances by the grace of God and trusted in the gospel.

A light dispersed the darkness that had shadowed Augustine's mind and heart for so long. Now he was coming to know God. A new perspective on life and the world accompanied his growing awareness of the Creator and Redeemer of all things. Extraordinary feelings of affection for God were welling up inside of him; they displaced the destructive desires that had enslaved him for years. Truth and love had triumphed, and he was transformed.

At the age of thirty-one, after his long and arduous search, Augustine discovered the deep meaning of happiness in God. Unsurprisingly, then, he spent the rest of his years using his remarkable intellectual gifts and limitless energies to understand more about life's chief good and helping others on their way to him.

## Confessions for the Masses

> "... the Confessions *is a history of the schooling of the heart in love.*"
>
> Peter Brown, Introduction to Confessions[3]

Augustine offered this account of his life in his famous spiritual autobiography titled *Confessions*. He wrote this book in A.D. 397 while he was

---

3. Peter Brown, introduction to Augustine, *Confessions*, trans. Frank Sheed (Indianapolis: Hackett Publishing Company, Inc., 1992), p. xvii.

bishop of Hippo in North Africa, some eleven years after his conversion to Christ. One of the church's classic texts, its value lies not only in its theological and spiritual insights, but also in its brutally honest depiction of Augustine's life, warts and all. Most of us are too proud or weak to reveal our flaws forthrightly to others. Augustine, however, with great humility, bared his heart and soul before the whole world in an act of unsparing self-revelation that is rarely, if ever, found in the canon of human literature.[4]

Augustine no doubt wrote his book for his own benefit, but he also had larger purposes in mind. He believed there was something about his own journey that was typical of most everyone, everywhere. Most of us, he believed, live lives very similar to his own, despite differences in detail. He felt his story was *not* unique, but an example of struggling, discontented human beings looking earnestly for the happy life . . . just like we are. He wandered about in confusion trying to figure out what life was all about . . . just like we do. He attached himself in love helter-skelter to those things he thought would make him happy . . . just as we do. He discovered that the things he loved for happiness' sake didn't last very long . . . just as they don't for us. He realized how his various desires and habits deceptively enslaved him in a miserable life. His toiling for fulfillment resulted in nothing but frustration. No matter how hard he tried, he still felt empty and depressed. Sound familiar?

## Ignorance and Disordered Love in the World

*"For my people have committed two evils: they have forsaken Me, the fountain of living waters, to hew for themselves cisterns, broken cisterns that can hold no water."*

Jeremiah 2:13

Most people think that happiness and satisfaction reside primarily in their ardent love for things of this world. These disordered loves segue rather easily into disordered lives, and both are rooted in a commonplace igno-

---

4. Benjamin Breckinridge Warfield, "Augustine and His Confessions," in *Calvin and Augustine,* ed. Samuel G. Craig, foreword J. Marcellus Kik (Philadelphia: The Presbyterian and Reformed Publishing Company, 1956, 1974), p. 332.

rance of our chief good. We must expose and critique the reasons why we are baffled about the foundations of the happy life.

## Ignorance of the Chief Good

> *"Unhappiness is not knowing what we want and killing ourselves to get it."*
>
> Don Herold, American humorist (1889-1966)[5]

According to St. Augustine, there are at least four types of people in search of a happy life. Of the four, the first three cannot be happy, each for a particular reason. The fourth kind of person is a candidate for happiness, but a significant question must be answered to obtain it. In each instance, Augustine insists that happiness is deeply connected to the things we love. He begins by describing the three kinds of unhappy people:

> But the title happy cannot, in my opinion, belong either [1] to him who has not what he loves, whatever it may be, or [2] to him who has what he loves if it is hurtful, or [3] to him who does not love what he has, although it is good in perfection.[6]

The first person cannot be happy because he does not possess the things he wants most in life. Such a person lacks what he treasures, and what he treasures could be a person, a place, or a thing. For example, it's hard to be happy if you desire to live in your dream home in the Rocky Mountains with your soulmate . . . but instead occupy a shack on a God-forsaken piece of real estate all by yourself. Your dangling carrots are out of reach! So Augustine is right: you can't be happy if you don't have whatever it is you love most in life.

A second kind of person can't be happy either, but for a different reason. In this case, you have what you love and it makes you happy, but what you have that makes you happy isn't good for you! Your treasure is really

---

5. Quote available at http://en.thinkexist.com/quotes/don_herold/ (accessed March 20, 2007).

6. Augustine, "Of the Morals of the Catholic Church," in the *Nicene and Post-Nicene Fathers,* ed. Philip Schaff, vol. 4 (Peabody, Mass.: Hendrickson Publishers, Inc., 1994), p. 42 (Chap. 3).

trash, death in disguise. You can't be happy if what you love is ultimately destructive. As Alan Jackson sings in a country-western favorite:

Everything I love is killing me,
Cigarettes, Jack Daniels and caffeine;
And that's the way you're turning out to be;
Everything I love, gonna have to give up,
'Cause everything I love is killing me.[7]

The third type of unhappy person lives an ironic life. You have what it takes to be happy, but you don't care a thing for it. You regard your treasure as if it were trash. A Mercedes is at your disposal, but you prefer your go-cart. Shouldn't you enjoy your filet mignon over precious beef jerky? You dismiss the true source of satisfaction, and foolishly turn your attention to lesser things. Augustine is spot on once again: you have what it takes to be happy, but you just shrug your shoulders.

According to Augustine, then, there are three kinds of people who can't be happy: "For the one who seeks what he cannot obtain suffers *torture,* and one who has got what is not desirable is *cheated,* and one who does not seek what is worth seeking for is *diseased.*"[8] Tortured, cheated, and diseased people aren't happy people because, respectively, they lack what they love, love what they shouldn't, or don't love what they should.

If these people aren't happy, can anyone be? Augustine says yes. He explains it like this: "I find, then, a fourth case, where the happy life exists, — when that which is man's chief good is both loved and possessed."[9] Augustine's claim, counter to the currents of contemporary culture, is that there is an objective reality that is the chief good for all human beings — philosophers call it the *summum bonum* — and that genuine happiness depends upon your knowing what it is, having it in your life, and loving it with all your heart. Naturally, then, the most important question is this: *What is our chief good?*[10]

---

7. "Everything I Love," by Carson Chamberlain and Harley Lee Allen, © 1996 Universal — Songs Of PolyGram Int., Inc. and Coburn Music, Inc. (BMI). Used By Permission. All Rights Reserved.

8. Augustine, "Of the Morals of the Catholic Church," p. 42 (Chap. 3, emphasis added).

9. Augustine, "Of the Morals of the Catholic Church," p. 42 (Chap. 3).

10. Augustine, "Of the Morals of the Catholic Church," p. 42 (Chap. 3).

**Theological Reasons for Our Ignorance**  In inquiring about our *chief good* we are also inquiring about our *total good*, because we want to understand all the things that are necessary for the happy life. We want the complete story, not an abridged version of it, in our quest to know what's best for us as human beings. We want the chief good and other goods, rightly ordered. We want both first and second things, the first things in first place, the second things in second place, and the second things rightly related to first things and the first things rightly related to second things. As C. S. Lewis says, "You can't get second things by putting them first; you can get second things only by putting first things first. From which . . . would follow . . . the question, What things are first?"[11] That's exactly our question: what is our chief, and by implication, total good?

The first problem we encounter is that many people don't believe there is a chief good that objectively applies to all people everywhere. There are a plethora of possibilities about how we can live our lives, and none of them should be questioned (unless they are harmful to others). Then there is this matter of our ignorance. It's not popular to speak negatively of human nature, but we must acknowledge our impoverished intellectual condition and face up to our deficiencies. If we are ignorant of our ignorance, then how much more ignorant can we be?

Actually, there is a good theological reason for this. Our revolt against God is the reason for the blindness of our minds and hearts — theologians call it the *noetic* or intellectual effects of sin. We don't know who God is. We also are confused about the origin and nature of the universe. We don't know where we are in terms of our location here on earth. We are puzzled about who we are as persons and why we are even here. We don't know what's gone wrong with the world or what remedy there might be. Life is one great big blooming, buzzing confusion, to borrow a phrase from William James.

The Bible addresses our cognitive incompetencies frequently. In the Old Testament, the prophet Jeremiah is blunt about our blindness: "Every man is stupid, devoid of knowledge" (10:14). He continues in verse 23: "I know, O Lord, that a man's way is not in himself; Nor is it in a man who walks to direct his steps." One reason for this, he says, is that we have forgotten God "and trusted in falsehood" (Jer. 13:25). This "weeping" prophet,

11. C. S. Lewis, "First and Second Things," in *God in the Dock: Essays on Theology and Ethics*, ed. Walter Hooper (Grand Rapids: Eerdmans, 1970), p. 280.

as he is known, sums up our destitute mental condition in these straight-forward words:

> The heart is more deceitful than all else
> And is desperately sick;
> Who can understand it? (Jer. 17:9)

In the New Testament, Jesus alluded to our overall intellectual short-comings when, in speaking to religious leaders, he said, "If a blind man guides a blind man, both will fall into a pit" (Matt. 15:14). He knew we lived in darkness, and for this reason he claimed to be the light of the world, so that in him we might have the light of life (John 8:12).

Paul in Romans 1:18-25 says we suppress the truth in unrighteousness, our speculations about life are futile, and our hearts are foolish and dark-ened. We have exchanged the truth about God for a lie. Still, we think we are wise, even though we're deceived! In 1 Corinthians 1, Paul also teaches that the world's wisdom, of which it is unreasonably proud, is ultimately foolishness, since it omits the knowledge of God (vv. 18-31). In the second chapter of this letter, he states that spiritual truth is foolishness to us and we cannot understand it because of our unspiritual condition. In 2 Corin-thians 4:4, Paul adds the thought that demonic powers have also blinded our minds to prevent us from knowing the truth about Christ. Finally, in Ephesians 4:17-19, Paul teaches that we live in mental futility, darkness, and ignorance, along with hardness of heart. Overall, these texts give us a realistic, if depressing, description of our cognitive condition. It's cer-tainly not very flattering.

This biblical teaching helps explain why many prominent thinkers over the centuries have also acknowledged the difficulty we have in dis-covering and knowing the truth. Plato, for example, said we are foolishly deceived about reality, as if we were all born in a darkened cave. Aristotle taught that though we all long to know, we are seriously perplexed when it comes to knowing the means and ends of all our actions. Ancient skep-tics asserted that neither our senses nor our reason are capable of knowl-edge as trustworthy guides to truth. Augustine stated that the human race has fallen into a terrifying abyss of rebellion against God that gener-ates all our errors and wrong desires. Thomas Aquinas acknowledged the weaknesses of the human intellect that must be healed and completed by God's grace if we are to know and believe the truth. John Calvin asserted that the fallen mind is lost as if it were in a labyrinth; he called it an "idol factory" that leads us astray. Francis Bacon argued that our minds are subservient to false intellectual gods that prevent us from discovering the truth. Immanuel Kant believed that our minds are limited to knowing how things appear to us and not as they are in themselves. Friedrich Nietzsche was convinced that our personal perspectives were all we could know about life. Finally, pragmatist Richard Rorty has argued that "truths" do not mirror reality, but are merely practical tools we need to complete our tasks. The skeptical motto of the French humanist Michel Montaigne sums up this survey rather nicely: *"Que sais-je"* — "What do I know?"

If we are incarcerated in a kind of knowledge prison, we can understand why there is so much jibber-jabber about the happy life. As Henry Drummond put it, "half the world is on the wrong scent in pursuit of happiness."[12] Drummond was probably rather generous in limiting the hoodwinked to only half of us!

It's easy to traverse the crowded pathway to happiness, since everybody, it seems, is walking there. The next thing you know, however, you realize you are plodding down the proverbial boulevard of broken dreams. Jesus gave the warning: "for the gate is wide and the way is broad that leads to destruction, and there are many who enter through it" (Matt. 7:13). Your family and friends, your acquaintances and contacts, however winsome or persuasive they may be, just might be the deluded crew leading you straight into a ditch. Or if you prefer to take the credit all by yourself, then you might ask, as Augustine once did, "what am I to myself but a guide to my own self-destruction?"[13]

**Cultural Reasons for Our Ignorance**  Not only are we unconscious of our chief good for theological reasons; what we falsely imagine the happy life to be is also nurtured by "the informing ambience" that governs the

12. Henry Drummond, *The Greatest Thing in the World* (New York: Thomas Y. Crowell Company Publishers, n.d.), p. 16. I do not mean to suggest that various thinkers, past or present, have not discovered and conveyed some things about beatitude that are helpful. They have. But I am asserting that though occasionally apt, they lack the proper framework and deeper insights we need to make better sense of our happiness deficit and what to do about it.

13. Augustine, *Confessions*, trans., intro., notes Henry Chadwick, Oxford World's Classics (New York: Oxford University Press, 1992) p. 52 (§4.1).

places where we live.[14] Our situation is aggravated by at least three additional factors. First is the multiplicity of worldview perspectives on happiness surrounding us. Second is the influential content of our culture, especially of the popular kind. Third, there is the resulting confusion of real and apparent goods. All three of these factors frustrate our discovery of the happy life.

First, *views of happiness don't arise out thin air, but are derived from the content of basic worldviews.* Ideas about happiness arise from worldview convictions about God, reality, humanity, truth, goodness, history, death, and other important issues of life. The possibility of a "feasible felicity," says Wilfred McClay, *"is a matter of having the right expectations,"* and having the right expectations depends upon a view of the world. "In a word," McClay states, "what we believe about the world's structure and meaning will determine what we think happiness is, and how we can act to gain it for ourselves. What we *believe* provides the basic structure of what we *expect.*"[15]

Sigmund Freud's materialism and C. S. Lewis's Christian theism, for example, made significant theoretical and practical differences in their respective outlooks on life and views of happiness. According to Armand Nicholi, "When we observe Freud's life and the life of Lewis before and after his conversion, we can't help but observe how one's worldview has a profound impact on one's capacity to experience happiness."[16] Worldviews and happiness views are joined together such that this matter of mirth depends on whether we are theists, deists, pantheists, polytheists, atheists, materialists, nihilists, existentialists, spiritualists, pagans, and so on. Each hypothesis about the world logically entails a notion of the happy life, as this chart suggests:

14. Wendell Berry, "Imagination in Place," in *The Way of Ignorance and Other Essays* (Emeryville, Calif.: Shoemaker & Hoard, 2005), p. 48.

15. Wilfred M. McClay, "The Paradox of the Pursuit of Happiness," *Implications: Reflections and Provocations on Faith and Life* (December 2006). Available at: www.ttf.org/index/journal/detail/paradox-of-happiness (accessed March 27, 2007). This is an abridged version of McClay's "A Short History of Happiness," also available at: www.ttf.org/index/journal/detail/short-history-of-happiness.

16. Dr. Armand M. Nicholi Jr., *The Question of God: C. S. Lewis and Sigmund Freud Debate God, Love, Sex, and the Meaning of Life* (New York: The Free Press, 2002), p. 125.

| Worldview | View of Happiness |
|---|---|
| Theism | Loving God as Creator and Redeemer |
| Deism | Be good, revere a transcendent God |
| Pantheism | Living in harmony with the divine cosmos |
| Polytheism | Placating the gods and goddesses |
| Naturalism | Exalting self and enjoying the world |
| Materialism | Pleasures and consumption |
| Existentialism | Authenticity by choices |
| Spiritualism | Consciousness expansion, meditation |
| Paganism | Devotion to gods of self, sex, the occult, the environment, technology, etc. |

The diversity of prominent worldviews in our culture explains why we are inundated by so many outlooks on happiness — and hence our bewilderment. This situation begs the question about the truthfulness of any of them. Does any worldview get it right? For our purposes, this question leads directly to a second one: Does any worldview provide a viable view of the happy life? These questions have implications for each of us. What is your worldview, and what does it say about happiness? Now is the time to do some perhaps overdue introspection, since, as Socrates put it, "the unexamined life is not worth living." G. K. Chesterton didn't necessarily have happiness in mind when he wrote about the importance of worldviews, but what he has to say has a direct effect on it:

> But there are some people, nevertheless — and I am one of them — who think that the most practical and important thing about a man is still his view of the universe. . . . We think the question is not whether the theory of the cosmos affects matters, but whether in the long run, anything else affects them.[17]

Second, *immersion in contemporary culture, especially of the popular kind, radically influences our perceptions of happiness.* With worldview assumptions in the background, our cultures feed us a steady diet of messages and images about the good life that we are more than eager to consume. Culture is like a buffet line, offering us a variety of items to fulfill our hunger and

---

17. G. K. Chesterton, *Heretics,* in *The Complete Works of G. K. Chesterton,* ed. David Dooley, vol. 1 (San Francisco: Ignatius Press, 1986), p. 41.

thirst for happiness. Various selections on the cultural menu can gratify just about every taste and desire. It takes so little to entice a starving or dehydrated person to eat and drink! As Proverbs 27:7 says,

> A sated man loathes honey,
> But to a famished man any bitter thing is sweet.

If this proverb is referring to spiritual matters, it suggests that we famished ones have been offered many bitter things in sweet disguises to satisfy our contentment cravings. To borrow words from a story about Elisha in the Old Testament, "There is death in the pot" (2 Kings 4:40). At least Elisha's companions could tell what they were eating.

Yet we seem oblivious to the waste we are consuming. "One of the most salient features of our culture," writes philosopher Harry Frankfurt, "is that there is so much bullshit."[18] Yes, you read that right — there is so much "bullshit" in our culture.

Now please don't think me profane in quoting this — it's actually quite biblical. That word might actually be used in the most appropriate translation of Philippians 3:8. There Paul refers to the natural and spiritual privileges of his culture that once served as the sources of meaning and purpose in his life as basically "bullshit." "More than that," writes the Apostle, "I count all things to be loss in view of the surpassing value of knowing Christ Jesus my Lord, for whom I have suffered the loss of all things, and count them but *rubbish* in order that I may gain Christ." The italicized word in Greek is *skubala,* and it is rather politely translated in English as "refuse," "dung," or by the word "rubbish," as it is here. In fact, *skubala* is an offensive term that refers to the muck of excrement, rotten food, decomposing corpses, dirt, and trash: "Nastiness and decay are the constant elements of its meaning; it is a coarse, ugly, violent word implying worthlessness, uselessness, and repulsiveness."[19] If we use it in this verse, we can understand what Paul's culture promoted as the means to happiness, and how Paul himself, once he knew and believed differently, regarded it all.

For Frankfurt, "bullshit" proliferates in a culture when people are forced to talk about things without knowing what they are talking about.

---

18. Harry G. Frankfurt, *On Bullshit* (Princeton: Princeton University Press, 2005), p. 1.

19. *The New International Dictionary of New Testament Theology,* vol. 1, s.v. "Dirt, Filth, Refuse." This description was written by J. I. Packer.

It spreads when skepticism flourishes and the possibility of knowing objective truth is denied. "It is just this lack of connection to a concern for the truth — " Frankfurt says, "this indifference to how things really are — that I regard as the essence of bullshit."[20] Television satirist Stephen Colbert calls this same condition "truthiness," or the tendency to accept something as true not because it has rational support, but rather on intuition because it feels good and fits with or confirms our prejudices.[21]

Drawing on this, I propose that most of the views on happiness we get from our culture are "bullshit" ("truthiness," you have to admit, doesn't have nearly the same thrust). Many people are talking about this topic without knowing what they are talking about. Many people are telling us what happiness is without caring about the truth. Relativism and skepticism have fostered a pragmatic mindset that is more concerned about what works than what's right. We live in a "Pinocchio nation"[22] and have built our lives on lies. How odd it is that we rarely notice. Fish don't realize they are wet, and we apparently don't realize what we are swimming in, either. Surely it's time to take notice, to save the human fish from drowning.[23] Does anyone have the courage to address this situation? Apparently Frankfurt does:

> The realms of advertising and public relations, and the nowadays closely related realm of politics, are replete with instances of bullshit so unmitigated that they can serve among the most indisputable and classic paradigms of the concept. And in these realms there are exquisitely sophisticated craftsmen who — with the help of advanced and demanding techniques of market research, of public opinion polling, of psychological testing, and so forth — dedicate themselves tirelessly to getting every word and image they produce exactly right.[24]

20. Frankfurt, *On Bullshit*, pp. 63-64, 33-34.

21. Colbert's notion of "truthiness" was discussed by Rod Dreher, "Fact or Fiction?" *The Dallas Morning News*, June 24, 2007, Section P, pp. 1, 4-5. For more information on this trendy term, see http://www.macmillandictionary.com/New-Words/060213-truthiness.htm (accessed June 26, 2007).

22. Devlin Donaldson and Steve Wamberg, *Pinocchio Nation: Embracing Truth in a Culture of Lies* (Colorado Springs: Pinon Press, 2001).

23. I have borrowed the idea about saving fish from drowning from the title of a novel by Amy Tan, *Saving Fish from Drowning* (New York: G. P. Putnam's Sons, Penguin Group, 2005).

24. Frankfurt, *On Bullshit*, pp. 22-23.

Popular culture is particularly responsible for the proliferation of much of the refuse that surrounds us, especially in the way it communicates perceptions of the happy life. Though parents and the home, clergy and the church, and teachers and the schools retain some influence in shaping minds, hearts, and lives today, especially those of the young, a virtually omnipresent popular culture — administered so powerfully through the media of television, music, movies, magazines, the internet, and so on — often outdoes them all! Furthermore, popular culture is fueled by a prevailing advertising industry that not only sells products and generates astounding wealth, but also more importantly shapes our identities and desires and profoundly influences our lives.[25]

Celebrities — over which we have "gone goofola"[26] — are too often our true authority figures, with real but unrecognized parental, clerical, and educational influence across the whole cultural gamut. What they think, say, do, and wear frequently affect our thoughts, words, deeds, and fashions as well. As role models for young and old alike, they establish mindsets, shape dreams, motivate pursuits, and prompt behaviors. We also adopt their very projections of the happy life. Evoking the language of worship, Amanda Parsons says, "Those of us who are fans, we use these celebrity lives in ways that transform our own. I sometimes think that these are our gods and goddesses, these are our icons, and their stories become kind of parables for how to lead our lives."[27]

As parents, clergy, and educators in disguise, celebrities teach a specific curriculum, even though we rarely if ever recognize their words, stories, songs, and performances as such. They train us well about things like sex, food, fashion, money, possessions, achievement, prestige, and power. Since their teachings come through a variety of creative means — Plato thought the arts were the most morally and socially influential of all means of persuasion — they have unique power to shape the mental and moral imaginations of their devoted student-fans. That's us!

The pressure to give in to the sway of popular culture is intensified by the implicit grading scale that subtly assesses all of us in terms of our so-

25. See Sam Van Eman, *On Earth as it is in Advertising: From Commercial Hype to Gospel Hope* (Grand Rapids: Brazos Press, 2005).

26. Steve Allen, quoted in Craig Detweiler and Barry Taylor, *A Matrix of Meanings: Finding God in Popular Culture*, Engaging Culture Series, ed. William A. Dyrness and Robert K. Johnston (Grand Rapids: Baker Academic, 2003), p. 89.

27. Quoted in Detweiler and Taylor, *A Matrix of Meanings*, p. 91.

cial, moral, physical, economic, and sexual standing. It's basically a peer-pressure, pass/fail system of evaluation. If you fit in, you pass; if you don't fit in, you fail. Better yet, if you pass and fit in, you're cool and accepted. Worse yet, if you don't pass and fail to fit in, you're a loser and a reject. The pressure from all four points of the social compass to conform our lives and search for the good life to the mindset, values, and behaviors promoted by popular culture is virtually irresistible.

Now please don't misunderstand me: this is not a plea to reject all expressions of popular culture outright. Far from it. Cultural engagement is good, but it has to be done with wisdom and discernment. Jesus, after all, didn't run from the culture of this world; rather, he became human "and moved into the neighborhood," as a paraphrase of John 1:14 puts it.[28] Furthermore, God's common grace endows all people regardless of their spiritual condition with extraordinary gifts, talents, and abilities in every department of life. This widespread, unmerited favor of God accounts for the creative, fruitful labors of so many people in the world and for the genuine expressions of truth, goodness, and beauty we see and enjoy — even, yes, in popular culture.

Still, a considerable amount of falsehood, evil, and ugliness have polluted the cultural waters we regularly imbibe, especially affecting younger people and shaping their dreams for a happy life. As the Roman poet Horace once remarked,

> New vessels will for long retain the taste
> Of what is first poured into them.[29]

If hot coffee is the first drink poured into a new beverage container, any liquid dispensed from it thereafter — like water at a picnic — will retain the aroma and flavor of coffee. Likewise, the cultural content that is poured early on into the minds and imaginations of young people will indelibly affect them. Conscientious parents do their best to guard their children's cultural intake, recognizing its power to lastingly form their hearts and minds. As essayist and mother Caitlin Flanagan wrote in the January 2006 edition of *The Atlantic*, "The 'it takes a village' philosophy is a joke,

---

28. *The Message* by Eugene Peterson.

29. Quoted in Augustine, *Concerning the City of God against the Pagans*, trans. (1972) Henry Bettenson, intro. (1984) John O'Meara (New York: Penguin Books, 1984, reprint 1987), p. 8 (§1.3).

because the village is now so polluted and so desolate of commonly held, child-appropriate moral values that my job as a mother is not to rely on the village, but to protect my children from it."[30] The best of parents face an extraordinary challenge to keep their kids from being inundated by an ever coarsening and destructive popular culture. Depictions of the eroticized young female and the perpetually adolescent, macho male in the PBS Frontline video "Merchants of Cool" demonstrate the media's decisive power to shape the aspirations and dispositions of young people with alarming clarity.[31]

Older folks are not immune to its influence, either. In fact, adults are just as susceptible in mind, heart, and body to the swamp of popular culture as their younger counterparts are. Judge not the younger, lest the older be judged! Popular culture is a great leveler in terms of its influence, regardless of age. The bottom line is this: popular culture is notoriously potent and a major source of the "bullshit" that shapes our lives and influences our understanding of the happy life.

The third factor that affects our take on the happy life is the outcome of the previous two. The variety of worldview perspectives on happiness and the weight of our culture context *often causes us to confuse real and apparent goods*. We must beware of happiness look-a-likes. There are a lot of really good impersonators out there. We can all too easily confuse what we desire with what is desirable, satisfy the superficial and starve the essential traits of our nature, love absolutely what we should love relatively, and love relatively what we should love absolutely. We can be on a fool's errand after fool's gold. As William Cowper writes, "What is base no polish can make sterling."[32] The psalmist's question is best: "How long will you love what is worthless and aim at deception?" (Ps. 4:2). U2's lyrics convey the inevitable result: "I still haven't found what I'm looking for."[33] Fooled as we are about the happy life, is it any wonder that we succumb in our stupidity to disordered love?

30. Caitlin Flanagan, " Are You There, God? It's Me, Monica," *The Atlantic*, January 2006.

31. Information on "Merchants of Cool" is available at: http://www.pbs.org/wgbh/pages/frontline/shows/cool/ where it can be viewed at no charge. Accessed May 29, 2007.

32. William Cowper, "The Winter Walk at Noon," Book 6 in *The Task*, in *Cowper: Poetical Works*, ed. H. S. Milford, 4th ed., corrections and additions Norma Russell (London: Oxford University Press, 1967), p. 241 (lines 989-90).

33. U2, "I Still Haven't Found What I'm Looking For," *The Joshua Tree*, Island Records Inc., 1987.

## Disordered Love

*"O why are we so haggard at the heart,*
*so care-coiled, care-killed . . . so cogged, so cumbered."*

Gerard Manley Hopkins,
"The Leaden Echo and the Golden Echo"[34]

As we discussed in chapter one, out of extravagant love God created us to be happy in a proper relationship with him and his creation — our chief and total good. Our fallen condition has done nothing but increase the fervency of our quest to regain the felicity we lost when we rejected God and went our own way. As we have seen so far in this chapter, both sin and our social setting eclipse our knowledge of the happy life. Now we tend to think that we can find it in this world on its own by ourselves without God, especially through the things we love.[35] When we detect our limitations, feel needy or incomplete, or have a *Sehnsucht* experience, we attach ourselves in love to various things we hope and pray will supply the happiness we desire and satisfy that mysterious longing that has been summoning us from afar.

Pascal understood our situation well. Recognizing that we substitute astronomical bodies, food, animals, sex, science, pleasure, and many other things for God, he writes, "He [God] only is our true good, and since we have forsaken him, it is a strange thing that there is nothing in nature which has not been serviceable in taking his place. . . . And since man has lost the true good, everything can appear equally good to him . . . though so opposed to God, to reason, and to the whole course of nature."[36]

There are many things we can love, and all of them fit our nature and meet our needs. We need and love other *people* to offset loneliness and provide companionship. We need and love *places* to offset homelessness and

---

34. Gerard Manley Hopkins, "The Leaden Echo and the Golden Echo," in *A Hopkins Reader*, ed. and intro. John Pick (Garden City, N.Y.: Image Books, Doubleday & Company, Inc., 1966), p. 68.

35. My discussion of disordered love is indebted at several points to Samuel E. Stumpf's analysis of this theme in his *Philosophy: History and Problems*, 4th ed. (New York: McGraw-Hill, 1971), pp. 144-46.

36. Blaise Pascal, *Pensées*, trans. W. F. Trotter, *Great Books of the Western World*, ed. Robert Maynard Hutchins, vol. 33 (Chicago: William Benton, Publisher, Encyclopedia Britannica Inc., 1952), p. 244 (#425).

afford a sense of belongingness and security. We need and love *things* like food that satisfies our hunger, water that quenches our thirst, houses that provide shelter, clothing that supplies covering and protection. We need and love *rest, recreation, and play* to overcome weariness and boredom and to supply experiences of adventure and excitement. We need and love *ideas* for our minds to displace ignorance, and *work* to make meaningful contributions through our lives. We also naturally love, nourish, and cherish *ourselves*. Our love for *animals* belongs here as well. Human life is a coupling life.[37] We want to become one with the thing we love, to be joined intimately to whatever we believe will bring us happiness, peace, and joy.

All these things we need and love are good because God in his goodness made them. All these things are also *delectable*, since they possess a God-given attractiveness that naturally draws us to them. All the entities in God's creation are legitimate objects of our love and valid sources of satisfaction if we understand them correctly and love them *in the right way*.

Each thing we love is different because of the way God made it. According to Augustine, "There is a scale of value stretching from earthly to heavenly realities, from the visible to the invisible; and the inequality between these goods makes possible the existence of them all."[38] God is one thing, angels are another, as are people, terriers, red oaks, squash, rocks, and dirt. Each item fits in God's overall scheme of creation. The nature of things in the hierarchy is unchangeable, and so is the kind of satisfaction it can provide when we are related to it through love.

Because of these actual differences in things, the outcome of loving each actual thing will be different. There is a divinely designed fit between our needs, the character of the things that can satisfy them, and the way we should love them in order to be satisfied. Even though each thing God made is good, delightful, legitimate, and a source of satisfaction as an object of our love, we "must not expect more from it than its unique nature can provide."[39] We must give love and praise to things apportioned to their worth.[40]

Problems don't arise because we need things, or because we love

37. Augustine, *On the Trinity*, trans. Arthur West Haddan, revised, annotated, intro. W. G. T. Shedd, *Nicene and Post-Nicene Fathers*, ed. Philip Schaff, First Series, vol. 3 (Peabody, Mass.: Hendrickson Publishers, 1994), p. 124 (§8.10.14).

38. Augustine, *The City of God*, pp. 453-44 (§11.22).

39. Stumpf, *Philosophy: History and Problems*, p. 145.

40. Cowper, "The Winter Walk at Noon," book 6 in *The Task*, p. 236 (line 756).

things, or because of the things themselves that we love and need. Problems arise when we fail to grasp the *nature* of the objects that we need and love, the *manner* in which we love them, and the *expectations* we have regarding the outcome of our love. Many of us fail to grasp the unique character of each object, the place it should hold, and the purpose it is to fill in our lives. People "do not observe the value of . . . things in their own sphere and in their own nature; their position in the splendor of the providential order and the contribution they make by their own special beauty to the whole material scheme, as to a universal commonwealth."[41]

Since we fail to recognize what things are, what they are intended to do for us, and how we should love them (thanks to our spiritually and culturally induced ignorance), we love them unintelligently, excessively, and unrealistically — that is, in the manner of disordered love. Augustine used the sobering words "cupidity" and "concupiscence" (*cupiditas* and *concupiscentia*) to describe this misdirected form of "love" and "desire." He used the word "curiosity" (*curiositas*) to refer to a consuming interest in created things without reference to their Creator.[42] If cupidity, concupiscence, or curiosity happens — and if these aren't the distinguishing features of human life, then I don't know what are — then the happiness we hoped to obtain from loving these things the way we do is sure to be frustrated. After all, things can only impart what they possess. Hear the wisdom of Oswald Chambers:

> If we love a human being and do not love God, we demand of him every perfection and every rectitude, and when we do not get it, we become cruel and vindictive; we are demanding of a human being that which he or she cannot give. There is only one Being who can satisfy the last aching abyss of the human heart and that is the Lord Jesus Christ. Why our Lord is apparently so severe regarding every human relationship is because He knows that every relationship not based on loyalty to Himself will end in disaster.[43]

41. Augustine, *The City of God*, pp. 453-54 (§11.22).

42. *Augustine Through the Ages: An Encyclopedia*, ed. Allan D. Fitzgerald, O.S.A. (Grand Rapids: Eerdmans, 1999), s.v. "Concupiscence." For more on the theme of "curiosity" in Augustine, see Paul Griffiths, "The Vice of Curiosity," *Pro Ecclesia* 15 (2006): 47-63.

43. Oswald Chambers, *My Utmost for His Highest* (Westwood, N.J.: Barbour and Company, Inc., 1935), p. 154 (July 30). Available at http://www.myutmost.org/07/0730.html (accessed July 23, 2007).

Furthermore, since the objects we love are made specifically to meet specific needs, we cannot substitute one thing for another and expect fulfillment. We should love God, people, animals, places, and things the way God, people, animals, places, and things should be loved. Nothing but frustration lies ahead if this order is reversed. Happy, then, is the person who comprehends and loves all things in their proper places in their proper ways. As Augustine says, rightly ordered love or charity *(caritas)* is the secret of a holy and fulfilling life:

> [It] requires one to be capable of an objective and impartial evaluation of things; to love things, that is to say, in the *right order* so that you do not love what is not to be loved, or fail to love what is to be loved, or have a greater love for what should be loved less, or an equal love for things that should be loved less or more, or a lesser or greater love for things that should be loved equally.[44]

Unfortunately, we don't understand things as clearly, nor love things as skillfully, as we should. As C. S Lewis points out in *Mere Christianity*, in our feverish attempts to satisfy our cravings for happiness, the fulfillment promised by things like love, travel, or study (add whatever you have tried to this short list) inevitably escapes us. "There are all sorts of things in this world," Lewis writes, "that offer to give it to you, but they never quite keep their promise."

One erroneous response to this disappointment Lewis dubs "The Fool's Way." Such a person, he says, "goes on all his life thinking that if only he tried another woman, or went for a more expensive holiday, or whatever it is, then, this time, he really would catch the mysterious something we are all after."[45] Precisely what is wrong with "The Fool's Way"? The fool's way leaves God out of the picture, for neither physical nature nor human nature on their own are the goods by which we are made complete.

The greatest disordered love of all is our confident but false hope that our love for things in the world, despite their goodness and desirability, can satisfy the need we have for loving union with God. This was the greatest evil in Augustine's pre-Christian life, and its consequences were

44. Augustine, *Teaching Christianity (De Doctrina Christiana), The Works of Saint Augustine for the 21st Century*, intro., trans., notes Edmund Hill, O.P., ed. John E. Rotelle, O.S.A, Part 1, vol. 11 (Hyde Park, N.Y.: New City Press, 1996), p. 118 (§1.27, 28; emphasis added).

45. C. S. Lewis, *Mere Christianity* (New York: The Macmillan Company, 1958), p. 105.

severe. "My sin," he confessed, "consisted in this, that I sought pleasure, sublimity, and truth not in God but in his creatures, in myself and other created beings. So it was that I plunged into miseries, confusions, and error."[46] Given our own ignorance and the deceptions of our surrounding culture, it is very easy for us to be forgetfully intoxicated with the creation but without the Creator, especially as "lovers of self, lovers of money . . . [and] lovers of pleasure rather than lovers of God" (2 Tim. 3:2-4).[47]

## The Two Cities

*"The loves of a few men move the lives of many. History itself seems to turn in one direction rather than another with the turning of an emperor's heart."*

The Great Ideas: A Syntopican, vol. 1, s.v. "Love"

Disordered love is not only a mistake made in our personal lives; it is a major motivating force behind the dynamics of history as well. Two cities created by two kinds of love, Augustine argued, were the engines of the human drama. On the one hand, there is the earthly, self-centered love of the city of man (*civitas mundi*) that pridefully seeks to dominate all things for the sake of its own well-being and glory. On the other hand, there is the heavenly, other-centered love of the city of God (*civitas Dei*) that is directed in humility toward the well-being of others and the glory of God. Augustine's description of these two competing spiritual commonwealths is worth reading all the way through.

> We see then that the two cities were created by two kinds of love: the earthly city was created by self-love reaching the point of contempt for God, the Heavenly City by the love of God carried as far as contempt of self. In fact, the earthly city glories in itself, the Heavenly City glories in the Lord. The former looks for glory from men, the latter finds its highest glory in God. . . . In the former, the lust for domination lords it over its princes as over the nations it subjugates; in the other both those put in authority and those subject to them serve one another in love, the

46. Saint Augustine, *Confessions*, pp. 22-23 (§1.20.31).
47. The image of forgetful intoxication of the creation without its Creator is found in Augustine, *Confessions* (§2.3).

rulers by their counsel, the subjects by obedience. The one city loves its own strength shown in its powerful leaders; the other says to its God: "I will love you, my Lord, my strength."

Consequently, in the earthly city its wise men who live by men's standards have pursued the goods of the body or of their own mind, or of both. . . . In the Heavenly City . . . man's only wisdom is the devotion which rightly worships the true God. . . .[48]

The manner and expectations we have for the things we love, then, is the force that explains what occurs in the world, individually and corporately, both the good and the bad. As we shall see in the next chapter, the results of disordered love in the world are catastrophic — idolatry, the seven deadly sins, addictions, crime, warfare. An entire theology, moral philosophy, and philosophy of history from a Christian perspective is properly rooted in love.

## Ignorance and Disordered Love in the Church

*"Brethren, do not be children in your thinking; yet in evil be in-fants, but in your thinking be mature."*

1 Corinthians 14:20

As we indicated briefly in chapter one, the world's maladies of ignorance and disordered love too often have their mirror image in the church as well — the same problems, just in reverse. People in the world embrace the creation to the exclusion of the Creator, but many in the church embrace the Creator to the exclusion of the creation. In search of the happy life, neither group can figure out how to love God and the world at the same time *well*. If the world's resulting problem is one of hedonism (which worships bodily life and its pleasures), then the church's problem is often one of Gnosticism (which depreciates creation, bodily life, and its pleasures). The world's "this-worldliness" is matched by the church's "other-worldliness." If non-Christians can be so earthly-minded that they are of no heavenly good, then Christians can be so heavenly-minded that they are of no earthly good (forgive the clichés, please). For the complete story,

48. Augustine, *The City of God*, pp. 593-94 (§14.28). See also the discussion in *Augustine Through the Ages: An Encyclopedia*, s.v. "Love."

then, we should say a word about the church's own version of ignorance and disordered love, because they have practical effects.

## Ignorance in the Church

> *"My people are destroyed for lack of knowledge."*
>
> Hosea 4:6

People in the church often lack an understanding of the biblical teaching of creation and the divinely ordained importance and purpose of the material world. Creation isn't the most important teaching in Scripture, but it is the setting for the Christian story. It is the stage upon which the divine drama of creation, the fall, and redemption takes place. God's very good creation is what sin has marred and what Christ has saved. Herman Bavinck's words tell the story succinctly: "And the essence of the Christian religion consists in the reality that the creation of the Father, ruined by sin, is restored in the death of the Son of God and recreated by the grace of the Holy Spirit into a kingdom of God."[49]

In our ignorance of creation we misunderstand ourselves, failing to grasp our *embodiment* as whole persons made in the image and likeness of God. We misconstrue the spiritual role God intended for *food* to play in human experience. We also forget the place of *land* in the purposes of God for Israel, for the church, and in the new creation. We have also lost the significance of Christ's *incarnation* as God in the flesh. We don't understand the character of our future as *resurrected persons*. We are misinformed about the *physical character of eternity,* as we anticipate an insubstantial, heavenly realm in the skies rather than a solid and sublime union of heaven and earth in which God will make all things new.

There are several reasons for our ignorance of the material dimensions of the Christian faith. Biblically, we detach the Old Testament from the New Testament and forget that Christianity is a religion of creation as well as redemption. Theologically, we lose sight of the fact that Jesus is the cosmic Christ who not only redeemed but also created all things, and is the Savior not only of souls but also of bodies and of the entire world as

---

49. Herman Bavinck, *Reformed Dogmatics: Prolegomena*, ed. John Bolt, trans. John Vriend, vol. 1 (Grand Rapids: Baker Academic, 2003), p. 112.

well. Philosophically, we succumb to a destructive dualism that favors the sacred over the secular, the eternal over the temporal, the soul over the body, grace over nature, faith over reason, instead of honoring the wholeness and value of these intrinsically related pairs. Logically, we focus on our favorite components of the Christian faith rather than grasping their meaning in the context of the larger biblical story. Socially, we focus on defending creation against evolution but forget to pay attention to the meaning of what we are so zealous to defend. The bottom line is that the Christian vision of creation is clouded and the church's love for God's world is sadly deficient. This is especially distressing since the teachings enumerated above show that Christianity, of all the world's great religions, is the most materialistic.[50]

## Disordered Love in the Church

> *"Do not handle, do not taste, do not touch!"*
>
> Colossians 2:21

If *slothfulness* is a deficient love for the Creator, then *scornfulness,* I suggest, denotes a deficient love for creation. The word fits, since it refers to a feeling of contempt or disdain for something because of its perceived inferiority or worthlessness. Whether it is the world as the alleged domain of the devil, or the body as the assumed source of temptation, or the culture as the apparent cause of worldliness, or education as the perceived root of error, or history as the supposed scene of corruption, people in the church have been inclined to dismiss these realms as undeserving of their time, interest, and attention in light of kingdom work, higher callings, and heavenly perspectives. Grieving over the loss of a loved one is a case in point. If we grieve vigorously, it might betray an excessive, earthly love for some creature or some aspect of creation. Grief, presumably, is not a sign of godliness.

Augustine, for example, felt ashamed of his bereavement over the death of his childhood friend and even for the loss of his own mother. When his young companion died of a fever, Augustine confessed "the

---

50. William Temple, quoted in Richard H. Schmidt, *Glorious Companions: Five Centuries of Anglican Spirituality* (Grand Rapids: Eerdmans, 2002), p. 262.

uncleanness of such affections" for him in his *Confessions* because his grief
was allegedly too great. When his mother died, he momentarily held back
his tears and checked his son's weeping for his deceased grandmother.
Ashamed at his human emotions, and grieved at his grief as an unshak-
able habit, Augustine eventually broke down for less than an hour, making
his tears for his mother a pillow for his heart. But he wept only before
God, since he was convinced that others observing him would misinter-
pret his sorrow as unchristian. Nonetheless, he still felt constrained to
confess his private tears and the sin of his grief to God, and to ask the readers of his *Confessions* not to despise him, but to pray for him for having too
much earthly affection for his mother.[51]

This, I'm afraid, illustrates scornfulness as a disordered love of *deficiency* for God's creatures and creation. Christians do not grieve as those
who have no hope. Still, they grieve, and they do so because they recognize that what they had and loved was worth having and loving, and what
they have now lost is worthy of heartache. Job reacted like this to his
losses. So did Jesus. Nicholas Wolterstorff's *Lament for a Son* and C. S.
Lewis's *A Grief Observed* show us a better way.[52]

In addition to this depreciation of grief as symptomatic of scornfulness, there are other unnatural, dehumanizing tendencies that grow out of
a failure to rightly love the creation in relation to its Creator. In *angelism*,
we denigrate the body and its needs in an attempt to become more like
non-physical beings of pure spirit. In *legalism*, we feel the need to add culturally based if not unbiblical requirements to our list of Christian duties
to produce an enhanced if not unrealistic version of holiness before God.
In *pietism*, we misunderstand the comprehensive character of biblical faith
and limit the application of Christian spirituality to the practice of personal spiritual disciplines such as prayer, Bible study, fellowship, and
evangelism. In *dualism*, we separate ourselves from secular and temporal
affairs for exclusive involvement in church-related activities of eternal significance. In *stoicism*, we attempt to live in an unaffected manner above the
historical circumstances of life to show ourselves to be more than conquerors in Christ. In *pragmatism*, we highlight achievements and results
but forget that truth is foundational to genuine humanity, success, and

51. See the stories in Augustine's *Confessions*, §4.6 and 12.9
52. Nicholas Wolterstorff, *Lament for a Son* (Grand Rapids: Eerdmans, 1987); C. S. Lewis,
*A Grief Observed*, new ed. (San Francisco: HarperSanFrancisco, 2001).

fruitfulness. In *barbarism,* we assume that our lack of cultural concern or intellectual naiveté is a badge of spiritual honor.

These are seven deadly sins of a false, disembodied spirituality — traits unfortunately honored in many Christian communities, but erroneously based on an insufficient love for God's handiwork and its proper place in the happy life. This has resulted in costly cultural disengagement. It has also limited the expression of the fullness of believers' God-given humanity. It has been an example of a diminished, unappealing view of Christianity in the eyes of a critical world. If I choose to follow Christ, must I become an angelic, legalistic, pietistic, dualistic, stoic, pragmatic, and barbaristic sort of super-saint? God forbid!

## The War of the Mind and Heart

*"Ideas are dangerous."*

G. K. Chesterton, *Heretics*[53]

The human mind and heart, then, are a battlefield of ideas and affections, the greatest Armageddon, the true holy war. There are no conscientious objections or exemptions. This is the chief struggle over the chief good. We are blinded to it in our sin, and we are deceived about it by the droppings of our cultures. Because we fail to understand things as they are, we love in a wrong way and with false hopes. In our blindness, our loves are woefully disordered. As we think in our hearts, so are we (Prov. 23:7).

A parallel problem occurs in the church, except in reverse. Christians too often fail to understand and love the creation just as non-Christians fail to love the Creator. Whether it's a disordered love of excess, as in the world, or of deficiency, as among believers, an inordinacy of slothfulness or scornfulness, "Look what a mess we've made of love!"[54]

In this battle of battles, waged naively and unsuccessfully, there are, of course, casualties. Many of us are seriously wounded in the fight. Our ignorance and wrong desires — powerful and pathological as they are — have defaced us and left our lives in shambles.

---

53. G. K. Chesterton, *Heretics* (New York: Devin Adair, 1950), p. 299.
54. See the lead quote at the beginning of this chapter.

## CHAPTER THREE

# Disordered Lives:
# Seven (and Even More) Ways to Die

*"Precious, precious, precious!" Gollum cried. "My Precious! O my
Precious!"*

J. R. R. Tolkien, *The Return of the King*

## Introduction

Gollum was a Hobbit, though he certainly didn't look like one. According
to J. R. R. Tolkien's description in the prologue to *The Fellowship of the Ring*,
Hobbits were a pleasant sort of folk, short in stature to be sure. They
"dressed in bright colours, being notably fond of yellow and green; but
they seldom wore shoes, since their feet had tough leathery soles and were
clad in thick curling hair, much like the hair of their heads, which was
commonly brown. . . . Their faces were as a rule good-natured rather than
beautiful, broad, bright-eyed, red-cheeked, with mouths apt to laughter,
and to eating and drinking. And laugh they did, and eat, and drink, often
and heartily, being fond of simple jests at all times, and of six meals a day
(when they could get them). They were hospitable and delighted in parties,
and in presents, which they gave away freely and eagerly accepted."[1] This

---

1. J. R. R. Tolkien, "Prologue," *The Lord of the Rings* (Boston: Houghton Mifflin Company,
1994), p. 2. Page numbers in parentheses are from this book.

appealing description makes Hobbithood seem enviable. But it doesn't sound anything like Gollum.

Gollum's original name was Trahald. It meant "burrowing or worming in" and was anglicized as Sméagol. He became so altered in how he looked and lived that he was virtually unrecognizable as a member of the Stoor breed of Hobbits. By the time he encountered Bilbo and Frodo, he was extremely thin and wiry, black-skinned and flatfooted, with sparse, wispy hair, long thin hands, and bulging, insipid eyes. His acute hearing compensated for his poor vision. He was strong, and he could move about and climb as silently and quickly as a fly.[2] In Tolkien's words, "He was a loathsome little creature: he paddled a small boat with his large flat feet, peering with pale luminous eyes and catching blind fish with his long fingers, and eating them raw. He ate any living thing, even orc, if he could catch it without a struggle" (p. 11).

What accounts for Gollum's transformation from a homey Hobbit into such a monstrosity? Why did he become so corrupt, misshapen, and flat-out ugly? The answer is this: his disordered love. Gollum's obsession for the One Ring, the Great Ring, the Ruling Ring of power overtook him and disfigured his entire being. "My precious," he called it, and he talked to it, even when it wasn't with him (p. 11). At the very end, Sam Gamgee can only marvel at "the agony of Gollum's shriveled mind and body, enslaved to that Ring" (p. 923). His addiction to his "precious" prevailed, and it thoroughly debauched him.

As Gandalf the wizard declared, "He could not get rid of it. He had no will left in the matter" (p. 54). Then the unthinkable happened. Gollum lost the ring inadvertently, and it fell into Frodo's hands with a commission to destroy it. Gollum's passion for his treasure overcame every hatred and fear, and he ventured out of his cave to intercept it before Frodo could complete his task. At long last, when they arrived together at Mount Doom, Gollum's ghastly, yet pitiful, nature is disclosed in a final fight with Frodo, as Sam looks on:

> Suddenly Sam saw Gollum's long hands draw upwards to his mouth; his white fangs gleamed, and then snapped as they bit. Frodo gave a cry, and there he was, fallen upon his knees at chasm's edge. But Gollum,

2. Robert Foster, *The Complete Guide to Middle-Earth: From The Hobbit to The Silmarillion* (New York: Ballantine Books, a Del Rey Book, 1971, 1978), p. 218.

dancing like a mad thing, held aloft the ring, a finger still thrust within its circle. It shone now as if verily it was wrought of living fire.

"Precious, precious, precious!" Gollum cried. "My Precious! O my Precious!" And with that, even as his eyes were lifted up to gloat on his prize, he stepped too far, toppled, wavered for a moment on the brink, and then with a shriek he fell. Out of the depths came his last wail *Precious*, and he was gone (p. 925).

Mythical characters like Gollum — who "have their insides on the outside" and "are visible souls"[3] — possess a remarkable power of illumination. Gollum's distorted life in body and soul is a poignant example for us of the consequences of disordered love. His inverted affections had mastered and maligned him. His "precious" did him in. What he was inwardly he became outwardly — a weird, ugly, unhappy, and ultimately tragic little figure, destroyed in his own desires. As we are about to see, there's a little, or perhaps lot, of Gollum in all of us.

## Gollums 'R' Us

*"I have not much hope that Gollum can be cured before he dies, but there is a chance of it."*

Gandalf in J. R. R. Tolkien's *The Fellowship of the Ring*[4]

Because of his obsession with the ring, Gollum was no longer the Hobbit he was supposed to be. Neither are we the kind of people we are supposed to be when our ignorance and disordered loves generate multi-faceted disorders in our lives. Should we fail to refer all things to God, we can easily become obsessed with a variety of "precious" objects in their apparent grandiosity as if they were the lucky charms of our happiness. If we are convinced that someone or something is what we have been looking for all our lives, you can be sure we will pursue it full throttle with high hopes of success. If it yields to our quest, then we enjoy what it has to offer, at

3. C. S. Lewis, "Tolkien's *The Lord of the Rings*," in *C. S. Lewis on Stories and Other Essays on Literature*, ed. Walter Hooper (New York: A Harvest/HBJ Book — Harcourt Brace Jovanovich Publishers, 1982, 1966), p. 89.

4. J. R. R. Tolkien, *The Fellowship of the Ring*, in *The Lord of the Rings* (Boston: Houghton Mifflin Company, 1994), p. 58.

least for a while. If our love is unrequited and we remain unsatisfied, then we redouble our efforts until we obtain our final goal. Whether the success of our search is short-lived (which it will be) or a partial or total disappointment (that's eventually certain, too), then we become unrelenting until we get what we want, even if, unbeknownst to us, the same letdown awaits us again.

Since finding felicity feels like a matter of life and death, and our very existence depends upon it, we keep on looking, keep on striving, keep on hoping, keep on demanding that something, somewhere will finally work. Is it him? Is it her? Is it this? Is it that? Is it here? Is it there? Is it now? Is it then? What is it? Where is it? In the midst of the experience of needing some happiness somehow, we quietly change, and not normally for the better. Our indefatigable "love" can be transmogrified into a concealed form of cruelty that demands fulfillment. If it festers, it can leave a wide swath of destruction in its path, as C. S. Lewis explains.

> We may give our human loves the unconditional allegiance which we owe only to God. Then they become gods: then they become demons. Then they will destroy us, and also destroy themselves.[5]

In other words, disordered love isn't really love at all when in our diseased hearts it becomes demonic in its demands. If God's love for us and our love for God do not control us, then who knows what we might say or do to insure our self-preservation and to satisfy our mental needs and bodily obsessions, especially since our sense of peace and purpose are dependent upon them? Should these sins convert into habits and addictions, as they often do, they can foster crime or even warfare, if we think violence is necessary to remove obstacles to get what we want. In failing to worship God, then, we open the door to the worst of sins, and all hell breaks loose in our lives and in the world through us.

---

5. C. S. Lewis, *The Four Loves* (New York: Harcourt, Brace, Inc., 1960), pp. 19-20.

## Idolatry

*". . . do not go after other gods to your own harm. . . ."*

Jeremiah 7:6 (E.S.V.)

To be fair, not every disordered love terminates in blatant idolatry. Jumbled-up love can just be, well, jumbled-up love, stopping short of actual hardcore veneration. In fact, the problem may not be too much love for something, but too little love for God by comparison. Again, C. S. Lewis has a good word on this:

> It is probably impossible to love any human being simply too much. We may love him too much in proportion to our love for God; but it is the smallness of our love for God, not the greatness of our love for the man, that constitutes the inordinacy.[6]

Of course, the first two of the Ten Commandments and the Greatest Commandment of all warn us about this lack of love for God and seek to secure his supremacy in our lives.

> You shall have no other gods before Me. You shall not make for yourself an idol, or any likeness of what is in heaven above or on the earth beneath or in the water under the earth. You shall not worship them or serve them; for I, the LORD your God, am a jealous God, visiting the iniquity of the fathers on the children, on the third and the fourth generations of those who hate Me, but showing lovingkindness to thousands, to those who love Me and keep My commandments. (Exod. 20:3-6)

> You shall love the LORD your God with all your heart and with all your soul and with all your might. (Deut. 6:5)

Nonetheless, idolatry, as the chief of sins and the number one cause of God's judgment on people and nations, is still prevalent in the world today. Though some people worship actual idols, its contemporary form is typically more subtle. Frederick Buechner describes it as "ushering God out once and for all through the front door," but then replacing "him with something spirited in through the service entrance." For Buechner,

---

6. Lewis, *The Four Loves*, p. 170.

Idolatry is the practice of ascribing absolute value to things of relative worth. Under certain circumstances, money, patriotism, sexual freedom, moral principles, family loyalty, physical beauty, social or intellectual preeminence, and so on are fine things to have around; but to make them the standard by which all other values are measured, to make them your masters, to look to them to justify your life and save your soul is sheerest folly. They just aren't up to it.[7]

If we show God the exit stage right, then other things will necessarily enter our lives stage left to put a foundation under our feet (that is, until a hardship occurs, and we call upon God as our heavenly butler for a quick fix). Otherwise, we forget God amidst a multitude of legitimate pleasures in life — "Golf is life: The rest is just details." These things excite us and give us a sense of meaning and purpose, until their insufficiency is revealed. Meanwhile, we live as practical atheists rather than as adoring theists, but with a steep price to pay for our defection in the short or long run.

Interestingly enough, the Bible portrays the error of idolatry in sexual and political terms.[8] On the one hand, God is our exclusive *lover,* our only spouse, our true partner. We are bound to him, as it were, by the ties of spiritual marriage. In idolatry, however, we divert our attention and affection, and become intimate with a *rival lover* who breaks up our relationship with God. Idolatry is *spiritual adultery,* and it arouses God's jealousy until he wins us back. Read Ezekiel 16 and 23 for rather torrid descriptions of Israel's spiritual adultery and its results.

On the other hand, God is our ultimate *king,* our real ruler, our exclusive lord. We are bound to him, as it were, by covenant as subjects in his kingdom, and owe him complete loyalty and obedience. In idolatry, however, we divert our allegiance and service, and submit ourselves to a *rival leader* of dubious authority who opposes the rule of God. Idolatry is *political treason,* and it provokes God's judgments until we repent, and acknowledge him as king once again. Read Jeremiah 11 for a blunt description of the results of the political unfaithfulness of God's people.

God, then, is our spouse and sovereign, and claims exclusive rights to our love and loyalty. If we succumb to idolatry, we are guilty of infidelity

7. Frederick Buechner, *Wishful Thinking: A Seeker's ABC,* rev. and exp. ed. (San Francisco: HarperSanFrancisco, 1993), p. 49.

8. *New Dictionary of Biblical Theology,* ed. T. Desmond Alexander and Brian S. Rosner (Downers Grove, Ill.: InterVarsity Press, 2000), s.v. "Idolatry."

and disloyalty, if you will, "sexually" and "politically," as we opt for alternative lovers and lords. Idolatry has many consequences, not the least of which is God's frightening displeasure and judgment. "For the LORD your God is a consuming fire, a jealous God" (Deut. 4:24).

Idolatry is also extraordinarily dangerous and damaging in personal ways. "The gods we worship," said Emerson, "write their names on our faces; be sure of that. Therefore it behooves us to be careful what we worship, for what we are worshipping we are becoming."[9] In the words of the psalmist, "Those who make [idols] . . . will become like them,/Everyone who trusts in them" (Ps. 115:8). Though God made us so that people might see him through us, our idolatry changes our countenance and character, and we reflect the dastardly traits of the false gods we adore. Sooner rather than later, we can take on a Gollum-like visage reflecting the deadliest sins of all.

## The Seven Deadly Sins

*"Seven deadly sins. Seven ways to die."*

from the film *Seven*[10]

The list of the seven deadly sins was originally formulated to protect monks and nuns from misbehavior in monasteries and nunneries. Yet it was quickly apparent that they applied to regular people in everyday life whether they were in religious orders or not. Sin is no respecter of persons. The disorder of idolatry translates naturally into a disordered life of depravity no matter who or where we are.

As a catalog of only seven vices — pride, envy, anger, sloth, avarice or greed, gluttony, and lust — it is obviously not exhaustive in scope. Nonetheless, as Geoffrey Chaucer writes in *The Canterbury Tales,* they are the "principal sins" or "the chief sins and the trunk from which branch all others." Murder, for example, is anger's son. Theft is the daughter of greed. Adultery is the offspring of lust. The seven deadlies are causes, other sins their effects.

---

9. This frequently used quote is attributed to Emerson and is thought to be found in his notebooks, but its precise location is virtually impossible to establish.

10. From The Internet Movie Data Base, http://www.imdb.com/title/tt0114369/taglines (accessed June 5, 2007).

Pride, envy, and anger are primarily internal and spiritual in character, the cold, chilly sins that exalt the self and separate us from others. Since on occasion they seem justifiable, they have an air of respectability. Sloth, avarice, gluttony, lust are bodily in nature. As the so-called warm, torrid, or sultry sins of self-indulgence, they have garnered a more negative reputation.

Though each sin is unique in its character and consequences, they are "all leashed together" to form an intertwining whole, and pride is the source of them all. As Chaucer says, "For from this root [of pride] spring certain branches, as anger, envy, acedia or sloth, avarice . . . gluttony, and lechery. And each of these principal sins has its branches and its twigs. . . ."[11] Pride, then, is the primary cause, and the other sins are its multiple effects.

Most importantly, the seven deadly sins are disordered loves. The seven deadly sins disorder our lives. Pride, envy, and anger flow from an obsession with the self. Avarice, gluttony, and lust originate in excessive love for money, food, and sex. Since these things rank high in our hearts, love for God ranks low, and this deficiency of affection for him is called sloth. If Gollum's ring was his "precious," then these sins disclose what is precious to us as well. Our dear treasure is in our pride, envy, anger, sloth, avarice, gluttony, and lust, and in our treasure we discern our hearts, for where your precious treasure is, there is your heart also (Matt 6:21). On its throne sits the self.

**Pride**   This deadly sin and disordered form of life consists of an immoderate love of self. It is the haughty attitude of people who believe that they are the most important persons in the universe, even though it may be rooted in fear and insecurity. Prideful people feel they are better than others because of their superior abilities, achievements, position, and so on. As a result, they also feel contempt for those beneath them. Pride, in brief, amounts to "inordinate self esteem."[12] As U2's Bono sings, "Some people got way too much confidence baby"![13]

C. S. Lewis points out that pride is "the essential vice, the utmost evil," in relation to which all other sins are mere "fleabites" by comparison. It is,

---

11. Geoffrey Chaucer, *Canterbury Tales*, trans. J. U. Nicolson, illustrated Rockwell Kent, intro. Gordon Hall Gerould (Garden City, N.Y.: Garden City Publishing Company, Inc., 1934), pp. 565-66 (Parson's Tale).

12. *The Compact Edition of the Oxford English Dictionary*, vol. 2, s.v. "Pride."

13. U2, "Original of the Species," from the CD *How to Dismantle an Atomic Bomb*, Interscope Records, 2004.

he says, "the complete anti-God state of mind." If we feel superior to everyone and everything else, if we are consumed by extravagant self-love, and if we think that the universe revolves around our will and ways, then acknowledging God, much less bowing down in humble submission before him, is simply out of the question. Thus Lewis concludes, "As long as you are proud, you cannot know God."[14]

Pride is not only an "anti-God" attitude, but an "anti-others" one as well. In order to elevate ourselves, we must put down our associates and squelch their competition to our supremacy. If we are to be big, then others must be small. If others are made small, then we can be big. Pride, then, is essentially competitive and hostile — it abuses power and isolates us from others. It is a "spiritual cancer," as Lewis says, and it "eats up the very possibility of love, or contentment, or even common sense."[15] The point is clear in the King James Version of Proverbs 13:10: "Only by pride cometh contention."

As its twigs and branches, pride manifests itself in countless ways: in insubordination to God, in unteachability, in unrepentance, in excessive self-confidence, in heroic independence, in disobedience to authority figures, in bragging over one's accomplishments, in demeaning others and their successes, in expecting honor, in refusing it to others, in hiding one's true self and showing a false face, in claiming uncultivated virtues, in presumptuous undertakings, in trusting unreasonably in one's judgments, and on and on. Ironically, it can even "smuggle itself into the very centre of our religious life,"[16] in pride over our religion or religiosity. Pride is an obnoxious offense. How we despise it in other people. How rarely we detect it in ourselves. In Augustine's apt phrase, "For here is great misery, proud man!"[17] If you see yourself in a superior light accompanied by anti-God and/or anti-others states of mind, beware, then, of your *precious* pride.

**Envy** This deadly sin and disordered form of life arises directly out of our pride. As a book of cynical wit, *The Devil's Dictionary* defines "happiness" as "an agreeable sensation arising from contemplating the misery of

14. C. S. Lewis, *Mere Christianity* (New York: The Macmillan Company, 1958), pp. 94, 96.

15. Lewis, *Mere Christianity*, p. 97. This reflection on the competitive nature of pride is derived from pp. 95-96.

16. Lewis, *Mere Christianity*, p. 97.

17. Augustine, *On the Catechising of the Uninstructed*, trans. S. D. F. Salmond, in *Nicene and Post-Nicene Fathers*, ed. Philip Schaff, First Series, vol. 3 (Peabody, Mass.: Hendrickson Publishers, Inc., 1994), p. 287 (§4.8).

another,"[18] but this is really a better definition of envy. The Germans call it *Schadenfreude* — the pleasure we take in the misfortune of others. On the one hand, envious people feel blessed when others mourn, and on the other, they mourn when others are blessed. Why should others enjoy what I don't? Why shouldn't I enjoy what others do?[19] We feel bad when others succeed; we feel better when others fail; we feel best when we succeed and others fail. Soaking self-centeredness is foundational to envy. The poet William Cowper assumes as much:

> Each vainly magnifies his own success.
> Resents his fellow's, wishes it were less.[20]

Envy has both vertical and horizontal trajectories. It resents God as the giver of good gifts, the good gifts he gives, and the ones who get his good gifts. "Is your eye envious because I am generous?" asks Jesus in the parable of the vineyard (Matt. 20:15). As Dorothy Sayers observes, "Envy cannot bear to admire or respect; it cannot . . . be grateful."[21]

You may have felt more than a bit disconsolate when your friends showed up in that beautiful new car, or told you about their three-week vacation, or invited you to see their dream home, or announced that a new baby was on the way (especially if you are desperately trying to get pregnant). The successful can drive the less successful crazy and spur efforts to equal or better them. Janis Joplin's memorable refrain reminds us of our envious bent and the desire we have to settle the score:

> Oh Lord, won't you buy me a Mercedes Benz?
> My friends all drive Porsches, I must make amends.
> Worked hard all my lifetime, no help from my friends,
> So Lord, won't you buy me a Mercedes Benz?[22]

---

18. Ambrose Bierce, *The Devil's Dictionary* (Hertfordshire: Wordsworth Reference, 1996), p. 114.

19. Dorothy Sayers, "The Other Six Deadly Sins," in *The Whimsical Christian: Eighteen Essays* (New York: Collier Books, Macmillan Publishing Company, 1987), p. 171.

20. William Cowper, "Tirocinium: or, A Review Of Schools," in *Cowper: Poetical Works,* ed. H. S. Milford, 4th ed., corrections and additions Norma Russell (London: Oxford University Press, 1934), p. 252 (lines 476-77).

21. Sayers, "The Other Six Deadly Sins," p. 174.

22. "Mercedes Benz," by Janis Joplin, Michael McClure, and Robert Neuwirth, © 1971, renewed © 1999 Strong Arm Music (ASCAP) admin. By Wixen Music Publishing, Inc. All rights reserved.

Envy's destructive strategies are limited only by our imaginations. We can backbite, detract, grumble, murmur, divide, accuse, malign, resent, hate, lie, gossip, invert, belittle, slander, criticize, annoy, listen and assent to libel, damn with faint praise, share secrets, betray weaknesses, and so on. The envious will do whatever it takes to debunk the envied — to pull them down, to raise us up. Debunking others is envy's defining mission, "the consuming desire to have everybody else as unsuccessful as you are."[23] King Saul, for example, couldn't stand it when the women of Israel heaped greater praises on his younger rival David for his military victories than they did for his own. Saul envied David greatly and sought to kill him (1 Sam. 18:7-9, 15-16, 29). Yes, envy can even beget murder. It rarely rests at the emotional stage for long. If you wince or wither at another's success and despise the giver, the gifts, or the gifted, beware of your *precious* envy.

**Anger** This deadly sin and disordered form of life is fueled by pride and envy combined. Its Latin root means "to strangle." Of course, there is such a thing as righteous anger or indignation. It occurs when we are infuriated by wickedness and justly motivated to do something about it.[24] Jesus was rightly incensed at rank unbelief (Mark 9:19) and justly motivated when he cleared the Temple of its desecrators (Mark 11:15-18). In both cases, he was angry at sin, but there was no sin in his anger. As Paul urges us, "be angry and yet do not sin" (Eph. 4:26; cf. Ps. 4:4). We too can react fairly and force-fully to wrong situations in the world for goodness' sake. "The person who is angry," Aristotle said, "at the right things and towards the right people, and also in the right way, at the right time and for the right length of time, is [to be] praised."[25]

On the other hand, as the third of the seven deadlies, unrighteous anger is a selfishly motivated vice, fusing reckless feelings, thoughts, and actions. If we feel we have been ignored, forgotten, bullied, slighted, tricked, humiliated, teased, disrespected, belittled, or wronged — in short, if we feel we have been mistreated in any way — we are filled with anger of varying degrees, and our first thought is to exact vengeance on people who have threatened or hurt us. We plot a course to get even. Though we

---

23. Buechner, *Wishful Thinking: A Seeker's ABC*, p. 24.

24. Chaucer, *The Canterbury Tales*, p. 518 (The Parson's Tale §33).

25. Aristotle, *Nicomachean Ethics*, trans. Terence Irwin (Indianapolis: Hackett Publishing Company, 1985), p. 105 (§4.5).

think our anger serves justice, what we really want is punishment, revenge, or retribution. A viciously angry person "cannot be sated unless somebody is hounded down, beaten, and trampled on, and a savage war dance executed upon the body."[26] As Chaucer said, "truly, almost all the harm that any man does to his neighbor comes from wrath."[27]

Anger is the wrecking-ball of humanity. "An angry man stirs up strife," says Proverbs 29:22, "and a hot-tempered man abounds in transgression." Anger's strife and transgressions — its branches and twigs — include gossip, slander, malice, abusive speech, lying, quarrels, fighting, spousal abuse, divorce, child abuse, parental disrespect, workplace violence, sexual assault, murder, homicide, racism, sexism, terrorism, genocide, warfare, and more. Anger destroys families, friendships, neighborhoods, community groups, churches, cities, and nations. Anger can consume us rather than the objects of our anger. In expressing it, "what you are wolfing down is yourself."[28] How different life on this planet would be if our fury subsided!

In the Sermon on the Mount, Jesus condemns this deadly sin of unjust anger, knowing it can explode verbally and violently in heinous name-calling ("You fool!") and in murder with malice aforethought. Anger is so serious it will condemn you in court and can send you to hell (Matt. 5:21-22). Paul taught that anger and its offspring must be decisively set aside and resolved before the sun goes down (Col. 3:8; Eph. 4:26). If you are filled with rage and it is tempting you to take action, beware your *precious* anger.

**Sloth**   This deadly sin and disordered form of life is a lack of love for God and the things of God. Sloth is not just old-fashioned laziness. It is a distinctively spiritual or religious sin that demotes God's role in our lives and replaces him enthusiastically with other things. It is a sin of spiritual lethargy and dejection. When we are in the throes of spiritual lethargy, God bores us or seems insignificant, whereas other loves capture our interest and attention, excite and energize us. Sloth as spiritual sluggishness is also called the noon-day demon, since we sometimes find it hard to turn to God in much the same way as we find it difficult to return to work after a

---

26. Sayers, "The Other Six Deadly Sins," p. 161.
27. Chaucer, *The Canterbury Tales*, p. 519 (The Parson's Tale §33).
28. Buechner, *Wishful Thinking: A Seeker's ABC*, p. 2.

hearty lunch. In such spiritual dejection, we are disappointed that God is our chief good.[29] Either we feel he has let us down and can no longer be trusted, or we simply prefer that the happy life be found in other things besides him. We don't want God messing with our favorite loves or our busy lives. Sloth prefers a transcendent, deistic God who keeps to himself rather than an immanent, theistic God who is involved in history and human affairs.

Our lack of love for God can make us spiritually lazy, morally negligent, and intellectually idle. Slothful people forget church, avoid Scripture, refuse repentance, rarely pray, reject fellowship, don't witness, shun service, deride duty, rebuff suffering, scorn theology, evade thought or meditation, and in general are repulsed by religion and the religious life. Churchgoers are not immune to the "slugabed sin of sloth," and it seems to be one of the greatest transgressions in our culture of "whatever." In general, sloth "believes in nothing, cares for nothing, seeks to know nothing, interferes with nothing, enjoys nothing, loves nothing, hates nothing, finds purpose in nothing, lives for nothing, and remains alive for there is nothing it would die for."[30] Sloth, then, is a sin of omission in that it fails to find God supremely significant and attractive so as to pursue him enthusiastically.[31]

Sloth also frees us to pursue whatever we truly love in life, heedless of the claims of faith upon us. Since sloth is right in the middle of the seven deadly sins, it is their hinge point — it makes the other six sins possible. By dethroning God and enthroning ourselves, we can be absorbed in greed, gluttony, and lust, or whatever else our hearts desire. Sloth, in other words, makes a self-centered, hedonistic life possible.

We do our own human dignity a grave disservice if we find our fulfillment in things less than God himself. How tragic is the one who finds the meaning of life in a dog rather than in God. How sad to center life in clothes rather than in Christ. Superficiality, after all, is symptomatic of slothfulness. As Josef Pieper writes in rather dense terms, sloth means "that man denies his effective assent to his true essence, that he closes

29. Thomas Aquinas, *Summa Theologica*, trans. Fathers of the English Dominican Province, rev. Daniel J. Sullivan, *Great Books of the Western World*, ed. Robert Maynard Hutchins, vol. 20 (Chicago: William Benton, Publisher, Encyclopedia Britannica, Inc., 1952), p. 566 (§2.2.Q35).

30. Sayers, "The Other Six Deadly Sins," p. 176.

31. Peter Kreeft, *Back to Virtue: Traditional Moral Wisdom for Modern Moral Confusion*, foreword Russell Kirk (San Francisco: Ignatius Press, 1992), p. 154.

himself to the demand that arises from his own dignity, that he is not in-clined to claim for himself that grandeur that is imposed on him with his essence's God-given nobility of being."[32] In other words, idols are insuffi-cient and unsuitable as the image and likeness of God.

Eventually things catch up with us, as we recognize the connection between our slothfulness and the despair in our lives. Sloth makes us tardy in turning to God and enjoying all things in him.[33] Upon his delayed conversion at age thirty-one, a formerly slothful Augustine cried out in re-gret, "Too late have I loved Thee, O Thou Beauty of ancient days, yet ever new! Too late I loved Thee!" His great regret was that God was his "tardy joy."[34] If you don't think God is worth your while and your ambitions are elsewhere, beware your *precious* sloth.

**Avarice**   This deadly sin and disordered form of life — better known as greed — consists of an inordinate love of money, wealth, and possessions. We have a voracious desire for more and more cash in order to have more and more things. Avarice literally means "to crave" and is related to the word "avid," and the avaricious are certainly avid in their craving for mate-rial gain. One commercial asks: "What's in your wallet?" The Bible asks, "What's in your heart?" Many of us would have to answer that our wallets are in our hearts! We suffer from the financial virus of "affluenza," living, as we are, in a "wonderland of wares."[35] We have been taught that greed is good and money is what matters in life.

Total U.S. consumer debt has risen above two trillion dollars at this writing.[36] This fact certainly reflects our obeisance to the almighty dollar,

32. Josef Pieper, *A Brief Reader on the Virtues of the Human Heart*, trans. Paul C. Duggan (San Francisco: Ignatius Press, 1991), p. 51.

33. Chaucer, *The Canterbury Tales*, pp. 527-29 (The Parson's Tale §54-59).

34. Augustine, *The Confessions*, trans. Edward B. Pusey, *Great Books of the Western World*, ed. Robert Maynard Hutchins, vol. 18 (Chicago: William Benton, Publisher, Encyclopedia Britannica, Inc., 1952), p. 81 (§10.27) and p. 9 (§2.2).

35. Jessie H. O'Neill has diagnosed and offered a prescription for this "disease" of affluenza in her book, *The Golden Ghetto: The Psychology of Affluence* (The Affluenza Project, 1997). For more on this theme, see O'Neill's website at: http://www.affluenza.com (accessed August 9, 2006). The phrase "wonderland of wares" is from George R. Collins, *Outline of Business*, part 2, *Pocket Library of the World's Essential Knowledge*, vol. 10 (New York: Funk and Wagnalls Company, 1929), p. 54.

36. See The Federal Reserve Board Statistical Release at http://www.federalreserve.gov/releases/G19/Current/. The Bank of England has reported that British consumers owe more

with its fiscal and social purchasing power. After all, avarice is not just about money and stuff, but has as much, if not more, to do with self-esteem, security, status, and power. We measure our human worth by our net worth, and great wealth and great egos often go together. Our bank accounts are our refuge and strength, a very present help in time of trouble. Those who admire the rich are many, and the rich rule over the many who admire them.[37] The new Golden Rule is brutally simple: those who have the gold make the rules.

The capitalistic economic system, which has long dominated the West and has now gone global, has its pluses and its minuses. On the plus side, it is responsible for enhancing the material conditions of life, for which we can be very grateful. On the minus side, it has made us look pretty silly as human beings. In his book *Consumed: How Markets Corrupt Children, Infantilize Adults and Swallow Citizens*, Benjamin Barber notes that triumphant capitalism has produced an ethos of "induced childishness: an infantilization that is closely tied to the demands of consumer capitalism in a global market economy." Prosperity has its benefits, but it may keep "kidults," "rejuveniles," "twixters," and "adultescents" from ever growing up.[38] The only difference between men and boys, so it is said, is the price of their toys (and the same probably goes for women, too).

Our consumerism and materialism have also generated interesting social and spiritual paradoxes. On the one hand, our prosperous conditions have undermined the work ethic and virtues that are necessary to generate the wealth we now enjoy. If these values are withering away, what then will the economic future hold? On the other hand, our obsession with consumption and material abundance has created a spiritual vacuum of astronomical proportions in countless numbers of people.[39] As a result, many are reevaluating the basic purposes of their lives on a spiritual level and are reconsidering the role that wealth should play in the quest for the happy life.

---

than one trillion pounds on bankcards, mortgages, and loans. See http://news.bbc.co.uk/1/hi/business/3935671.stm (both websites accessed June 8, 2007).

37. See Deut. 8:17; Job 31:25; Ps. 49:6; Prov. 14:20; 10:15; 18:11; 22:7.

38. Benjamin Barber, *Consumed: How Markets Corrupt Children, Infantilize Adults and Swallow Citizens* (New York: W. W. Norton, 2007), p. 3.

39. Taken from George F. Will's review of Brink Lindsey's *The Age of Abundance: How Prosperity Transformed America's Politics and Culture* (New York: HarperCollins, Publisher. 2007), in *The New York Times Book Review*, June 10, 2007, pp. 16-17.

What people are finding out about wealth, often through difficult personal experiences, are lessons the Bible has taught all along. For example, making money can be extremely taxing, but losing it is a piece of cake — hard come, easy go (Prov. 23:4-5). Furthermore, money won't make you happy no matter how much you have; it won't buy you love, and it has never been able to provide peace to a weary and restless soul (Eccles. 5:10; Song of Solomon 8:7). It's stupid to give up God for gold (Luke 12:13-21). The irony of avarice is that if you win, you lose — this is why Paul said the love of money is a root of all sorts of evil (1 Tim. 6:10). If you find yourself in the bondage of golden handcuffs, beware your *precious* avarice.

**Gluttony**    This deadly sin and disordered form of life is dominated by an unreasonable love for food, drink, and intoxicants. Interestingly enough, the root of this word refers to the throat and means "to gulp down or swallow." Gluttony is the habit of eating and drinking too voraciously or too scrupulously, especially to the point of wastefulness. We can be either too immoderate or too meticulous about either the quantity or the quality of what we put into our stomachs. Either way, our bellies become our gods as we live in subservience to the demands of hunger and thirst. It is especially pernicious if those in need are neglected as a result.

As indicated, there are two basic types of gluttony. First, there is the typical *gluttony of excess*. The indulgences associated with the Greek and Roman festivals of Dionysus or Bacchus (the god of wine) may come to mind. Or we might think about the monstrously large portions of food and beverage served at many restaurants, or the general overindulgence for which so many of us have been guilty. Gorging and guzzling are selfish and repelling traits in any person.

If eating, drinking, and being merry to excess are national pastimes, it can literally show. While obesity isn't necessarily the result of gluttony, it may play a role in the lives of people who are overweight. Thirty percent of U.S. adults twenty years of age and older — over sixty million people — are obese. Among children and teens between the ages of six to nineteen, over nine million young people are overweight.[40] Currently, nearly fourteen million Americans — one in every thirteen adults — abuse alcohol

---

40. From the Centers for Disease Control and Prevention at http://www.cdc.gov/nccdphp/dnpa/obesity/ (accessed June 8, 2007).

or are alcoholic.[41] Gluttony is dependent on social and economic contexts (I saw no overweight people in Cuba on a recent visit there, for example), and cultures of superabundance like our own do allow gluttony and gluttony-based obesity to proliferate.

The gluttony of excess is matched by the second, equally notorious *gluttony of delicacy*, as it has been called. We can think too much and be too concerned about food and drink, and look forward to our meals with too much anticipation — what shall we eat, and when, and where, and how? Based on a list from Thomas Aquinas, we can commit this more refined version of gluttony by eating too early and often, too eagerly and greedily, too expensively and elegantly, and too fastidiously and fussily.[42] In a Screwtape letter, C.S. Lewis asks, "But what do quantities matter provided we can use a human belly and palate to produce querulousness, impatience, uncharitableness, and self-concern?"[43] Gluttonies of excess or delicacy seem especially insidious in a world where there is so much need and thousands die daily from malnutrition.

Whatever the form, the Scriptures don't smile on gastronomic or bibulous self-indulgence (Prov. 23:2, 20-21; Eccles. 6:7; Hab. 2:5; Matt. 6:25; Luke 12:19; Phil. 3:18-19). Gluttony can affect our physical well-being, impede the functioning of our faculties, and prevent us from fulfilling our daily duties and callings in life. Who can calculate the health risks, personal pain and embarrassment, economic burdens, family stress and breakdown, crime and corruption, and other civic and social liabilities that our obsessions with food and drink have fostered?

There is another profound reason for the Bible's concern about gluttony. Regardless of its quantity or quality, food and drink will never fill our hearts and souls. We eat meal after meal after meal, and still get hungry and thirsty again. The meaning and satisfaction we are seeking through it also eludes us. We wind up just as empty as we were before. Who can eat or drink or have enjoyment without God (Eccles. 2:25)? As Frederick Buechner writes, "A glutton is one who raids the icebox for a cure for spiritual malnutrition."[44] So, if in high hopes you keep your nose

41. From The National Institute on Alcohol Abuse and Alcoholism (NIAAA), http://www.niaaa.nih.gov (accessed June 8, 2007).

42. *The Catholic Encyclopedia*, s.v. "Gluttony."

43. C. S. Lewis, *The Screwtape Letters and Screwtape Proposes a Toast*, with a new preface by the author (New York: The Macmillan Company, 1961), p. 86 (Letter 17).

44. Buechner, *Wishful Thinking: A Seeker's ABC*, p. 35.

buried in your dish and you seek too much comfort in your cups, beware your *precious* gluttony.

**Lust**   This deadly sin and disordered form of life springs from unchecked sexual desire. Formerly, lust was a benign term that referred to pleasure or delight in general. Now we use it to refer to an inordinate craving for sexual experiences. Lustful desire generates such recognizable subspecies as fornication, adultery, prostitution, pornography, incest, rape, pedophilia, bestiality, sodomy, and what seems like an ever-proliferating list of further desires. It is possible to live lustfully even in marriage, if the sexual relationship between spouses is self-centered, abusive, or limited to loveless physical gratification. Lust is associated with fancier names like lasciviousness (undue interest in sex) or licentiousness (selfish, aggressive sexual behavior), and it is the source of both. This is why Jesus taught that the act of adultery and the commandment forbidding it needed to be traced back to its root cause: "everyone who looks at a woman with lust for her has already committed adultery with her in his heart" (Matt. 5:28).

Few gifts of God have been more thoroughly desecrated than our sexuality. If demonic influence lies behind our libidinous escapades, Lewis's Screwtape articulates the strategy well: "All we can do is to encourage the humans to take the pleasures which our Enemy [God] has produced, at times, or in ways, or in degrees, which He has forbidden."[45] We are deeply susceptible to enjoying divinely ordained sexual pleasures in illicit ways, for two basic reasons.[46] The first is simply the tantalizing physical appeal that such experiences hold — the mere "wow" factor of human sexuality. The second is more serious. Men and women live out of their lusts because they are numb, bored, and discontent. If money, food, and other stimulants have failed to satisfy, or if life in a destitute spiritual, social, or cultural environment has failed to fulfill, then perhaps sex is the savior that that can excite or save the soul. Hugh Hefner apparently thinks so, and he's certainly not alone. If lust is lord, maybe it can give us the peace and purpose we crave. As Bruce Marshall wryly observed, "the young man who rings the bell at the brothel is unconsciously looking for God."[47]

---

45. Lewis, *The Screwtape Letters*, p. 41.
46. Sayers, "The Other Six Deadly Sins," p. 158.
47. According to The American Chesterton Society, this quote is falsely attributed to

But sex on its own is a poor substitute for God. Whether we use love to get sex or sex to get love, it is insufficient to satisfy the deeper yearnings of our souls and bodies. God intentionally designed the fireworks of sexuality to point us to the dynamic character of his own love for us. God is not only King of kings and Lord of lords, but also the Lover of all lovers, and only his love will fulfill us.

The problem is, we really don't believe this. We still think sex is the be-all, end-all. We have, however, paid a price for our mistake. The consequences of the sexual revolution have been great in both body and soul. In the U.S., the Centers for Disease Control estimate that nineteen million sexually transmitted disease infections — chlamydia, gonorrhea, syphilis, and others — occur annually, almost half of them among young people between the ages of fifteen and twenty-four. In addition to the physical and psychological consequences, these diseases also entail a tremendous economic toll, estimated at about $14.1 billion annually.[48] By the end of 2003, an estimated 1 to 1.2 million persons in the United States were living with HIV/AIDS, with twenty-four to twenty-seven percent unaware of their HIV infection. In 2005, 38,096 cases of HIV/AIDS in adults, adolescents, and children were diagnosed in thirty-three states, and the CDC has estimated that approximately 40,000 persons in the United States become infected with HIV each year.[49]

In addition to this hard data, the psychological damage resulting from lust is incalculable. Who knows how many broken souls, broken hearts, broken relationships, broken marriages, broken lives, broken families, broken churches, and broken communities have resulted from our inability to control our bodily desires? How much disappointment and despair, chaos and confusion, disorder and destruction has lust produced? Who knows what the economic, criminal, sociological, educational, political, legal, and religious fallout has been from our sexual imprudence? If you

---

G. K. Chesterton (as well as St. Francis and St. Augustine), but actually comes from Bruce Marshall, *The World, The Flesh and Father Smith* (Boston: Houghton Mifflin, 1945), p. 108. Information available at: http://www.chesterton.org/qmeister2/qmeister.htm (accessed June 26, 2007).

48. See Centers for Disease Control and Prevention, STD Surveillance 2005, at http://www.cdc.gov/std/stats/trends2005.htm (accessed June 22, 2007).

49. Centers for Disease Control and Prevention, "A Glance at the HIV/AIDS Epidemic." Available at http://www.cdc.gov/hiv/resources/factsheets/At-A-Glance.htm (accessed June 22, 2007).

think that true happiness is always waiting in the next sexual encounter, beware your *precious* lust.

## The Disordered Life of the Seven Deadly Sins

*"This momentary joy breeds months of pain;*
*This hot desire converts to cold disdain."*

Shakespeare, *The Rape of Lucrece*[50]

Combined, the disordered loves of pride, envy, anger, sloth, avarice, gluttony, and lust would amount to one incredibly disordered, egotistical, narcissistic, self-absorbed life. The secret thoughts of such a person's heart would be exceedingly vain.

> I am the most important person in the world, and every one else is my subordinate. Indeed, all are my inferiors. People should not excel me, but if they do, I will bring them down that I might be lifted up. Woe to any one who should offend me, for I will certainly get my revenge. I am indifferent toward God and my love and energies are directed toward the fulfillment of my personal desires. I get money that I might acquire and retain what I want. I eat and drink beyond satiation. The bodies of my lovers give me pleasure.

Instead of glamorizing us, the seven deadly sins "gollumize" us head to toe in betrayed promises of the happy life. We think that pride, envy, anger, sloth, avarice, gluttony, and lust are seven ways to live, when, in fact, they are seven ways to die. The wages of sin is death (Rom. 6:23), and, as we have seen, that's not simply an abstract biblical decree. What would the world be like if it were filled with people like this? Maybe like the one we have!

You would think that our disordered lives based on disordered loves would cause us to wake up and see what we're doing to ourselves. Shouldn't our frustrations force us to recognize that the things we seek to fulfill us just won't cut it, and can't? Unfortunately, the more they resist us, the more we

---

50. Shakespeare, "The Rape of Lucrece," in *William Shakespeare: The Complete Works*, 2nd ed., gen. eds., Stanley Wells and Gary Taylor, intro. Stanley Wells (Oxford: Clarendon Press, 1986, 2005), p. 245 (lines 690-91).

pursue them, until we find ourselves in heavy dependence upon them and are held captive to our objects of desire. We become slaves of what we want and have to have. But we are rather s . . . l . . . o . . . w to notice that we are sinking in the quicksand of habits and addictions, making a bigger and bigger train wreck of our lives.

## Habits and Addictions

*"A habit, I say, is longtime training, my friend,*
*And this becomes men's nature in the end."*

Euenus in Aristotle's, *Nicomachean Ethics*[51]

Etymologically, the word "habit" literally means "to have and to hold." It refers to repeated actions and behaviors we are often not aware of that end up determining the condition, course, and even destiny of our lives. "Addiction" is derived from original terms that mean "to favor" and "to say over and over again." It denotes a mental or physical dependence on someone or something we think we can't live without, generally with harmful effects. Whether we are conscious of it or not, we want our habit patterns and addictive behaviors to give us some pleasure, to relieve a little stress, and to bring peace of mind. Our genetic makeup, medical condition, personal experiences, and cultural contexts no doubt contribute to forming whatever our habits and addictions may be, and we should never underestimate the influence of these factors in considering them.

We must also realize, however, that various spiritual factors also dispose us to ongoing or irresistible behaviors, and are their deepest source. The original roots of our habits and addictions lie in our excessive and unreasonable loves for things that we believe will be sources of contentment and the pathways to a happy life. Slothful of God, we have made idols out of ourselves in our pride, envy, and anger, and we have become dependent upon and committed to money, food, and sex to satisfy and save us. When they don't, we keep at them as if they would. They hold us tight in their grip as they subtly shape us and determine where we are headed in our lives. Sow a love, reap an action; sow an action, reap a habit; sow a habit, reap an addiction; sow a habit and an addiction, reap a character; sow a

---

51. Aristotle, *Nichomachean Ethics*, p. 198 (§1152a).

character, reap a destiny; sow a destiny and reap an eternity — one way or another.

Before he was converted, Augustine was virtually addicted to sex, over which he fought a great battle within. He wanted to do what was right, yet he kept doing the very thing he hated, "held fast," as he said, "not in fetters clamped upon me by another, but by my own will, which had the strength of chains."

> Because my will was perverse it changed to lust, and lust yielded to become habit, and habit not resisted became necessity. These were like links hanging one on another — which is why I have called it a chain — and their hard bondage held me bound hand and foot.[52]

Augustine's disordered loves and desires led to choices and behaviors that eventually became his habits and necessities. These were like links in a chain that kept him in bondage. What he thought would bring him happiness — his sexual experiences — actually brought him hell. He could not free himself. He escaped only by the grace of a redeemed set of loves and desires in the God-given gift of a new will.

Our story is similar. Sin within leads us to decisions and actions repeated so often that after a while we can't resist them anymore. We still believe these things hold the key to a better life, whether in the form of alcohol or psychoactive drugs, work, food, pornography, sex, people, shopping, gambling, television, movies, music, sports, the Internet — you name it. When we recognize the destructive consequences of these uncontrollable behaviors, we resolve to do something about it, but typically with little improvement. Life away from the bottle is rarely achieved by willpower alone. Smokers fare little better. According to the U.S. Department of Health and Human Services, "nearly half of all smokers try to quit in a given year. . . . Only two to three percent of smokers . . . manage to stop smoking for one year."[53] Meanwhile, the fallout from our habits and addictions has hit the giga-range physically, psychologically, socially, and

---

52. Augustine, *Confessions*, trans. F. J. Sheed, intro. Peter Brown (Indianapolis: Hackett Publishing Company, 1992), p. 164 (§8.5).

53. This point and the economic statistic below is from a report by the U.S. Treasury titled "The Economic Costs of Smoking in the United States and the Benefits of Comprehensive Tobacco Legislation." Available at http://www.ustreas.gov/press/releases/reports/tobacco.pdf (accessed July 24, 2007).

economically. The cost of smoking to the U.S. economy is about $130 billion per year.

To what do your disordered loves incline you? What habits and addictions hold you captive? How have they disordered your life? Barring an experience of grace, are you on a pathway to destruction rather than paradise? Beware your *precious* habits and addictions.

## Crime and Warfare

> *"I grant that, men continuing what they are,*
> *Fierce, avaricious, proud, there must be war."*

William Cowper, "Table Talk"[54]

According to Augustine, in the disordered loves of the seven deadly sins we seek happiness in the self, in our neighbors, or in bodily things for their own sake without God. These sins first corrupt us, and in the pitiful state of our shameful corruption, we will lash out in violence, if that's what it takes to get what we need and want. For Augustine, this is the source of criminal behavior.

Shriveled up on the inside after years of frustration and pain, we may turn to criminal acts to overcome obstacles to our satisfaction or to insure the success of our self-centered pursuits. Staggering spiritual impoverishment and rampant desire, resulting in habits and addictions, beget criminal behavior. "They waste their small means in luxury," Augustine writes, "and subsequently, *under pressure of want*, break out into thefts and burglaries, and at times even into highway robberies, and so they are suddenly filled with fears both numerous and great; and men who a little before were singing in the house of revelry, are now dreaming of the sorrows of the prison."[55]

Crimes like homicide, arson, battery, blackmail, kidnapping, terrorism, perjury, extortion, espionage, solicitation, and fraud may be necessary to eliminate barriers to our desires. Crimes like physical assaults, burglary, sexual abuse, embezzlement, forgery, identity theft, piracy, rape, smuggling, stalking, tax evasion, treason, and vandalism will be necessary

---

54. Cowper, "Table Talk," in *Cowper: Poetical Works*, p. 1 (lines 9-10).

55. Augustine, *On the Catechising of the Uninstructed*, p. 300 (§16.24), emphasis added.

*to get that thing or person we love and want.* We may attack a human being or institution we perceive as a threat in order *to protect* what we already have and love. We may physically harm or even murder an enemy out of revenge, or a superior out of envy, all for *the sake of validating the self.* We may even perpetrate violence for *the pathological pleasure of watching others suffer.* The disorder of crime, in short, may come to seem necessary to get what we love in order to find peace and be happy.

Nations go to war for similar pernicious reasons: the unjust *acquisition* of peoples, lands, resources; the selfish *protection* of what they already possess; the empty *validation* of national honor; and the pure *baseness* of wicked leaders. As the enlargement of the soul, a state's behavior toward other states in warfare mimics the purposes and patterns present in criminal activity. Both are a reflection of the disorders in human nature. As we read in James 4:1-2, "What is the source of quarrels and conflicts among you? Is not the source your *pleasures* that wage war in your members? You *lust* and do not have; so you commit murder. You are *envious* and cannot obtain; so you fight and quarrel" (emphasis added).

Likewise, in describing the Corcyraean Revolution, the ancient Greek historian Thucydides, who lived from about 460-400 B.C., wrote in his famous *History of the Peloponnesian War,* "The cause of all these evils was the *lust* for power arising from greed and ambition; and from these *passions* proceeded the violence of parties once engaged in contention."[56] Augustine also explained the real evils of war in terms of disordered love: "The real evils in war are *love* of violence, revengeful cruelty, fierce and implacable enmity, wild resistance, and the *lust* of power, and such like."[57] How much longer will wars rooted in mixed-up pleasures, lust, envy, greed, and ambition continue? Joe Portnoy has an answer: "Wars will go on as long as men's hearts are as they are."[58]

Beware, then, if you are entertaining a thought to commit a crime or

---

56. Thucydides, *The History of the Peloponnesian War,* trans. Richard Crawley, rev. R. Feetham, *The Great Books of the Western World,* ed. Robert M. Hutchins, vol. 6 (Chicago: Encyclopedia Britannica, 1952), p. 437 (§3.82), emphasis added.

57. Augustine, "Reply to Faustus the Manichaean," trans. Richard Stothert, in *Nicene and Post-Nicene Fathers,* ed. Philip Schaff, First Series, vol. 4 (Peabody, Mass.: Hendrickson Publishers, Inc., 1994), p. 301 (§22.74), emphasis added.

58. Andrew Carroll, photographs by Maggie Steber, "War Letters: The Lives Between the Lines," *National Geographic,* November 2005, p. 85.

go to war, if you have the power to do so, to obtain or protect what seems ultimately *precious* to you!

## Vanity of Vanities

*"For who can eat and who can have enjoyment without Him?"*

Ecclesiastes 2:25

Because of ignorance and wrong desire, we have thoroughly disordered our lives and made a mess of the world. Disordered love generates disordered lives, and disordered lives generate disordered families, and disordered families generate disordered communities, and disordered communities generate disordered cities, and disordered cities generate disordered states and nations, and disordered states and nations produce a disordered world, just like the one we have today. Our disordered love and disordered lives are the roots, then, of our disordered world, all directed in feverish devotion to the discovery of the happy life. We should have known better by now about the futility of our efforts directed to this blessed end.

One reason why we should have known better is found in the Old Testament book of Ecclesiastes. For millennia, it has stood out like the Rock of Gibraltar in its clear declarations that all of our strenuous attempts to anchor our happiness in human or earthly pursuits apart from God are vain and futile. An empty life without God generates a queasy, unsettled "earth-sickness" of saddening and maddening proportions. We are worn out with what the Germans call *Weltschmerz*, or world-weariness. Still, we try to treat our earth-sickness and world-weariness homeopathically with more earth-stuff or more worldliness, to no avail.

The folly of treating the disease with more of the disease is the message of Ecclesiastes. The purpose of this book is to expose the real meaninglessness of all our hypothetical meanings, the actual purposelessness of all our supposed purposes, the true emptiness of all our alleged fulfillments, and the actual sadness of all the things we think bring us joy.[59] In short, Ecclesiastes unmasks the nihilism of our lives. In the sober-

---

59. See Peter Kreeft's illuminating discussion of Ecclesiastes along these lines in his *Three Philosophies of Life: Ecclesiastes: Life as Vanity, Job: Life as Suffering, Song of Songs: Life as Love* (San Francisco: Ignatius Press, 1989), pp. 13-58.

ing words of the author, "Thus I considered all my activities which my hands had done and the labor which I had exerted, and behold all was vanity and striving after wind and there was no profit under the sun" (Eccles. 2:11).

Still, we continue to place our whole hope of a satisfying life in things that can never satisfy us on their own. Or as Ecclesiastes itself puts it, our virtually unlimited love "under the sun" for pleasure, laughter, wine, houses, vineyards, gardens, parks, trees, lakes, servants, flocks, herds, silver, gold, song, sex, knowledge, and fame as the final sources of the good life amount to nothing. Ecclesiastes exposes the inevitable outcome of our assumptions about life, reduces all our pretension to absurdity, and reveals the *"whole false happiness"* of our lives.[60]

Augustine summarizes the catastrophic human condition in a list of realistic woes that demonstrated to him, as it should to us, exactly where our ignorance and wrong desires have led us:

> Carking anxieties, agitations of mind, disappointments, fears, frenzied joys, quarrels, disputes, wars, treacheries, hatreds, enmities, deceits, flattery, fraud, theft, rapine, perfidy, ambition, envy, murder, parricide, cruelty, savagery, villainy, lust, promiscuity, indecency, unchastity, fornication, adultery, incest, unnatural vice in men and women (disgusting acts too filthy to be named), sacrilege, collusion, false witness, unjust judgment, violence, robbery, and all other such evils which do not immediately come to mind, although they never cease to beset this life of man — *all these evils belong to man in his wickedness, and they all spring from that root of error and perverted affection which every son of Adam brings with him at his birth.*[61]

---

60. The quoted phrase is from Augustine, *On the Catechising of the Uninstructed*, p. 301 (§16.25), emphasis added.

61. Augustine, *Concerning the City of God against the Pagans*, trans. Henry Bettenson, intro. John O'Meara, Penguin Classics (New York: Penguin Books, 1984), p. 1065 (§22.22), emphasis added.

## Humor and Hope

*"There comes a time in the life of every man when he must take
the bull by the tail and squarely face the situation."*

W. C. Fields, in *And God Created Laughter*[62]

How should we respond to our ugly, depressing, "gollumized" human predicament? Should we redouble our efforts to figure things out and resolve
to create a better world? Should we toss in the towel, and consider it all a
hopeless mess? Perhaps some type of stoicism is the answer. "Whatever."
Might we simply crater to hedonism and live a prodigal life? Eat, drink and
be merry, for tomorrow we die? In the smoky lyrics of Peggy Lee's haunt-
ing song of personal disillusionment,

> Is that all there is, is that all there is
> If that's all there is my friends, then let's keep dancing
> Let's break out the booze and have a ball
> If that's all there is.[63]

Instead of these dead ends, let's try something else. In the midst of
the vanity, futility, frustration, and pain, I propose a response of laughter
and humor. Contradiction is often at the heart of humor. "The comic is
present," said philosopher Søren Kierkegaard, "in every stage of life . . . ,
because where there is life there is contradiction, and wherever there is
contradiction, the comic is present."[64] I think we need to laugh at the jarring discrepancy between our exhausting efforts to discover the happy
life and our abysmal failure to achieve it. We've been "searching for riches
in abandoned mines,"[65] and we need to laugh at our stupidity and foolishness. Humor is the best way out of this hole in the ground. It hurts if
you *don't* laugh. "God writes a lot of comedy," says Garrison Keillor,

62. Quoted in Conrad Hyers, *And God Created Laughter: The Bible as Divine Comedy* (Atlanta: John Knox Press, 1987), p. 11.

63. "Is That All There Is," © Sony/ATV Music Publishing LLC. All rights administered
by Sony/ATV Music Publishing LLC, 8 Music Square West, Nashville, Tenn. 37203. All rights
reserved. Used by permission.

64. Søren Kierkegaard, *Concluding Unscientific Postscript to* Philosophical Fragments,
ed., trans., intro., and notes Howard V. Hong and Edna H. Hong, vol. 1 (Princeton: Princeton
University Press, 1992), pp. 513-14.

65. Brooks Williams, "Restless," from the CD *Skiffle-Bop*, Signature Records, 2001.

". . . the trouble is, he's stuck with so many bad actors who don't know how to play funny."[66]

Therefore, let us laugh as Abraham and Sarah did when in their old age God told them they would have a son — he was a mere one hundred and she a sprightly ninety (Gen. 17–18). In laughing at a promise barely believed, she conceived and gave birth to Isaac, and both of them realized in the end that nothing was too difficult for God.

Let us then trust God to do what we can't do for ourselves in the midst of our impossible circumstances, especially when it comes to learning the deep meaning of happiness. The laughter of faith is at the center of the divine comedy, for there is salvation from sin and our brokenhearted loves and lives only in the gospel of our Lord and Savior Jesus Christ.

66. Cited at http://www.brainyquote.com/quotes/authors/g/garrison_keillor.html (accessed June 28, 2007).

## CHAPTER FOUR

# The Gospel:
# From Futility to the Living God

*"Lisping our syllables, we scramble next*
*Through moral narrative, or sacred text;*
*And learn with wonder how this world began,*
*Who made, who marr'd, and who has ransom'd man."*

William Cowper, "Tirocinium:
or, A Review of Schools"[1]

## Introduction

"Jesus wept." Yes, this is the shortest verse in the Bible (John 11:35), but such a trivial fact hardly exhausts its deeper meaning and significance. In this tiny two-word text — a mere proper noun and past-tense verb — we discover the primary motivation of Jesus' ministry and the core of the Christian gospel.

When Jesus "burst into tears,"[2] he was approaching the grave of his

---

1. William Cowper, "Tirocinium: or, A Review of Schools," in *Cowper: Poetical Works*, ed. H. S. Milford, 4th ed., corrections and additions Norma Russell (London: Oxford University Press, 1967), p. 245 (lines 125-28).

2. Leon Morris, *The Gospel According to John: The English Text with Introduction, Exposition and Notes*, The New International Commentary on the New Testament, gen. ed. F. F. Bruce (Grand Rapids: Eerdmans, 1971), p. 558, n. 71.

beloved friend Lazarus. His sisters Mary and Martha were among his fa-
vorites as well. Jesus had been informed earlier that Lazarus was seriously
ill. But for reasons he only knew at the time, he stayed where he was for
two more days instead of rushing immediately to his friend's aid. When he
finally arrived at Bethany, where this small family of siblings resided, the
lamentation over the loss of Lazarus was well underway. People were
coming from all over to join in on the grieving process and to offer comfort to the bereaved sisters. Neither Martha nor Mary could understand
why Jesus had delayed his coming. They didn't hesitate to express their ex-
asperation with him, since they knew he could have saved their brother's
life. As Jesus observed their disappointment, the intensity of their grief,
and the many tears that were being shed, he himself was deeply moved
and troubled within. He began to weep also. The abundance of Jesus' tears
prompted many observers to comment on his great love for Lazarus. Others, on the other hand, continued to voice criticism of his tardy arrival.

Undoubtedly Jesus wept because he had lost a friend to death. He also
shed tears out of sympathy for his surviving sisters. Had he responded in
any other way, it would have been heartless and even strange. Jesus was no
stoic.

At the same time, Jesus wept over Lazarus not only out of sorrow and
sympathy, but for another reason as well. He was mad. He was angry. He
was filled with rage. Twice in the story we read that Jesus was emotionally
disturbed and troubled within (vv. 33, 38). The original wording indicates
that there was something about the heartrending scene before him that
evoked his indignation, as his eyes flooded with tears and fell from his
cheeks.[3] The paraphrase of verse 38 in *The Message* describes Christ's con-

---

3. As B. B. Warfield puts it in an outstanding essay on "The Emotional Life of Our
Lord," *The Person and Work of Christ*, ed. Samuel Craig (Philadelphia: The Presbyterian and Reformed Publishing Company, 1970), p. 115, "What John tells us, in point of fact, is that Jesus
approached the grave of Lazarus, in a state, not of uncontrollable grief, but of irrepressible
anger. He did respond to the spectacle of human sorrow abandoning itself to its unre-
strained expression, with quiet, sympathetic tears: 'Jesus wept' (verse 36 *sic*). But the emo-
tion which tore his breast and clamored for utterance was just rage." Several prominent
New Testament scholars concur with Warfield's reading of this text, including John Calvin,
*Commentary on a Harmony of the Evangelists: Matthew, Mark, and Luke*, trans. William Pringle,
vol. 17 (Grand Rapids: Baker Books, reprint 2003), pp. 439-43; B. F. Westcott, *The Gospel According to St. John: The Authorized Version with Introduction and Notes* (Grand Rapids: Eerdmans,
reprint 1975), pp. 170-72; Raymond E. Brown, *The Gospel According to John 1–12: A New Translation with Introduction and Commentary*, The Anchor Bible, gen. eds. William F. Albright and Da-

dition accurately: "Then Jesus, *the anger again welling up within him,* arrived at the tomb" (emphasis added).

What was it that prompted this geyser of indignation? Why was Jesus mad? What caused his deep, emotional disturbances? Specifically, it was death — the power of death, the stench of death, the abnormality of death — and the sickness that caused it and the grief that followed after it, that angered Jesus so greatly. The original language may even suggest that it caused him to make snorting sounds like a horse and his whole body to tremble.

Yet it was not just death and its causes and effects that turned Jesus inside out. It was also the underlying source of death: the devil, against whom his anger burned. Jesus was mad as hell at the devil — the enemy who was a murderer from the beginning and the father of all lies — because he was the one who was ultimately responsible for all the desolations and anguish inflicted on humanity and the earth. The death of Lazarus manifested the entire domain of evil and its reprehensible effects. It stood for nothing less than "the general misery of the whole human race."[4]

How contrary this situation was to the way God intended his people and his world to flourish in wholeness, peace, and blessing. Sin, Satan, and death had reduced the cosmos to chaos. The very good creation had become a deviant uncreation, and paradise was lost. In short, Jesus wept because of the vandalism of shalom.[5]

But Jesus had a plan all along. He had allowed Lazarus to die and his body to remain in the grave beyond any hope of a natural recovery in order to raise him from the dead.[6] When the pivotal moment arrived, he secured the removal of the stone from the deceased's grave — over Martha's protests of an impending stench. After offering a prayer to God, Jesus cried out with a loud voice, "Lazarus, come forth," and that's exactly what he did, looking perhaps as if he were competing in a sack race. Death was no match for Jesus' prevailing word, for "He who had died came forth, bound hand and foot with wrappings; and his face was wrapped around with a cloth." With gratitude (I would imagine), the

---

vid N. Freedman, vol. 29 (Garden City, N.Y.: Doubleday & Company, Inc., 1966), pp. 425-26, 435; Morris, *The Gospel According to John,* pp. 554-59.

4. Calvin, *Commentary on a Harmony of the Evangelists,* vol. 17, p. 439.

5. Cornelius Plantinga Jr., *Not the Way It's Supposed to Be: A Breviary of Sin* (Grand Rapids: Eerdmans, 1995), see chapter one.

6. Technically, Lazarus was "resuscitated," that is, brought back to regular physical life and not officially resurrected. Lazarus died again.

next thing Lazarus heard Jesus say was, "Unbind him, and let him go" (vv. 43-44).

Those present couldn't believe their eyes. What an amazing reversal of fortune — a *"eucatastrophe"* (good disaster) of the highest order.[7] Lazarus was alive again. Martha and Mary had their brother back. Laughter and shouts of joy replaced sadness and tears of grief. Life and hope prevailed. But what did it all mean?

This sign of release and renewal showed that Jesus was defeating the powers of sin and death that had stunk up the world and imprisoned people within it. It highlighted Christ's claim to be the resurrection and the life (John 11:25-26) and foreshadowed his victory over death on Easter Sunday. It indicated that new life is already available for those who believe in him. The commands "Lazarus, come forth. . . . Unbind him, and let him go" illustrate the purposes of conquest, release, and liberty for which Jesus came into the world. It was a sign that the restoration of shalom was underway.

Jesus was moved to redemptive action to salvage a world wrecked by sin and death. Sinners needed forgiveness. Falsehood needed correcting. Diseases needed curing. Demoniacs needed deliverance. Hunger and thirst needed satiation. Storms needed stilling. Death needed defeating. Life needed restoring. A short report on Christ's ministry in the book of Acts informs us that Jesus went about doing good, being full of the Holy Spirit and power (cf. Acts 10:38). In him we see the kingdom of God in dynamic action, the renewal of abundant or bountiful life, and the coming of a new creation. Paradise in Christ is regained.

Jesus' convivial lifestyle — for which his enemies falsely accused him of gluttony, drunkenness, and bad company — fit perfectly with his all-embracing purposes of cosmic revitalization. It stood in sharp contrast to the dehumanizing legalism and unappealing crabbiness of the conservative religious establishment, which was also marked by its glaring hypocrisy.

Jesus pronounced the blessing of happiness on his followers who submitted to him for salvation under his kingdom rule. Though the Greek

---

7. J. R. R. Tolkien, "On Fairy-Stories," in *Essays Presented to Charles Williams*, ed. C. S. Lewis (Grand Rapids: Eerdmans, 1947, paperback edition 1966, fourth printing, 1977), p. 81. Tolkien's word "eucatastrophe" literally means "good catastrophe" of a "sudden and miraculous grace."

word *makarioi* that introduces the beatitudes in the Sermon on the Mount is typically translated "blessed," several New Testament scholars are convinced that "'happy' is what Jesus [literally] said."[8] As J. B. Phillips puts it in his translation, "How happy are the humble-minded, for the kingdom of Heaven is theirs!"

These thoughts add up to a fresh perspective on why Jesus came to earth. Jesus as the Son of God was conceived in the womb of Mary, was born, lived, ministered, taught, died, rose again, ascended into heaven, assumed universal authority, sent the gift of the Holy Spirit, formed the church, and gave it its mission *not just so our souls could go to heaven when we die.* Rather Jesus came to redeem the world and to give meaning, fulfillment, and purpose in life to his disciples in his kingdom here on earth right now. In short, he came to renew shalom for his people and the entire creation. The final outcome of salvation — the proverbial icing on the cake — will be spending eternity with God and the company of the redeemed in the fully restored new heavens and new earth. Yes, really: all this, and heaven too.

## Hope for the Perpetually Unhappy

*"O Lord, you have made us for yourself, and our heart is restless until it rests in you."*

Augustine, *Confessions*[9]

If you have been following the many maps to happiness for years on end, but have gotten lost every time . . . if you are frustrated in your efforts to find contentment, but are living a life of "quiet desperation" . . . if the great things you have trusted in have failed, and you find yourself on the brink of despair . . . in short, if you are in a restless mess: isn't it time to consider a new map, try a new method, and look to a new object of hope? In Switchfoot's musical imagination, multiple disappointments

8. A. T. Robertson, *Word Pictures in the New Testament,* vol. 1 (Nashville: Broadman Press, 1930), p. 39. John Calvin also says the beatitudes embody the "true happiness" of Christ's disciples in his *Commentary on the Gospel According to John,* trans. William Pringle (Grand Rapids: Baker Books, reprint 2003), p. 259.

9. Augustine, *Confessions,* trans., intro., notes Henry Chadwick, Oxford World's Classics (New York: Oxford University Press, 1992), p. 3 (§1.1).

are blessings in disguise, since they amount to a "beautiful letdown" and force you to consider an option that may not have even been on your radar before:

> It was a beautiful let down
> When I crashed and burned
> When I found myself alone unknown and hurt
> It was a beautiful let down
> The day I knew
> That all the riches this world had to offer me
> Would never do.[10]

What will do, however, is Jesus Christ — the one who wept over Lazarus, the one who was angered at what sin, death, and the devil had done, the one who claimed to be the resurrection and the life, the one who came to restore shalom, the one in whom we discover the deep meaning of happiness now, and the one who is preparing a place for us with God forever. We should learn more about this Jesus, what he has done for us, and how we should respond in faith to him.

## Jesus in the Gospel of John

*"For God so loved the world, that He gave His only begotten Son, that whoever believes in Him shall not perish, but have eternal life."*

John 3:16

In the Gospel of John, where the story of Lazarus is found, Jesus performed many other miracles that revealed his divine identity and restored shalom to those in significant need. For example, he turned plain water into outstanding wine at a festive wedding celebration in Cana of Galilee (John 2:1-11). He healed a nobleman's son of a fatal fever (John 4:46-54). He cured a palsied man thirty-eight years in his sickness (John 5:1-9). He multiplied the capacity of only five loaves of bread and two fish to feed five thousand hungry men, plus women and children (John 6:1-14). He walked

---

10. Jonathan Foreman, "Beautiful Letdown," © 2003 Meadowgreen Music Company / Sugar Pete Songs. All rights reserved. Used by permission.

upon a stormy sea and calmed it (John 6:16-21). He healed a man of congenital blindness (John 9:1-41). He himself rose from the dead as a final validation of his identity and purpose (John 20:1-31). From this catalog of mighty deeds, Jesus was obviously concerned to address the many problems of insufficiency, sickness and disease, hunger and thirst, natural disturbances and death that afflict the human race. In surmounting these obstacles to human thriving, Jesus could say in John 10:10b that he had come that people might have life and have it abundantly — "more and better life than they ever dreamed of" *(The Message)*.

In this same Gospel, Jesus also makes seven important claims about himself that show him to be God-in-the-flesh. Together they indicate that his goal was to renew life and peace for his people. In each saying, he applies the chief Old Testament name of God to himself — the great "I AM" revealed to Moses at the burning bush (Exod. 3:14) — to indicate that he was God, and that everything we need and are looking for in life is found in and through him.

1. I am the bread of life; he who comes to Me will not hunger, and he who believes in Me shall never thirst (John 6:35).
2. I am the Light of the world; he who follows Me will not walk in the darkness, but will have the Light of life (John 8:12).
3. I am the door of the sheep (John 10:7).
4. I am the good shepherd; the good shepherd lays down His life for the sheep (John 10:11).
5. I am the resurrection and the life; he who believes in Me will live even if he dies, and everyone who lives and believes in Me will never die (John 11:25-26).
6. I am the way, and the truth, and the life; no one comes to the Father, but through me (John 14:6).
7. I am the true vine, and My Father is the vinedresser (John 15:1).

So, if you are spiritually hungry and looking for food and drink, if you are in the dark and need illumination, if you are confused and can't find the door, if you are fearful and needy, if you cry out for provision and protection, if you are scared of death and long for life, if you have lost your bearings and need to know the way, if you feel useless and want to be fruitful, then Jesus as the bread of life, the light of the world, the door of the sheep, the good shepherd, the resurrection and the life, the way, truth, and life, and the true vine — the great I AM — is the one for you!

## Who Is Jesus?

*"Who do people say that the Son of Man is? . . . But who do you say that I am?"*

Matthew 16:13, 15

What kind of person could make claims like these? Who is Jesus after all? What are people saying about him today? How do religious people portray him? Who do you think he is? His claims are so extraordinary that they raise questions not only about his identity but also about his very sanity.

Today, the popular media and academic culture offer many perspectives and lots of confusion about the person and mission of Jesus. Was Jesus really married with children? Did the church really suppress the truth about him in order to preserve its political power and social position, as *The Da Vinci Code* suggests? Were Jesus' words and deeds in the New Testament Gospels falsely reported, was his resurrection a hoax, and was his body eaten by dogs, as members of the Jesus Seminar allege? Should we conceive of Jesus as a mere spinner of tales, a winsome wisdom teacher, or a wandering cynic sage, as students of the Gnostic and apocryphal gospels propose? Historically speaking, these views of Jesus miss the truth by miles.[11]

---

11. There are many good books that convey historic, orthodox perspectives on Jesus and offer helpful responses to recent, unconventional views of his identity and purpose. The classic work is C. S. Lewis, *Mere Christianity* (New York: Macmillan, 1943). A popular apologetic work is Lee Strobel, *The Case for the Real Jesus* (Grand Rapids: Zondervan, 2007). The following three works are semi-popular in content: Luke Timothy Johnson, *The Real Jesus* (New York: HarperSanFrancisco/HarperCollins Publishers, 1996); Gregory A. Boyd, *Cynic, Sage or Son of God?* (Wheaton: BridgePoint/Victor, 1995); N. T. Wright, *The Challenge of Jesus* (Downers Grove: InterVarsity Press, 1999). N. T. Wright has also produced three scholarly volumes of a projected five- or six-volume series on the life of Jesus and New Testament theology: *The New Testament and the People of God* (Minneapolis: Fortress, 1992); *Jesus and the Victory of God* (Minneapolis: Fortress, 1996); *The Resurrection of the Son of God* (Minneapolis: Fortress, 2003). For a spiritual approach to the life and work of Christ, see Philip Yancey, *The Jesus I Never Knew* (Grand Rapids: Zondervan, 1995). For a discussion of contemporary cultural portrayals of Jesus, see C. Marvin Pate and Cheryl L. Pate, *Crucified in the Media: Finding the Real Jesus Among Today's Headlines* (Grand Rapids: Baker Books, 2005).

While the public debate over Jesus will no doubt continue, somehow a rather lackluster portrait of Jesus has also insinuated itself in the minds and imaginations of many people in many walks of life. Who is responsible for this bland perspective on Christ? How has such a deadening view of him developed? Where do these boring depictions come from?

Certainly not from those who knew him! As Dorothy Sayers states, "Not Herod, not Caiaphas, not Pilate, not Judas ever contrived to fasten upon Jesus Christ the reproach of insipidity; that final indignity was left for pious hands to inflict."[12] Sadly, much of the blame may be laid for anemic views of Jesus at the feet of Jesus' devoted followers, who have somehow emasculated him and diluted his reputation. Too many preachers proclaim and too many parishioners embrace a featureless Christ. Yet as Sayers writes elsewhere, "To those who knew Him, however, He in no way suggested a milk-and-water person; they objected to Him as a dangerous firebrand."[13]

## Christ the Firebrand

*"They were utterly astonished, saying, 'He has done all things well.'"*

Mark 7:37

A fresh reading of all four Gospels proves that Christ was a firebrand indeed. Controversy and suspense surrounded him even before he was born, certainly while he was alive, and after his death right up to the present. His actual paternity was a matter of suspicion, and his birth attracted the attention of peasants, dignitaries, and even angels. Within two years of his nativity, one insecure politician pursued a program of infanticide to prevent his possible rise to power. By the age of twelve, he was already confounding the religious leaders of the land with his questions and insights, as he manifested the signs of a special divine calling. His developing wisdom and maturity astounded all who knew him, even as he simulta-

---

12. Dorothy L. Sayers, "Introduction" to *The Man Born to Be King: A Play-Cycle on the Life of Our Lord and Saviour Jesus Christ* (San Francisco: Ignatius Press, 1990, originally published 1943), p. 30.

13. Dorothy L. Sayers, *Creed or Chaos?* (Manchester, N.H.: Sophia Institute Press, 1949, 1974), p. 7.

neously labored for almost two decades as a master carpenter, no doubt. When he was thirty years old, he aligned himself with the morally rigorous ministry of a prophet of strange dress and a bizarre diet by submitting to his call for repentance and baptism. From then on, he taught with unmistakable authority, performed amazing signs and wonders, and gathered to himself a motley crew of followers quite diverse in background and temperament. Eventually, one betrayed and another denied him. They all abandoned him at his greatest moment of need.

Jesus challenged the authority and character of both politicians and religious leaders, calling an elite Roman ruler a crafty "fox" on one occasion, and castigating the Scribes and Pharisees as "hypocrites." For some, he hung out with the wrong crowd and allegedly ate and drank too much. Toward the end of his life, he had the audacity to clear the temple precincts of their entrepreneurial corruption in a dramatic flourish. He also showed himself more than capable of handling the verbal challenges of his enemies with remarkable intellect. To top things off, he often applied messianic and divine titles to himself, and he claimed to deserve the same kind of love and glory due only to God. He taught that his death would be a sacrifice that would defeat sin and evil, and that he would rise in conquest of death three days later. A month or so afterward, he ascended into heaven to the right hand of God's throne, from which he rules everything in heaven and on earth with unquestionable authority and power.

Jesus also had a softer side that certain situations elicited — "the meekness and gentleness of Christ" — seen, for example, when he lovingly restored a beloved daughter to life, when he mercifully forgave an adulterous woman of her sexual sin, when he kindly raised a widow's son from the dead, when he tenderly made provision for his mother even while hanging on the cross. Yet, as the above indicates, he could also be as tough as nails. In him we see the perfect blend of virtues.

Who, then, was Jesus, and what was he like? Colorless? Wishy-washy? Never. Notorious? Controversial? Indeed. Intelligent? Gifted? Absolutely. Tenderhearted? Kind? Most certainly. As Sayers concludes, "He was emphatically not a dull man in His human lifetime, and if He was God, there can be nothing dull about God either."[14]

14. Sayers, *Creed or Chaos?* p. 7.

## God Incarnate

*". . . God's infinity*
*Dwindled to infancy."*

Gerard Manley Hopkins, "The Blessed Virgin"[15]

That Jesus is both God and man — that is, the God-Man (and in neither nature dull nor boring) — is exactly what the church has taught for over two millennia. His "divinity-in-humanity" or "humanity-in-divinity" is the mystery of the incarnation. This great theological word *incarnate* literally means "in the flesh." It conveys the idea that Jesus Christ as a person was the perfect and permanent union of humanity and deity without either of these natures being impaired.[16] The incarnation is significant not only because it makes God known to people, but also because it makes people known to people. In Christ we see what God is really like, and we also see what we are really like, or at least what we are supposed to be like. Jesus is truly God and truly human. When I was a college freshman, I once asked a history professor about the greatest event in all of human history. He drew on his Catholic heritage and replied without missing a step: "The incarnation of the Son of God."[17]

Five important New Testament passages on the incarnation — three from the Gospels and two from Paul's letters — present this mystery of Christian teaching that God "was revealed in human flesh" in the person of Jesus Christ (1 Tim. 3:16).

> "Behold, the virgin shall be with child and shall bear a Son, and they shall call His name Immanuel, which translated means, *'God with us.'*" (Matt. 1:23; cf. Isa. 7:14)

> "And behold, you [Mary] will conceive in your womb and bear a son, and you shall name Him Jesus. He will be great and will be called the Son of the Most High; and the Lord God will give Him the throne of His

15. Gerard Manley Hopkins, "The Blessed Virgin Compared To The Air We Breathe," in *A Hopkins Reader*, ed. and intro. John Pick (Garden City, N.Y.: Image Books, Doubleday & Company, Inc., 1966), p. 70.

16. Taken from *The Oxford Dictionary of the Christian Church* (1997), s.v. "Incarnation."

17. Dr. Bede Karl Lackner, professor emeritus of history, University of Texas at Arlington, Arlington, Texas.

father David; and He will reign over the house of Jacob forever, and His kingdom will have no end." (Luke 1:31-33)

"In the beginning was the Word, and the Word was with God, and the Word was God. . . . And the Word became flesh, and dwelt among us, and we saw His glory, glory as of the only begotten from the Father, full of grace and truth." (John 1:1, 14)

"Have this attitude in yourselves which was also in Christ Jesus, who, although He existed in the form of God, did not regard equality with God a thing to be grasped, but emptied Himself, taking the form of a bond-servant, and being made in the likeness of men." (Phil. 2:5-7)

"But when the fullness of time came, God sent forth His Son, born of a woman, born under the Law." (Gal. 4:4)

His virginal conception and birth into the world at a specific time and place in history through his mother Mary are no small miracles. These events bring the biblical narrative in its presentation of "Who made, who marr'd, and who has ransom'd man"[18] to its climax. His nativity in Bethlehem signals the fulfillment of the Old Testament promises of redemption, the purpose of which was to salvage the creation from the death-dealing effects of human rebellion against God. Creation's fall is healed in Christ's redemption.

Of course, Jesus' birth into the world as the God-Man is the event we celebrate at Christmastime. The second verse of Charles Wesley's famous yuletide carol "Hark! the Herald Angels Sing" expresses this highpoint of the biblical drama with precise and poetic words:

Christ, by highest heav'n adored, Christ, the everlasting Lord!
Late in time behold him come, off-spring of the Virgin's womb.
Veiled in flesh the Godhead see; hail, th' incarnate Deity.
Pleased as man with men to dwell, Jesus, our Emmanuel.[19]

This hymn is an eighteenth-century rendition of the teaching about Jesus that was established by the church in the fifth century. Christian

18. William Cowper, "Tirocinium: or, A Review of Schools," in *Cowper: Poetical Works*, p. 245 (line 128).

19. Charles Wesley, "Hark! the Herald Angels Sing," *Trinity Hymnal*, rev. ed. (Atlanta/Philadelphia: Great Commission Publications, 1990), p. 203.

leaders had wrestled intensely over Christ's identity for roughly the first four hundred years of the church's existence. After much controversy and prayer, it settled on a proper doctrine of Christ at the Council of Chalcedon in A.D. 451. His full deity and humanity, his sinlessness, and the reason for his incarnation through Mary are explained in the first section of this historic statement of Christian belief articulated at Chalcedon:

> Therefore, following the holy fathers, we all with one accord teach men to acknowledge one and the Same Son, our Lord Jesus Christ, at once complete in Godhead and complete in manhood, truly God and truly man consisting of a reasonable soul and body; of one substance with the Father as regards his Godhead, and at the same time of one substance with us as regards his manhood; like us in all respects, apart from sin; as regards his Godhead, begotten of the Father before all ages, but yet as regards his manhood begotten, for us men and for our salvation, of Mary the Virgin, the God-bearer.

How Christ's divine and human natures are properly related in Jesus as a single person are the subjects addressed in the second part of this definitive creed.

> One and the same Christ, Son, Lord, Only-begotten, recognized in two natures, without confusion, without change, without division, without separation; the distinction of natures being in no way annulled by the union, but rather the characteristics of each nature being preserved and coming together to form one person and substance, not as parted or separated into two persons, but one and the same Son and Only-begotten God the Word, Lord Jesus Christ; even as the prophets from earliest times spoke of him, and our Lord Jesus Christ himself taught us, and the creed of the Fathers has handed down to us.[20]

Such a high view of Christ's divinity and humanity has its roots in the Old Testament prophets, in Jesus' own teaching, and in the writings of the Apostles and church fathers. Its lofty concepts help to make sense of the phenomenal personality we meet in the Gospels and the New Testa-

---

20. Taken from *The Book of Common Prayer and Administration of the Sacraments and Other Rites and Ceremonies of the Church, Together with The Psalter or Psalms of David,* According to the Use of The Episcopal Church (The Church Hymnal Corporation and The Seabury Press, 1977), p. 864.

ment letters. It far surpasses the diminished versions of him in *The Da Vinci Code,* the Jesus Seminar, and the Gnostic and apocryphal gospels. The Scriptures and the church have proclaimed Jesus Christ as God incarnate in the context of the Trinity as the foremost person in the universe and the most significant figure in human history.

## Jesus Is Lord?

*"Thomas answered and said to Him, 'My Lord and My God.'"*

John 20:28

Each of us must make up our minds about who Jesus is and what he has done. The one thing you can't say about Jesus is that he was just a great moral teacher, like a Jewish version of Socrates, Plato, or Aristotle, or some other great teacher. If he was just a teacher like other teachers and a man like other men, then how could he have said the grandiose things he said about himself with a straight face? How could he have done the miraculous things he did and only be human?

If he was merely a man and a great teacher, and yet said what he said and did what he did, then he'd be either a deluded lunatic or a demonic fiend. If he was the former, he would have misled people accidentally. If he was the latter, he was purposively deceptive. In either case, he would have been the greatest liar and the hugest hoax in recorded history.

Fortunately, another option is possible. As C. S. Lewis asserts, "You must make your choice. Either this man was, and is, the Son of God: or else a madman or something worse. You can shut Him up for a fool, you can spit at Him and kill Him as a demon; *or you can fall at His feet and call Him Lord and God.*"[21] The one thing we can't do, though many do it, is to call Jesus a great human teacher. This is not a viable alternative. Indifference or neutrality toward Jesus is not an option, either. The approach of making no decision one way or the other is, in fact, a decision.

Lunatic, liar, or Lord? On the basis of Jesus' humbling crucifixion, the apostle Paul was convinced of this last option and believed all would embrace it soon or later:

---

21. C. S. Lewis, *Mere Christianity* (New York: The Macmillan Company, 1958), p. 41 (emphasis added).

For this reason also, God highly exalted Him, and bestowed on Him the name which is above every name, so that at the name of Jesus every knee will bow, of those who are in heaven and on earth and under the earth, and that every tongue will confess that *Jesus Christ is Lord,* to the glory of God the Father. (Phil. 2:9-11, emphasis added)

## The Kingdom of God

*"The 'Kingdom of God' is . . . the manifestation and effective assertion of the divine sovereignty against all the evil of the world."*

C. H. Dodd, *The Parables of the Kingdom*[22]

In Christ as God incarnate — the great I AM in the flesh — the kingdom of God has come into the world to save it. Whereas eternal life is featured in John's Gospel, Jesus' message of the kingdom is on center stage in Matthew, Mark, and Luke. Despite its prominence in Scripture and its wide use as a phrase in the church, the concept of the kingdom is often misunderstood. Many think it is heaven, where Christians go when they die. Some equate it with the church. Others think of it as a future realm of blessing that will last for a thousand years on earth (the millennial kingdom). Lots of people believe it is the presence of God in their hearts. Still others see it as a moral call to bring liberty and justice to all.

Is it up there? Down the road? Deep within? In an ethical achievement? In some institution? Each of these views may contain a smidgen of truth, but all of them are wide of the mark. There is a better, biblical way to understand what the "kingdom of God" and its parallel expression the "kingdom of heaven" mean.[23]

**The Definition of the Kingdom**  The original biblical words for "kingdom" (Hebrew: *malkut;* Greek: *basileia*) denote the dynamic and powerful activity of ruling or reigning. Secondarily they refer to the realm, sphere,

22. C. H. Dodd, *The Parables of the Kingdom,* rev. ed. (New York: Charles Scribner's Sons, 1961), p. 35.

23. Matthew in his Gospel uses the expression "kingdom of heaven" rather than "kingdom of God" out of deference to his Jewish readers who refused to employ the name of God openly.

or territory over which the rule or reign is dynamically and powerfully exercised. The kingdom of God, then, is best defined as the authoritative exercise of God's rule, reign, or sovereignty over and in the world.[24]

In Psalm 145:11-13, God's kingdom is identified as the expression of God's power, mighty acts, and dominion in all creation. Note the parallel meanings of the italicized words in this passage.

> They shall speak of the glory of Your *kingdom*
> And talk of Your *power;*
> To make known to the sons of men Your *mighty acts*
> And the glory of the majesty of Your *kingdom.*
> Your *kingdom* is an everlasting *kingdom,*
> And Your *dominion* endures throughout all generations.

To pray for the coming of God's kingdom in the Lord's Prayer in Matthew 6:10 is to pray for God's rule and will to be realized here on earth, just as it is where God is in heaven.

> Your kingdom come,
> Your will be done,
> On earth as it is in heaven.

On this basis, then, the kingdom of God and the kingdom of heaven are the energetic rule of God present in Jesus Christ and directed in power, dominion, and sovereignty against all the evil in the world. God established his kingdom at creation. Satan attacked it in the fall and established his rival reign. In Christ, God's empire has struck back to regain and restore the world and his people.

With this big picture in mind, we can understand why John the Bap-

---

24. *Theological Dictionary of the New Testament,* vol. 1, s.v. *"Basileus, Basileia, etc." Dictionary of New Testament Theology,* vol. 2, s.v. "King, Kingdom." In the *Dictionary of Jesus and the Gospels,* s.v. "Kingdom of God/Kingdom of Heaven," C. C. Caragounis declares, "The primary meaning of the Hebrew *malekut* (with synonyms), Aramaic *malku* and Greek *basileia* is abstract and dynamic, that is, 'sovereignty' or 'royal rule.' This is almost always the case in the [Old Testament] and Jewish literature when the term is applied to God. The sense of realm — a territorial kingdom — is secondary, arising out of the necessity for a definite locus as the sphere for the exercise of sovereignty." George E. Ladd, *A Theology of the New Testament,* rev. ed., ed. Donald A. Hagner (Grand Rapids: Eerdmans, 1974, 1993), p. 61, cites Ps. 103:19; Luke 19:12; 22:29; 23:42; John 18:36; Rev. 17:12 as indicative of this dynamic meaning of "kingdom."

tist as Jesus' forerunner created such a stir. Four hundred or more years had passed since a true messenger from God had burst onto the scene. Then all of a sudden, a big, burly, hair-shirted, locust-eating man announced with prophetic gusto that the Messiah was coming and God's rule and reign was approaching. "Repent," he cried out, "for the kingdom of heaven is at hand" (Matt. 3:2). Though some were reluctant, many responded to John's preaching and were baptized. Jesus was one of them, and shortly afterward he too began to preach and show that God's kingship was clearly registering its presence in the world. "The time is fulfilled," Jesus announced, "and the kingdom of God is at hand; repent and believe in the gospel" (Mark 1:15; cf. Matt. 4:17).

**The Redemptive Purpose of the Kingdom**    The arrival of God's redeeming rule in Christ at just the right time in fulfillment of Old Testament promises was certainly good news. It was the *gospel* of the kingdom of God. The things Jesus said and did — all his words and deeds — were indications that God's rule had broken into human history and that evil in all its forms was under attack. Jesus was entering into conflict with and emerging in triumphant conquest over all the wicked powers that had wrecked people's lives and torn up this planet where they lived.

In correcting falsehood and by teaching truth, God's kingdom in Christ is redeeming knowledge. In healing diseases, restoring health, raising the dead, and feeding the hungry, God's kingdom in Christ is redeeming bodies. In stilling storms and walking on water, God's kingdom in Christ is redeeming nature. In offering grace and forgiving sin, God's kingdom in Christ is redeeming lives. All of Jesus' sermons, discourses, and parables, all of his healings, miracles, resurrections, and provisions, all of his works of power in the natural world, all of his pronouncements of mercy and forgiveness together manifest the presence of the kingdom of God in its initial victory over wickedness and the opening sign of the establishment of a new creation.

Jesus' exorcisms were a case in point. Though his enemies argued that he cast out demons by demonic power, Jesus showed how illogical such an accusation was. Why would Satan use his own authority against himself? "Any kingdom," he stated, "divided against itself is laid waste; and any city or house divided against itself will not stand" (Matt. 12:25). Instead, he performed these merciful acts of deliverance by God's Spirit, and this, he said, was positive proof that God's redeeming rule had arrived in the world: "But if I cast out demons by the Spirit of God," Jesus asserted, "then the kingdom of God has come upon you" (Matt. 12:28).

In this context, Jesus explained why he came in a quick parable: "Or how can anyone enter the strong man's house and carry off his property, unless he first binds the strong man? Then he will plunder his house" (Matt. 12:29). Satan is the "strong man," and Christ says he came to tie him up so that he might take back the property he had illegitimately acquired. In short: everything belonged to God in the beginning; Satan took it over; Jesus binds him up in order to take it back. As we read in 1 John 3:8, Jesus came "to destroy the works of the devil."

**The Mystery of the Kingdom**  This, however, was not what most people in Jesus' day were anticipating. He was not the kind of messiah they were expecting. The non-military, apolitical, and un-ethnic nature of his kingdom was simply contrary to Jewish expectations and dreams. Even John the Baptist wondered whether Jesus was the real messiah and whether he and his followers should look for someone else.

What accounts for this perplexity? Jesus read the Old Testament differently than his Jewish brothers and sisters did. His interpretation of God's messianic kingdom was quite dissimilar to his peers'. The kingdom's humble origins, its presence in redemptive words and deeds, its fulfillment through suffering and sacrifice befuddled his followers. Yet it conformed to the true Old Testament vision for the future and fulfilled the deeper divine purposes of redemption in history.

God's rule had indeed arrived inconspicuously in Jesus. "The kingdom of God," he said, "is not coming with signs to be observed; nor will they say, 'Look, here it is!' or, 'There it is!' For behold, the kingdom of God is in your midst" (Luke 17:20-21). He even pronounced a special blessing on those who did not stumble over him and the nature of his miracles and ministry (Matt. 11:2-6).

God's kingdom in Christ was a mystery. It arrived unexpectedly in a spiritual manner, in the person and work of Jesus Christ as a suffering servant. Jesus explained the mystery of the kingdom in several parables that revealed its true nature (Matt. 13; Mark 4; Luke 8). In the parable of the mustard seed and the pinch of leaven, he explained that the coming of the kingdom of God was virtually imperceptible because it was so small, visible only to the eye of faith. At the end of history, its true magnitude will be manifest clearly when the mustard seed becomes a huge plant and the pinch of leaven leavens the whole lump of dough.

Despite the kingdom's unpretentious presence, people should not underestimate its value as their most precious possession on earth. Like a man who sacrifices everything to acquire a treasure hidden in a field, or as a merchant who sells all he owns to purchase a priceless pearl, so each person must make any sacrifice necessary to submit to and enjoy the blessings of salvation in the hidden treasure and priceless pearl of God's kingdom.

Though people believed that this kingdom would be promoted by military might and political strategies, Jesus said it would be spread to others by the modest means of preaching. Like seed sown into various kinds of soil, so the word of the kingdom planted in various kinds of human hearts would yield various results. In some cases it would be fruitful; in some cases it would not. Since there would be both positive and negative responses to the message of the kingdom, this meant that the righteous and the wicked would unexpectedly co-exist side by side until the end, just as wheat and weeds (tares) remain together in a field until the time of the harvest.

The parables of the mustard seed and the leaven, of the hidden treasure and the costly pearl, of the sower and the soils, and of the wheat and the tares explain how God's kingdom entered the world in the simplicity of Christ's humble life, ministry, death, and resurrection. Despite its lack of ostentation, God's kingdom in Christ is the greatest human good. It is promoted by the preaching of the gospel. Believers and unbelievers will live together side by side in the world until God's kingdom fully comes and makes the final separation. And its greatest mystery of all is the cross.

**The Kingdom and the Cross**   Kings and queens in their pomp and circumstance expect to be served by their constituents. But Jesus, king of all kings, said that he "did not come to be served, but to serve and to give his life a ransom for many" (Mark 10:45). He knew that his life of faithful service would also culminate in his sacrificial death on the cross, but that it would be the superlative expression of the mystery of the kingdom of God in its triumph over evil.

Outwardly, there was nothing royal or kingly about Christ's death and its associated events. He was betrayed by one of his disciples; he was force-fully arrested and falsely tried by Jewish and Roman authorities; he was mercilessly beaten with rods and whipped within a centimeter of his life with a cat-o'-nine-tails; he was dressed in sarcastic robes; he was scornfully mocked, slapped, spat upon, and crowned with painful thorns; one of his followers denied him, and all the others deserted him; he was made to carry his own instrument of execution; he was stripped naked; he was nailed painfully to the cross through his hands and feet; he was ridiculed by soldiers and passers-by; he was verbally abused by a criminal crucified with him; he thirsted greatly and bled profusely; he felt God had abandoned him; he died of excruciating suffocation; he was pierced in his side by a soldier's sword; he was hastily buried in a borrowed grave.

What king in his right mind would submit to such indignities? Yet in his passion and death, Jesus is revealed at his kingly best. It has to be the greatest irony in history. Though it appears to be nothing but condemnation, defeat, death, and humiliation, in reality it turns out to be salvation, victory, life, and exaltation. In the condemnation of the cross, Christ paid the penalty for sin and obtained salvation. In the defeat of the cross, Christ conquered Satan and demons and triumphed over them. In death on the cross, Christ destroyed death itself, and he restored life by resurrection. In the humiliation of the cross Christ was exalted, because he won the victory over all his enemies! The mystery of the kingdom is the mystery of the cross: salvation through condemnation, victory through defeat, life through death, exaltation through humiliation. As the church fathers proclaimed, "The Lord rules from the cross" — *Christus Victor.* Thanks be to God!

Yet not all are thankful. For some Jews, the notion of a dying and rising Messiah was a stumbling block and a rock of offense. For some Gentiles, the idea that the world's salvation resides in a crucified and resurrected Jewish peasant who claimed to be God was utter foolishness. For many people, there was just no way that humanity's redemption, greatest good, and genuine happiness could be found in Jesus Christ. Many are of the same opinion still (1 Cor. 1:18-31).

God's paradigm, however, is quite different from ours. God's thoughts and ways are not our thoughts and ways. Accordingly, those who have trusted in Christ have discovered him, sometimes surprisingly, to be the power and wisdom of God, the source of salvation, peace, and contentment, and the basis of the deep meaning of happiness. God has been pleased through the apparent foolishness and weakness of the gospel of the kingdom to save those who believe, for in reality "the foolishness of God is wiser than men, and the weakness of God is stronger than men" (1 Cor. 1:25).

## Propitiation, Redemption, Reconciliation, Justification

*"But God demonstrates His own love toward us, in that while we were yet sinners, Christ died for us."*

Romans 5:8

In reflecting upon the kingdom-as-cross and the cross-as-kingdom, Paul and other New Testament writers describe its theological meaning and spiritual implications in several important ways. They draw on images from everyday life — the temple, the marketplace, personal relationships, and the courtroom — to convey the meaning of Christ's sacrifice and his kingdom victory on our behalf.

**Propitiation**  To begin with, temple sacrifices help us to understand Christ's death as a *propitiation* for our sin through his blood (Rom. 3:25; Heb. 2:17; 1 John 2:1-2; 4:10). Propitiation is an unfamiliar word, but it is really easy to understand. Our sin, of course, violates God's standards of righteousness, which makes him angry with us (cf. Ps. 7:11). His justice demands that an appropriate punishment be administered for our transgressions. As Numbers 14:18 states, "He will by no means clear the guilty." We are taught this, even know it intuitively, and keenly sense God's displeasure at our wrongdoing. We feel we must do whatever we can to satisfy God's justice and turn God's wrath away from us. "What can I do to make God happy with me?" or "How can I get right with God?" are our innermost thoughts. Despite all the good works and sacrifices, we fail to make appropriate restitution and eliminate God's real and felt antagonism toward us.

But this is exactly what Christ has accomplished on our behalf! Just as fines, incarceration, and other forms of punishment satisfy the demands of the law and avert the fury of the state toward us, so Christ's death satisfies the requirements of divine justice and eliminates his anger toward us. Jesus has placated God's sense of justice by offering his blood as an atoning sacrifice on our behalf. It makes us acceptable to him — that's what propitiation is. We don't have to secure God's favor or acceptance by our own efforts. Instead, we rely on what Jesus has accomplished for us. What relief this brings! Though this notion reminds us of God's wrath, it is actually a superlative expression of God's love. As 1 John 4:10 states, "In this is love, not that we loved God, but that He loved us and sent His Son to be the propitiation for our sins."

**Redemption**   We also understand the meaning of Christ's kingdom and cross in terms of the purchase and release of slaves from the marketplace as *redemption* (Rom. 3:24; 1 Cor. 1:30; Gal. 3:13; 4:5; Eph. 1:7, 14; 4:30; Col. 1:14; Titus 2:14; 1 Pet. 1:18; Heb. 9:12, 15; cf. 1 Cor. 6:19-20; 7:22-23). According to Scripture, we are in the unfortunate condition of slavery — slavery to sin (John 8:34; Rom. 6:16; 7:14), slavery to death (Rom. 6:23; Heb. 2:14-15), and slavery to Satan (Acts 26:18; Col. 1:13). Sin blinds us mentally and corrupts us morally, so that we live in bondage to deception and guilt. Sin also separates us from God and produces spiritual and physical death. Death imprisons us through fear, as we fret over our end and worry about an uncertain future. Satan not only employs sin and death, but also works through the enticements of "the world" to keep us subjected to his dominion of darkness. "Chains are the portion of revolted man, stripes and a dungeon," says poet William Cowper.[25] These powerful chains often control us apart from our conscious knowledge, much less our permission. How impotent we are to escape them by our own efforts. We need help to find a way out.

    This is why Christ came — to redeem us as the incarcerated ones from sin, death, and Satan, and all the misery this bondage causes in our lives. This deliverance was not without cost. A ransom had to be paid to secure our manumission. We could only be emancipated by the payment of a price, and that price was the blood of Jesus Christ. "In Him," writes the Apostle Paul, "we have redemption through his blood, the forgiveness of our sins, according to the riches of His grace" (Eph. 1:7). By His gracious sacrifice, we are released from our sin and guilt and are restored to God. Our fear of a damning death is eliminated. We are also set free from Satan's sway. Like Moses of old who led Israel out of Egypt, Christ is the leader of a new and even greater exodus. As Paul writes in Colossians

---

25. Cowper, "The Winter Morning Walk," book 5 of *The Task*, in *Cowper: Poetical Works*, p. 212 (lines 581-82).

1:13-14, "For He rescued us from the domain of darkness, and transferred us to the kingdom of His beloved Son, in whom we have redemption, the forgiveness of sins."

**Reconciliation**  The restoration of broken relationships provides yet a third image that helps us comprehend the work of Christ in terms of *reconciliation* (Rom. 5:10-11; 2 Cor. 5:18-21; Eph. 2:11-16; Col. 1:19-23). God created us to enjoy a relationship of love with himself. Our sin, however, created considerable friction. We were "alienated" from God and living in a state of hostility and enmity before God. Since we are engaged in the practice of evil deeds (even if we don't realize it), God regards us as enemies. He cannot tolerate our disobedience. We are far off from God, and he is far off from us. We need to be reunited with our maker, whom one day we will have to meet face to face and give an account of our lives. The only way we can be reconciled to God is if the primary cause of the conflict between us is removed. That cause, of course, is our sin. Just as an appropriate apology or restitution for an offense reconciles people who have been at odds, so Christ died on the cross to remove this barrier that has separated us from him.

Christ's death has reconciled everything to God. God made all things, all things were besmirched by sin, and Christ has reconciled all things to God by the blood of his cross. As Paul points out in Colossians 1:19-20, "it was the Father's good pleasure for all the fullness to dwell in Him [Jesus], and through Him to reconcile *all things* to Himself, having made peace through the blood of His cross; through Him, I say, whether *things on earth or things in heaven*" (emphasis added). In Christ, we can relate once again to God in peace, acceptability, and even friendship. This gracious message of reconciliation is proclaimed through God's ambassadors in urgent terms: "we beg you on behalf of Christ, be reconciled to God" (2 Cor. 5:20-21).

**Justification**  The courtroom provides the background to explaining Christ's sacrifice for us in legal terms as *justification* (Rom. 3:21-30; 5:1, 9; Gal. 2:15–3:29; Phil. 3:8-9). To understand this concept, picture yourself on trial in the Supreme Court where God is chief justice.[26] For such a legal task, God is preeminently credentialed and capable. Though remarkably

---

26. The reflections in this paragraph are based on various verses in Romans 1–3.

tolerant of our past infractions, now he impartially brings to light all the bad things we have ever said and done. They are not few in number. No wonder God's anger seemed to rain down on us from heaven. As the law is read and our sins revealed, we stand condemned before him. Our mouths are shut in any attempt at self-defense. We are held accountable for our wrongdoings. He judges us according to our deeds and sentences us to death. There are no excuses. Great regret and terror seize us simultaneously as we realize the error of our ways and the judgment that awaits us. Whether now or later, we know it is "a terrifying thing to fall into the hands of the living God" (Heb. 10:31).

We would go to our just punishment *if it weren't for the justifying work of Jesus Christ on our behalf.* He achieved this in two ways. First, he obeyed God's law fully and faithfully, and lived a perfectly righteous and obedient life (2 Cor. 5:21; 1 Pet. 2:22). This was the very thing we didn't do, and couldn't. Second, he bore the penalty of our moral failure through his death on the cross (Gal. 3:13; Col. 2:13-14). There was no way for us either to vindicate ourselves or pay for our own sins. "By the works of the Law," Paul says, "no flesh [i.e., person] will be justified" (Gal. 2:16). So Christ did it for us in our place! He is our substitute. He died on our behalf.

By Christ's blameless life and his sacrificial death, God's law has been fulfilled and the penalty for its violation has been paid. In this equation, sin and guilt are subtracted and Christ and his righteousness are added to our lives the moment we believe. Justification is not something we achieve, but something we receive, if we believe. Original sin was imputed or imparted to humanity; humanity's sin was imputed or imparted to Christ; Christ's righteousness is imputed or imparted to those who believe. This means peace with God! For if we are justified by faith, "we have peace with God through our Lord Jesus Christ" (Rom. 5:1).

So here is what Jesus accomplished for us. He satisfied God's justice and averted his anger. That's propitiation. He paid the ransom price to deliver us from bondage to sin, death, and Satan. That's redemption. He removed the enmity and alienation caused by our sin and restored us to fellowship with God. That's reconciliation. He fulfilled the law perfectly, canceled sin's penalty, and gave us the gift of righteousness. That's justification. The good news is that God's displeasure toward you has been removed and he accepts you fully, that you have been released from slavery to sin, death, and the devil, that your estranged relationship with God has been restored, and that you are perfectly righteous in his sight!

Here, then, is the central question you must consider: How will you respond to this great offer of salvation? What will you do with Christ in light of what Christ has done for you? How will you escape if you neglect so great a salvation?

## What Must I *Do* to Be Saved?

*"Believe in the Lord Jesus, and you will be saved, you and your household."*

Acts 16:31

Consciously or unconsciously, we have all made it the chief business of our lives to be saved. From almost the time we are born until the moment we die, we have been on a quest to figure out how we might deliver ourselves from our unpleasant or miserable circumstances, and find some kind of purpose, peace, and lasting felicity for our lives. People are continuously looking for some good news that makes life worthwhile. We need a gospel. We need salvation and we seek it every day, even if we don't think of it as such. The central question and quest of our lives is this: "Where is hope and happiness to be found?"

Many think they have found it, and they are on a mission to share it with others in an evangelistic sort of way, even if it's just a pyramid-marketing scheme. We are ambassadors for our "gospel," whatever it may be. Salesmen, advertisers, politicians, and others are enthusiastic in promoting their products and programs because they think what they have to offer is the sure and certain way to happiness. We believe and join in on the campaign. In this sense, everybody has a religion, even if it's religion in a disguise. Life is a quest for salvation in one way or another, whether we realize it or not.

The trouble, of course, is that our gospels are Christless gospels. Their benefits are partial and temporary, and leave us looking for something more. In fact, the deeper we move into our systems of homemade salvation, the worse things become. Our faiths falter, our hopes fade, our loves disappoint, our meanings fizzle, our freedoms bind, our contentment collapses, and our saviors fail to save. Jesus knew this would be the case, so he presents himself as our solution, along with serious warnings should we choose to ignore him.

Then Jesus said to His disciples, "If anyone wishes to come after Me, he must deny himself, and take up his cross, and follow Me. For whoever wishes to save his life will lose it; but whoever loses his life for My sake will find it. For what will it profit a man if he gains the whole world and forfeits his soul? Or what will a man give in exchange for his soul?" (Matthew 16:24-26; cf. Mark 8:34-38; Luke 9:23-25)

Christ's forthright words imply that the first significant step toward salvation is found in *repentance*. An "about-face" in your spiritual life rarely if ever happens if you have not first been struck in some significant way by the fear of God.[27] Under this frightening and yet motivating influence, the idea of repentance becomes sweet, since it is a signal of hope for real change. It begins with a profound alteration in our way of thinking. We realize we were wrong in the way we thought about God. The name of Jesus Christ wasn't just a swear word. In fact, Jesus' name is precious. He is the Savior and Lord of the world.

A change of mind also causes us to feel sorry for our sins, to regret our previous attitudes and behaviors, to be ashamed of our behaviors. Under this kind of conviction, grief washes over us as we recognize the error of our ways. How could I have thought the way I thought . . . so falsely? How could I have spoken the way I have spoken . . . so sacrilegiously? How could I have loved the way I have loved . . . so selfishly? How could I have lived the way I have lived . . . so foolishly?

In repentance, you make a 180-degree turn from yourself to Jesus Christ. As the passage above indicates, this involves denying yourself, taking up your cross, and following him. Denying yourself means forsaking your life of prideful independence from God. Taking up your cross means the crucifixion of your own selfish will and ways. Following Jesus means submitting to him in faith, no matter the cost.

There is a cost-benefit ratio in turning or not turning to Christ. To have it all, here and now, will cost you Jesus. Is it worth gaining the whole world, if it means forfeiting him? To have Jesus will cost you everything. Isn't it worth getting him, even if it means forfeiting the world? In the end, you will either save your life or lose it, depending upon your response to Jesus. What are you willing to give in exchange for your soul?

---

27. Augustine, *The Catechising of the Uninstructed*, trans. S. D. F. Salmond, in *Nicene and Post-Nicene Fathers*, ed. Philip Schaff, First Series, vol. 3 (Peabody, Mass.: Hendrickson Publishers, Inc., 1994), p. 288 (§5.9).

The key to Christ is faith. Not blind faith, but a faith that consists of knowledge, assent, and trust. You know who Jesus is and what he has accomplished. You assent in your mind to the truth of this knowledge about him. You trust in him totally to save you and become your Lord. You cast yourself wholeheartedly upon him as the King who conquered sin, death, and Satan. You rely upon him as the one who propitiates God on your behalf, redeems you from slavery to Satan, sin, and death, reconciles you to be friends with God, and gives you the gift of his righteousness to secure a perfect standing in God's sight. Salvation is God's gracious work for you, not your futile work for God. It's a matter of believing, not achieving. There is salvation in no one else, no other name in all creation by which you must be saved (Acts 4:12).

## What Does It *Mean* to Be Saved?

*"Who would have thought my shriveled heart*
*Could have recovered greenness?"*

George Herbert, "The Flower"[28]

Christianity knows nothing of a gospel of cheap grace — "grace without discipleship, grace without the cross."[29] It's like marriage: you give yourself totally to your spouse, and your spouse does likewise (or at least that's the ideal). Christ as our bridegroom expects nothing less from us (Eph. 5:22-33). Commitment to Christ is also like going to war or constructing a tower. No one of sound mind would undertake a military campaign or a building project unless the costs were clear (Luke 14:28-32). Salvation involves both conflict and construction, and you need to know what you are getting into before you get into it. The terms of the offer are clear. There is no fine print.

Evidence of a real commitment to Christ manifests itself in at least three ways. First, if we are converted to Christ, we will be baptized in water "in the name of the Father and the Son and Holy Spirit" (Matt. 28:19; see

28. George Herbert, "The Flower," in *The Works of George Herbert*, intro. and bibliog. Tim Cook, The Wordsworth Poetry Library (Hertfordshire, England: Wordsworth Editions, Ltd., 1994), p. 154.

29. Dietrich Bonhoeffer, *The Cost of Discipleship*, rev. ed., trans. R. H. Fuller, rev. Irmgard Booth (New York: Macmillan Publishing Co., Inc., 1963), p. 47.

also Acts 2:38; 22:16; Rom. 6:3-4; Gal. 3:27; Col. 2:11-12; 1 Pet. 3:21, etc.). Though the mode of baptism is disputed, its meaning is sufficiently clear. It is a public manifestation of our decision to become followers or disciples of Jesus. It identifies us with Christ's death, burial, and resurrection. It symbolizes that the penalty and power of sin have been broken and that we have been raised to newness of life in Christ. It is a sign of our citizenship in the kingdom of God that surpasses all other allegiances. Baptism is an exit and an entrance, both a funeral and a birthday. It has personal, public, and political meanings.

Second, becoming a Christian also means we are incorporated into the church as the body of Christ. The watermark of baptism is also a New Testament image used of the Holy Spirit, who "immerses" us into the body of Christ regardless of our ethnic background or social standing (1 Cor. 12:13). Spiritual integration into Christ's body is expressed concretely by active participation in a local church where God's word is proclaimed, the sacraments are administered, and we are submissive to the church's leadership and discipline. In this setting, we can grow in the grace and knowledge of our Lord and Savior Jesus Christ, learning what it means to be his well informed and transformed followers as we take our place in the community of faith, both serving and being served (2 Pet. 3:18; Gal. 4:19; Col. 1:28).

Finally, Christians must live in a manner worthy of the calling with which they have been called (Eph. 4:1). Faith alone justifies, but the faith that justifies is never alone. If it's genuine, it is always accompanied by good works. We must do what we know and behave as we believe. Otherwise, our hypocrisy would suggest that we have neither known nor believed as we should. We are saved by God's grace through faith, not by good works. Yet good works do show that we have been saved. Salvation and sanctification are two sides of the same coin. As Paul writes in Ephesians 2:8-10, "For by grace you have been saved through faith; and that not of yourselves, it is the gift of God; not as a result of works, so that no one may boast. For we are His workmanship, created in Christ Jesus for good works, which God prepared beforehand so that we would walk in them."

The assumption behind this text is that outward actions stem from inward conditions. A bad tree produces bad fruit, and a good tree produces good fruit. We can talk all we want, but how we live day to day speaks volumes about our condition within. As William Cowper puts it, "Nay —

conduct hath the loudest tongue. . . ./In the deed,/The unequivocal authentic deed,/We find sound argument, we read the heart."[30] What does your conduct say about you? What argument do your deeds make on your behalf? How do they interpret your heart? The gospel at its heart and core reorders our loves and our lives and enables us to taste shalom once again.

---

30. Cowper, "The Winter Morning Walk," book 5 of *The Task,* in *Cowper: Poetical Works,* p. 214 (lines 650, 652-53).

## CHAPTER FIVE

# Reordered Love:
# The Expulsive Power of a New Affection

*"'You must sit down,' says Love, 'and taste my meat.' So I did sit and eat."*

George Herbert, "Love Bade Me Welcome"[1]

## Introduction

"Hello, I'm Johnny Cash." With these words sonorously spoken, the "quintessential American troubadour"[2] introduces himself at the beginning of one of his most famous ballads, "Folsom Prison Blues." It's a classic about the woes of incarceration and the longing to be free. Hearing the lonely whistle of a nearby train and imagining its passengers enjoying an evening of exuberant activities only enhances the prisoner's regret and desire for emancipation. Their freedom — traveling, eating, drinking, and smoking to their heart's content — and his bondage drive him crazy, even though he knows he's getting what he deserves:

1. George Herbert, "Love Bade Me Welcome," in *The Works of George Herbert,* intro. and bibliography Tim Cook, The Wordsworth Poetry Library (Hertfordshire: Wordsworth Editions, Ltd., 1994), p. 176.
   2. Johnny Cash, with Patrick Carr, *Cash: The Autobiography* (New York: HarperSanFrancisco, HarperCollins Publishers, 1997), book flap.

But those people keep a movin',
And that's what tortures me.[3]

Cash's realistic way of singing about life in prison led many to believe that he was once a convict himself. Actually, he never was, as long as we ignore several overnight stays in the jailhouse for occasional misdemeanors. Despite his rough-and-tumble life, somehow Cash managed to escape doing hard time, at least literally. Metaphorically, by his own admission, he was locked up in the "penitentiary of his own soul."[4]

Indeed, Cash lived a notable and yet difficult life. Over his seventy-one years, he embodied multiple identities and roles, each authentic: "Songwriter. Six-string strummer. Storyteller. Country boy. Rock star. Folk hero. Preacher. Poet. Drug addict. Rebel. Sinner. Saint. Victim. Survivor. Home wrecker. Husband. Father. Klan target. Outlaw. Moviemaker. Jailbird. Jailhouse troubadour. Truth teller. Novelist. Salesman. War protestor. Patriot. Hell raiser. Heavenly guide."[5] A line in Kris Kristofferson's tribute song to Cash, "The Pilgrim," sums up his journey pretty well: "Takin' ev'ry wrong direction on his lonely way back home."[6]

From early on, Cash traversed the pathway of self-destruction. In the grip of self-hatred, fear, and loneliness, he was addicted to drugs and drink, and he was given to frequent fits of rage and violence. He marvels at the depths of selfishness to which he descended. Not unexpectedly, his first marriage ended in divorce. "You know," Cash confesses, "I had my years in the wilderness, had my years when the demons crawled up my back."[7] At the time, Cash could likely resonate with this famous cry of the heart: "My life, being such, was it life, O my God?"[8]

3. Johnny Cash, "Folsum Prison Blues," Sun Records, 1955; also in the album *Johnny Cash with His Hot and Blue Guitar*, Sun Records, 1957; *At Folsum Prison*, Columbia, 1968; Sony CD re-release, 1999.

4. Russell D. Moore, "Real Hard Cash," *Touchstone: A Journal of Mere Christianity* 18, no. 10 (December 2005): 18.

5. Dave Urbanski, *The Man Comes Around: The Spiritual Journey of Johnny Cash*, foreword Dan Haseltine (Relevant Books), pp. xv-xvi.

6. Quoted in Steve Turner, *The Man Called Cash: The Life, Love, and Faith of an American Legend* (Nashville: W Publishing Group, A Division of Thomas Nelson Publishers, 2004), p. xvii.

7. Johnny Cash, *My Mother's Hymn Book*, American Recordings 2004, liner notes, pp. 14-15.

8. Augustine, *Confessions*, trans. Edward B. Pusey, *The Great Books of the Western World*, ed.

Cash's story is particularly fascinating because of its spiritual dimension. He was a Christian, and had been since his childhood. "Beyond that," he admits, "I get complicated."[9] His parents bequeathed to him the legacy of a Baptist and Pentecostal faith, even though his father's testimony was often inconsistent. That plus the narrow focus of his spiritual heritage fostered a restlessness within him that eventually bubbled over into rebellion and waywardness.[10] Cash was a classic case of a prodigal Christian, who in dramatic fashion squandered his life in loose living. Under the pleasures, pressures, and pains of a show-business career, he deserted his first love for many years. For his departure from God, he paid a heavy price.

Eventually things changed. Cash longed for peace and contentment. He had tried everything, and everything he tried had failed him. To use his own words, he was "scraping the filthy bottom of the barrel of life."[11] Happiness for Cash was typically elusive. Having reached a crossroads, the choices before him were literally a matter of life or death. During the darkest nights of his soul, the old-time gospel hymns learned at his mother's knee still reverberated in his battered brain, summoning him back to God.

> Softly and tenderly Jesus is calling,
> Calling for you and for me;
> See, on the portals he's waiting and watching,
> Watching for you and for me.
> Come home, come home,
> Ye who are weary come home;
> Earnestly, tenderly, Jesus is calling,
> Calling, O sinner, come home![12]

This music, the sacrificial love of his second wife June Carter Cash, and the care and concern of indomitable friends were instrumental in his return to faith. "Eventually — slowly, with relapses and setbacks," Cash re-

---

Robert M. Hutchins, vol. 18 (Chicago: William Benton, Publisher, Encyclopedia Britannica, Inc., 1952), p. 14 (§3.2).

9. Cash, *Cash: The Autobiography*, p. 7.

10. Christopher S. Wren, *Winners Got Scars Too: The Life and Legends of Johnny Cash* (New York: The Dial Press, 1971), p. 48, cited in Urbanski, *The Man Comes Around*, p. 11.

11. Cash, *Cash: The Autobiography*, p. 169.

12. "Softly and Tenderly," Will L. Thompson, *Baptist Hymnal*, 1975 edition (Nashville: Convention Press, 1975), p. 190.

calls, "I regained my strength and sanity and I rebuilt my connection to God. . . . The greatest joy of my life was that I no longer felt separated from Him."[13] Had the prodigal not returned, like many entertainers in his generation, Cash would have probably died tragically as a younger man.

The Lord set this prisoner free, and Cash became free as the prisoner of the Lord. To be sure, he traversed the road ahead imperfectly. In Cash's own mind, he was at best "a C-minus Christian."[14] One of his biographers, however, grades him a little differently:

> Cash was an inspiration to Christians because of the candid way in which he discussed the problems that had affected his life. By admitting his mistakes he gave hope to the spiritually battered and abused. He also suggested a way of living the Christian life that was uncompromising yet compassionate, dedicated to timeless truths yet relevant to contemporary issues, in the world yet not of it, orthodox yet hip.[15]

Cash trekked through a deep wilderness of ignorance and wrong desire with painful consequences. In returning to Christ and the gospel, new loves and affections slowly but surely replaced his older ones. Cash's experience illustrates a common psychological process: old disordered loves will remain intact until new, reordered loves arrive to drive them out and take their place.

## "The Expulsive Power of a New Affection"

*"We see the world of mankind to be exceedingly busy and active;
and the affections of men are the springs of the motion. . . ."*

Jonathan Edwards, *Treatise on the Religious Affections*[16]

One of the primary effects of the gospel, whether we are coming to it for the first time or returning to it as Cash did, is the reordering of our deepest loves and desires. A nineteenth-century Scottish theologian and preacher

---

13. Cash, *Cash: The Autobiography*, p. 173.

14. Johnny Cash, *My Mother's Hymn Book*, liner notes, p. 10.

15. Turner, *The Man Called Cash*, p. 234.

16. Jonathan Edwards, *Religious Affections*, ed. John E. Smith, The Works of Jonathan Edwards, gen. ed., Perry Miller, vol. 2 (New Haven: Yale University Press, 1959), p. 101.

named Thomas Chalmers (1780-1847) examined the dynamics of this inner process in an address with the quaint title, "The Expulsive Power of a New Affection."[17] He wanted to know how our disordered love for things in the sinful world — the lusts of the flesh, the lusts of the eyes, and the boastful pride of life — can be dispersed from our hearts and be replaced with a rightly ordered love for God. He was convinced there were two basic ways to achieve this. The first was to demonstrate the *world's vanity* in such a way that our desires for its superficial enticements would be eradicated. On its own, the world and its attractions are shallow and empty, and when we see this, we will be repulsed and naturally withdraw our affections from it.

The second way to is to place *God in his grandeur* before our hearts as the object worthy of our love and devotion. We are not asked to give up loving one thing without being offered something better in its place. We "exchange an old affection for a new one" as an increasing awareness of the majesty of God dissolves our attachments to the world in our hearts (p. 301).

The method of vanity-exposure by itself, of course, is glaringly incompetent. We love by nature and need, and we must have objects to seek and satisfy us, even if the things we search for and secure are basically worthless. Since our desires are virtually bottomless, we will continue to be enthralled with "vanity fair" if there is nothing more compelling to replace it. Mere moral exhortation is also a futile way to disinfect the love of the world from our hearts. "Do not handle, do not taste, do not touch!" (Col. 2:21) are toothless spiritual demands if our very lives and happiness depend upon the things we can handle, taste and touch, and cherish. As Chalmers explains,

> Nothing can exceed the magnitude of the required change in a man's character — when bidden, as he is in the New Testament, to love not the world; no, nor any of the things that are in the world — for this so comprehends all that is dear to him in existence as to be equivalent to a command of self-annihilation. (p. 307)

17. Thomas Chalmers, "The Expulsive Power of a New Affection," in *20 Centuries of Great Preaching: An Encyclopedia of Preaching*, ed. Clyde E. Fant Jr. and William M. Pinson Jr., vol. 3, Wesley to Finney, 1703-1875 (Waco, Tex.: Word Books, 1971), pp. 300-314. Page numbers in parentheses are from this volume. This essay is available online at: http://www.newble.co .uk/chalmers/comm9.html (accessed July 2, 2007).

Our faculties of desire can never be destroyed and shouldn't be, but they can be redirected, as when one taste supplants another — like steak for hamburger. New affections for God in his greatness will jettison our old affections for the world in its inferiority, since the former is so much more alluring than the latter. To put it in the language of this book, reordered love for God will overcome our disordered love for the world only when we see and relish the beauty of God, manifested especially in Christ and his cross. To the eye of faith, nothing surpasses the glory of God incarnate and the triumph of his redemption! Such a radical shift in our affections has to be a work of grace if we are to be delivered from bondage to our former desires and enjoy the freedom Christ has given us.

For Chalmers, the alternatives were clear. *Either* we will love the world *or* we love God, but both loves cannot occupy the same heart simultaneously. "The love of God and the love of the world," he says, "are two affections, not merely in a state of rivalship, but in a state of enmity — and that so irreconcilable, that they cannot dwell together in the same bosom" (p. 307).

This either/or dichotomy could be misleading and needs some clarification. We should understand the expulsive power of a new affection in terms of loving both God and the world God made *in a right relation*, rather than being forced to choose between the two. We cultivate a new affection for God at the expense of *worldliness*, but not at the expense of the *world*. We cultivate a new affection for God at the expense of *corruption*, but not at the expense of *creation*. It's the corruption in creation and the worldliness in the world that should be expelled by a new affection for God, not affection or love for the creation or the world itself. A reordered love for God should reorder our love for the created world, not eliminate it.

In any case, until God is preeminently attractive to us and all things in life are loved in right relation to him, we will seek to satisfy our desires and find our happiness in a creation emptied of its Creator. Stuffing ourselves with earthly things, however, is bound to clog our arteries and cause constipation. C. S. Lewis would remind us that we are so content with our ordinary sources of happiness that we can't even imagine what better ones would be like:

> We are half-hearted creatures, fooling around with drink and sex and ambition when infinite joy is offered to us, like an ignorant child who wants to go on making mud pies in the slum because he cannot imag-

ine what is meant by the offer of a holiday at the sea. We are far too easily pleased.[18]

Johnny Cash gorged himself on "mud pies" in his early life, and they nearly killed him. We have dined on our own diets of dirt with predictable consequences. Escaping the miserable mud of the slums for a trip to the delightful sands of the sea requires following the route of reordered love.

## Reordered Love for God

*"We have heard, then, what and how much we must love; this we must strive after, and to this we must refer all our plans."*

Augustine, "Of the Morals of the Catholic Church"[19]

When a scribe asked Jesus what was the greatest commandment of all, he responded by quoting Deuteronomy 6:4-5, slightly changing the original Old Testament passage by adding the word "mind":

Jesus answered, "The foremost is, 'Hear, O Israel! The Lord our God is one Lord; and you shall love the Lord your God with all your heart, and with all your soul and with all your mind and with all your strength.'" (Mark 12:29-30; cf. Matthew 22:37-38; Luke 10:27)

In the greatest commandment, Jesus tells us *what* we are to love, *how* we are to love it, and by implication, *why*. Together this what, how, and why form the single primary reason for which the Bible, and indeed, people, exist.

**What We Are to Love**   The first thing Jesus tells us is *what* we are to love, and that, of course, is God. He assumed that his listeners knew something about the one whom they were to love, so he offered no real description of God. We, on the other hand, could use a little more information about who this God is and what this God is like.

18. C. S. Lewis, *The Weight of Glory and Other Addresses* (Grand Rapids: Eerdmans, 1949, 1965), p. 2.
19. Augustine, "Of the Morals of the Catholic Church," trans. Richard Stothert, in *The Nicene and Post-Nicene Fathers*, ed. Philip Schaff, New Series, vol. 4 (Peabody, Mass.: Hendrickson Publishers, 1994), p. 45 (§8.13).

If we approach God philosophically, we would employ reason and evidence to discover as much about him with our minds as we can. In this manner, some have argued in a purely rational way that God's total perfection implies his existence. If he is absolutely perfect, he can't lack anything, existence included. Others explain some feature of nature by appealing to God as its ultimate source. If the universe is an effect, then God must be its cause; if it's well designed, God must be its grand designer; if there is motion, God must be the prime mover; if there are degrees of perfection in beings, God must be the most perfect; if there are temporary, contingent beings, God must be their eternal, necessary ground. The infinitely perfect being based on these arguments is appropriately called God, the uncaused cause of all that is caused. This God of philosophy is also identified as the God of the Bible.

From a theological standpoint, we can form a systematic concept of God based on what many passages in the Scriptures say about him. In this tradition, the second chapter of *The Westminster Confession of Faith* offers a bracing description of God's attributes, God's self-sufficiency and sovereignty, and God's nature as trinity. It is worth quoting and contemplating at length.

> I. There is but one only, living, and true God, who is infinite in being and perfection, a most pure spirit, invisible, without body, parts, or passions; immutable, immense, eternal, incomprehensible, almighty, most wise, most holy, most free, most absolute, working all things according to the counsel of His own immutable and most righteous will, for His own glory; most loving, gracious, merciful, long-suffering, abundant in goodness and truth, forgiving iniquity, transgression, and sin; the rewarder of them that diligently seek Him; and withal [also], most just and terrible in His judgments; hating all sin, and who will by no means clear the guilty.
>
> II. God hath all life, glory, goodness, blessedness, in and of Himself; and is alone in and unto Himself all-sufficient, not standing in need of any creatures which He hath made, nor deriving any glory from them, but only manifesting His own glory in, by, unto, and upon them: He is the alone foundation of all being, of whom, through whom, and to whom are all things; and hath most sovereign dominion over them, to do by them, for them, or upon them whatsoever Himself pleaseth. In His sight all things are open and manifest, His knowledge is infinite, in-

fallible, and independent upon the creature; so as nothing is to Him contingent or uncertain. He is most holy in all His counsels, in all His works, and in all His commands. To Him is due from angels and men, and every other creature, whatsoever worship, service, or obedience He is pleased to require of them.

III. In the unity of the Godhead there be three persons, of one substance, power, and eternity: God the Father, God the Son, and God the Holy Ghost. The Father is of none, neither begotten, not proceeding; the Son is eternally begotten of the Father; the Holy Ghost eternally proceeding from the Father and the Son.[20]

We can also seek to understand God from the vantage point of his works. Just as we know and respond to people on the basis of the deeds they do in day-to-day life, so we also learn about God through the great things he has done in history. While God's deeds are many, they can be classified in the three major categories of creation, judgment, and redemption. God's sovereignty, wisdom, and power are revealed in his work as the maker of the heavens and the earth. God's holiness, righteousness, and justice are on display as the just judge of human sin and rebellion. God's mercy, love, and grace are manifested in his grand work of redemption in the person and work of Jesus Christ.

God is the Redeemer of this fallen creation, the Savior of this sin-shattered world. God delivers the creation from uncreation. God is the maker and re-maker of the heavens and the earth! God is what we are to love according to the greatest commandment, and the knowledge of God derived from philosophy, theology, and his works replaces our ignorance as the foundation upon which our loves for God are reordered. Some homemade, staccato-like verses that summarize the biblical narrative may give us a glimpse of the greatness of God as the one we are to love supremely.

Trinity — Father, Son, Holy Spirit.
Eternity, love, decrees.

Beginning, God, bang, *ex nihilo,* heavens, earth.
Formless, void, dark.

20. John H. Leith, ed., *Creeds of the Churches: A Reader in Christian Doctrine from the Bible to the Present,* 3rd ed. (Atlanta: John Knox Press, 1982), p. 197.

Spirit-dove, waters.
Light, land, sea.
Plants, trees, stars, moon,
Fish, birds, beasts, creepers.
Humanity, image, likeness, rule, subdue.
Male, female, blessing, dominion, be fruitful, multiply, food.
Man, garden, woman, marriage. *Shalom.*
* * * * * * * * *


Serpent, crafty. Not eat? Eaten.
Naked, fear, shame, guilt, hiding, blaming, deceived.

Judgment. Curse, belly, dust.
Children, pain, desire, husband, lord.
Toil, thorns, sweat, death, dust.
Knowledge, angel, exile. ~~*Shalom.*~~
* * * * * * * * *


Grace. Woman, seed, blows, heel, head.
"Eve," skins. Promise, covenant, prophecy, hope.
Cain, Abel, Seth, Noah, evil, ark, flood, nations, Babel.
Confusion, dispersal, despair.

Promise. Abraham, Isaac, Jacob, Judah.
Joseph, Moses, Caleb, Joshua.
Judges, Kings — Saul, David, Solomon.
Northern kingdom, southern kingdom.
Prophets — condemnation, consolation — exiles.
Return? How long?
* * * * * * * * *

Zacharias, Elizabeth, John: *Benedictus.*
Mary, Annunciation, virgin, conception, birth.
Immanuel.
Shepherds, star, magi, Herod, infanticide.
Egypt, Nazareth, carpentry.

Repent, baptism, temptation.
Kingdom, disciples, miracles, teaching.
Pharisees, Sadducees, lawyers, scribes.

Sweat, betrayal, kiss, denial.
Herod, Pilate, Annas, Caiaphas.
"Trials."
What is truth?
Scourging. *Ecce homo.* Barabbas. Sentencing.
Wood, thorns, nails, spear, blood, water.
Forgiveness, it is finished! death, tomb.

Alive! Appearances, ascension, throne.
Spirit, fire! Gospel.
Church, Peter — Jews, Paul — Gentiles. Epistles.
Faith, hope, love, preaching, sacraments, commission,
Holiness, vocation. *shalom.*
* * * * * * * * * *

Return, resurrection, judgments, wedding.
New heavens, new earth, gold, glory. *SHALOM!*
Maranatha.

**How We Should Love God** Jesus not only tells us we are to love God, but also explains *how much* we are to love him. In phrases that sound like they come straight from a telegram, Jesus says that love for God should be "with all our hearts, and with all our souls, and with all our minds, and with all our strength." These short phrases indicate that love for God includes emotional, spiritual, intellectual, and physical components. All together they mean that we are to love God completely and unconditionally — with everything we are, with everything we have, and in everything we do, no matter when, no matter where. As Augustine says, "In no time or place could it be wrong for a person to love God with his whole heart and his whole soul and his whole mind."[21]

We are to love God in body, soul, and spirit; in head, heart, and hand; in thoughts, words, and deeds. We are to love God in relation to food, clothing, shelter, money, wealth, possessions, houses, cars, and clothes. We are to love God at work, rest, and play. We are to love God at church, at school, at home, at the office, in the bedroom, in the law court, or on the

---

21. Augustine, *Confessions,* trans. Frank Sheed, intro. Peter Brown (Indianapolis/Cambridge: Hackett Publishing Company, Inc., 1993), p. 43 (§3.8). I changed the word "man" to "person" in this quote.

tennis court. We are to love God in the family, in friends, and among acquaintances. We to love God in the neighborhood, on the highway, in the
mountains, and at the beach. We are to love God during the morning, at
noon, in the evening, at night, on a weekday, on the weekend, on a holiday.
We are to love God in our occupations, on vacation, in avocation, in celebration, in desperation, in aspiration, in sickness and in health, whether
rich or poor, for better or worse, free or bound. We should be consumed
with the love of God in our persons, possessions, and pursuits, at every
place and at every time, just as Moses said we should:

> These words [concerning love for God], which I am commanding you
> today, shall be on your heart. You shall teach them diligently to your
> sons and shall talk of them when you sit in your house and when you
> walk by the way and when you lie down and when you rise up. You shall
> bind them as a sign on your hand and they shall be as frontals on your
> forehead. You shall write them on the doorposts of your house and on
> your gates. (Deut. 6:6-9)

How do we know if we love him? Is there any tangible way to measure
our affection for him? While love for God entails the previously mentioned emotional, spiritual, intellectual, and physical aspects, it is also vo-
litional in character. Submission to God's authority and obedience to his
will are indicators that we love him, especially when we are under fire and
even if we aren't. If you love God, you will keep his commandments, and if
you keep God's commandments, you love him. The reverse is also true. If
you don't love God, you won't keep his commandments, and if you won't
keep God's commandments, you don't love him (John 14:15, 21, 23; 15:10;
1 John 5:3). When we come to a fork in the road, subordination to God and
obedience to God's will indicate affection for him, and insubordination to
God and disobedience to his will indicate disaffection from him. While
important, feelings aren't the determining factors in this transaction. They
may or may not be present. Rather, submission and compliance or resistance and defiance are the litmus tests of love or lack of love for God. As
C. S. Lewis puts it, "The real question is, which (when the alternative
comes) do you serve, or choose, or put first? To which claim does your
will, in the last resort, yield?"[22]

22. C. S. Lewis, *The Four Loves* (San Diego: Harcourt, Inc., A Harvest Book, 1960, 1988),
pp. 122-23.

**Why We Should Love God**   The greatest commandment tells us we are to love God utterly, but it doesn't explicitly give us the reason why. Why, then, does he command this? The reason, I think, is because it is the very best thing for us — our chief good!

We don't love God because it meets some need in him. God is eternally self-sufficient, absolutely perfect, and lacking in nothing. As we read in the second chapter of *The Westminster Confession,* "God hath all life, glory, goodness, blessedness, in and of himself; and is alone in and unto himself all-sufficient, not standing in need of any creatures which He hath made."[23]

If God, then, is not the personal benefactor of the greatest commandment, then it stands to reason that we must be. God has commanded us to love him not for God's sake, but for ours. Given the way God has set things up, loving anything other than God as God is a major metaphysical and moral mistake. The greatest commandment protects us from the misery born of idolatry, that we might find our ultimate good and discover the deep meaning of happiness in God.

If we love God for this reason, then this is because God *first* loved us. The interesting point is that God loved us *first* for the very same reason — namely, that we might find our greatest good and happiness in him. God loved us for this purpose in creation. God has loved us for this purpose in redemption. The edenistic happiness of shalom that was lost in the fall has been restored for us to enjoy in Jesus Christ once again. The basic biblical pattern is happiness with God, unhappiness without God, and happiness regained with God again.

Our problem is that we have a very hard time believing this, even as Christians, and a very hard time letting go of what it would replace. We hang on to the comfort of the familiar with all we've got. To get us to love God and all things in him, God may have to use some tough love. Heartaches and difficulties — including tests, temptations, trials, sufferings, frustrations, and tragedies — are often the only forces strong enough to get our attention and move us in a different direction. Because of these struggles, we just might experience a revolution in our essential paradigms of love and happiness.

Experiencing pain, especially if it is severe, can raise significant questions about the love and justice of God. The main point here is that in the careful hands of the heavenly Father, pain becomes an instrument to arouse us and generate a major change in our lives. "God whispers to us in

23. Leith, ed., *Creeds of the Churches,* p. 197.

our pleasures," C. S. Lewis says, "speaks in our conscience, but shouts in our pains; it is His megaphone to rouse a deaf world."[24] Listen carefully. An increase in the divine decibels just might be the sign of a call to a reordered love for God. If you respond to the call, you just might discover that the nearness of God is your greatest good (cf. Ps. 73:28).

## Reordered Love for Self

*"Keep yourselves in the love of God. . . ."*

Jude 21

The scribe who asked Jesus about the greatest commandment in the law got a two-for-one deal, since that commandment has a twin: "The second is like it," Jesus continued, 'You shall love your neighbor as yourself'" (Matt. 22:39; 19:19; Mark 12:31; Luke 10:27; Rom. 13:9; James 2:8 cf. Lev. 19:18). If you look closer, however, you will see that there is a triple duty embedded in these commandments. We are to love God. We are to love our neighbors. We are also to love *ourselves*. Technically, we are not commanded to love ourselves in the second commandment. It just presupposes we do. If we are to love our neighbors as ourselves, then we must know how to love ourselves. So we must understand the Christian validity of self-love, how it can easily be disordered, and what a proper love for the self should look like.[25]

Sound bites from Scripture like "hate self" or "deny self" or "lose your life" or "take up your cross" have given the impression that Christianity loves self-abhorrence and abhors self-love. If it really did, who would want to become a Christian? Fortunately, it doesn't. Loving ourselves and our happiness — these are basically one and the same — is as natural and acceptable as breathing. It's just human nature to satisfy ordinary needs and desires. If I'm hungry, I eat. If I'm thirsty, I drink. If I'm tired, I sleep. If I'm clueless, I seek knowledge. If I'm poor, I work to get money. If I'm lonely, I find friends. If I'm sick, I go to the doctor. If I get a splinter or a headache, I head to the medicine cabinet for a pair of tweezers or a dose of aspirin.

24. C. S. Lewis, *The Problem of Pain* (New York: Macmillan, 1962), p. 93.
25. These reflections are partially inspired from Jonathan Edwards, *Christian Love and Its Fruits* (Grand Rapids: Sovereign Grace Publishers, 1971), pp. 78-79. This book was originally published as *Charity and Its Fruit*.

When needs like these make their presence known, we love ourselves . . . automatically. There is no need to command us to do so. We just do it.

Loving ourselves is not only natural; it is also scriptural. The Bible teaches that we who love God the Creator should also love his creation, and since we are part of his creation, we should also love ourselves. Furthermore, as the second great commandment mandates, we are to love our neighbors as we love ourselves. Self-love is the divinely ordained pattern for neighbor love. We love ourselves for our own sake, and we love ourselves for our neighbor's sake, and we love both ourselves and our neighbors in God for God's sake. In loving God first and foremost, we know how to love ourselves, and in knowing how to love ourselves, we know how to love our neighbor, not more or less than ourselves, but equally so. There is one single form of love distributed in three appropriate ways. Could this be a trace of our creation in the image of the Trinity?

Self-love is not only scripturally approved; it is also the underlying premise of every blessing offered and every warning issued in the Bible. The Scriptures motivate us to righteousness and warn us of wickedness because of the personal benefits or the possible liabilities associated with these respective behaviors. The entire system of rewards and punishments, blessings and curses, including the final destinies of heaven or hell, is based upon a fundamental principle of biblical self-interest and the inherent desire we have to further our own good, both temporally and eternally. We may not think about it, but the judgment is coming. For our own good, therefore, we should heed Paul's warning: "Therefore we also have as our ambition whether at home or absent, to be pleasing to Him. For we must all appear before the judgment seat of Christ, so that each one may be recompensed for his deeds in the body, according to what he has done, whether good or bad" (2 Cor. 5:9-10).

In attending to our own good, it is easy for self-love to slip into disorder. Self-love is disordered when we love ourselves too much compared to the way we love God; it is disordered when others get less love or more love than we have for ourselves, or when they get none at all. Self-love is also out of whack when we seek it exclusively in ourselves or in the world around us, especially in the lusts of the flesh, the lusts of the eyes, and the boastful pride of life. In disordered self-love, we try to gain the whole world, even if it costs us our souls. If we try to find and save ourselves in self-love, we end up losing ourselves, paradoxically. Our self-centeredness terminates in idolatry, the seven deadly sins, various habits and addictions, and in some cases we resort to the violence of crime and warfare. Self-love is good when it is in harmony with the love of God. Otherwise, we are headed for trouble. In searching for a mountaintop, we can wind up in a valley of despair.

Ironically, then, we must learn to love ourselves by not loving *our* selves.[26] We must seek happiness by not seeking *our* happiness. We must save ourselves by condemning ourselves. We must find it all by losing it all. This is why Jesus made demands of his would-be followers that seem exceedingly harsh at first blush.

> He who loves father or mother more than Me is not worthy of Me; and he who loves son or daughter more than Me is not worthy of Me. (Matt. 10:37)

> So then, none of you can be My disciple who does not give up all his own possessions. (Luke 14:33)

> If anyone comes to Me, and does not hate his own father and mother and wife and children and brothers and sisters, yes, and even his own life, he cannot be My disciple. (Luke 14:26)

> He who loves his life loses it, and he who hates his life in this world will keep it to life eternal. (John 12:25)

> If anyone wishes to come after Me, he must deny himself, and take up his cross and follow Me." (Mark 8:34)

Christ's call to hate the self and our family members is not because there is something wrong with them or because they are evil; after all, they are God's creation. Rather, it is a call for a "hatred" of the misplaced love for ourselves and family members that has blocked us from the love of God and the discovery of the deep meaning of happiness in him. Christ's demand that we give up our possessions is not because there is anything wrong with possessions or with possessing them. Instead, his call to give them up is because of the competition they pose to our affection for him. Christ's requirement that we deny ourselves and take up our crosses is not because we are worthless. Instead, it is directed at the elimination of the sin

---

26. Quoted in *Augustine Through the Ages: An Encyclopedia*, ed. Allan Fitzgerald, O.S.A. (Grand Rapids: Eerdmans, 1999), s.v. "Love."

and selfishness that has kept us from discovering the love of God and how to be happy in him. In these "hard sayings," then, we see that God wants to disabuse us of our disordered loves for ourselves, people, and possessions that we might first love him, and then learn to love these things in him.

We love ourselves rightly when we love God more than ourselves, when he is our chief good, and we refer all our plans and aim everything in our lives to him.[27] We really don't love ourselves or anyone or anything else if we don't love God. If we don't love God, we don't really love ourselves or anyone or anything else (appearances to the contrary notwithstanding). Loving ourselves in God is the greatest gift we can give and the best service we can offer to ourselves. Only then can we attend well to the needs of others. Charity begins at home.

- You only love yourself when God is your greatest good and you love God the most.
- Only when God is your greatest good and you love God the most will you truly love yourself.
- Only when you love yourself as you should in God will you be able to love your neighbor in God as you love yourself.

What we aim at in ourselves we ought to aim at in other people by assisting them toward God as their greatest good. If we love ourselves in order to find happiness in God, we should love others toward the very same end. As Augustine noted, "Following after God is the desire of happiness; reaching God is happiness itself."[28]

## Reordered Love for Neighbors

*"Beloved, if God so loved us, we also ought to love one another."*

1 John 4:11

Prior to the gospel, our sin just about snuffed out any genuine concern for other people. Our idolatry created space for reckless behavior toward oth-

---

27. Taken from Augustine, "Of the Morals of the Catholic Church," p. 55 (§26.48). I have also drawn on the discussion of self-love in *Augustine Through the Ages: An Encyclopedia*, s.v. "Love."

28. Augustine, "Of the Morals of the Catholic Church," p. 46 (§11.18).

ers, for without fear of God there is little respect for people. Our pride, envy, anger, sloth, avarice, gluttony, or lust rarely spared a soul. Our habits and addictions caused lots of pain to our nearest and dearest. Violence, even toward loved ones, was an option, if necessary, to get what we wanted. We weren't reticent to use and abuse other people as the means to our happiness. In our single-minded concern for our good, we just didn't care that much about the welfare of others.

Thanks to the grace of the gospel, our love for others has been reordered just as it has been reordered for God and ourselves. It's a package deal, for in loving God, we love our neighbors, and in loving our neighbors, we love God. This why the second greatest commandment is "like" the first. They are mutually implicated.

There are good reasons for this demand for neighbor love. It is an expression of love for God. It does the neighbor good. It challenges, fulfills, and gladdens the lover. It makes for a better world. Most importantly, we love our neighbors as ourselves because they are the image and likeness of God, as we also are (Gen. 1:26-27). Whatever the precise definition, this status is the source of our value and dignity as human beings. It is what distinguishes us from the animals and everything else in God's creation. Psalm 8 places us in a royal echelon just below God himself (vv. 5-8). Psalm 139:14 states that we are "fearfully and wonderfully made." We are fallen, but we are also great — a beast at times, but also beautiful. Human status as *imago Dei* is the grand rationale for neighbor love.

Christ's incarnation is the superlative confirmation of our dignity, and he verified this exalted status of ours in his teachings, ministry, and crucifixion. We are of more value than many sparrows, he said, and God's awareness of their plight, as well as his knowledge of the number of hairs on our heads, signals God's interest in and concern for us (Matt. 10:29-31). Jesus valued people as whole persons. He saved souls and he healed bodies, as we see in his pronouncements of forgiveness and in his multifaceted miracles of mercy. Our value as human beings is especially measured by Christ's death. In the calculus of heaven, God estimated that we were worth the gift of his only son, that we should not perish but have everlasting life. C. S. Lewis's words on human nobility are climactic:

> There are no *ordinary* people. You have never talked to a mere mortal. . . .
> But it is immortals whom we joke with, work with, marry, snub, and exploit — immortal horrors or everlasting splendors. . . . Next to the

Blessed Sacrament itself, your neighbour is the holiest object presented to your senses.[29]

If human beings are virtually holy, then how should we love them in practical ways that meet their needs and in such a way that they might find their greatest good in God and learn to love everything else in him? How should we love them so that they learn the deep meaning of happiness in their Creator and Redeemer? The New Testament contains many insights on these questions.

The Golden Rule is a good place to start. In the Sermon on the Mount, Jesus said, "In everything, therefore, treat people the same way you want them to treat you, for this is the Law and the Prophets" (Matt. 7:12; cf. Luke 6:31). Imagine what it would be like to live under certain circumstances, figure out how you would like to be treated in them, and when you come across others in those situations, treat them accordingly. Or if you have lived in certain circumstances and you remember how you wanted to be treated in them, when you come across others in those situations, treat them accordingly. Sharing a common human nature with others helps us to know what to do in these situations. Before we can understand or love another person, we must walk a mile in their shoes. But first we must take off our own.

President Kennedy used the Golden Rule in an anti-segregation speech in 1963 to foster better treatment of blacks by whites. Would they want to be treated as second-class citizens on the basis of skin color alone? The "heart of the question," Kennedy said, "is . . . whether we are going to treat our fellow Americans as we want to be treated."[30] To borrow an example from one of Jesus' parables, what if you were a traveler headed from Jerusalem to Jericho and were assaulted by robbers, stripped, beaten, and left for dead. How would you wish to be treated? As the priest and Levite did who passed by on the other side? Or as the good Samaritan did who felt compassion for you, dressed and bandaged your wounds, and took you to a nearby shelter for care at his own expense? As Jesus says at the end of the parable, "Go and do the same" (Luke 10:37). Obeying the golden rule, Jesus said, is so important it fulfills the theological and moral vision of the entire Old Testament.

29. Lewis, *The Weight of Glory*, p. 15.
30. Blackwell's *Encyclopedic Dictionary of Business Ethics*, s.v., "Golden Rule."

Christ's "new commandment" also gives us insight into the nature of reordered love for our neighbors. In John 13:34-35, Jesus said: "A new commandment I give to you, that you love one another, even as I have loved you, that you also love one another. By this all men will know that you are my disciples, if you have love for one another." We are to love others as ourselves, according to the second greatest commandment. We are to treat others as we would wish to be treated, to fulfill the Golden Rule. We are also to love others as Jesus has loved us, as this new commandment specifies.

The question, of course, is how did Jesus love us? The answer, in short, is by humble service and selfless sacrifice. Our baser instincts can incline us to aspire to greatness, to be first, to be served, to be in control. But these aspirations are manifestations of pride born of disordered love. Jesus offered an alternative model. When two of his disciples were bickering over special positions of authority and recognition in his kingdom, he explained his paradigm and offered himself as the prime example:

> Calling them to Himself, Jesus said to them, "You know that those who are recognized as rulers of the Gentiles lord it over them; and their great men exercise authority over them. But it is not this way among you, but whoever wishes to become great among you shall be your servant; and whoever wishes to be first among you shall be slave of all. For even the Son of Man did not come to be served, but to serve, and to give His life a ransom for many." (Mark 10:42-45)

In a countercultural way, Jesus affirmed that true greatness was not found in authority or power, but was a function of servanthood. He taught that to be in first place you must assume the last place of the slave. These inverted values were at the heart and core of Christ's own mission. He did not come in a high and mighty way to be served, but in a low and humble manner to serve, even to the point of death. Paul caught Christ's vision and explained it in Philippians 2:5-8:

> Have this attitude in yourselves which was also in Christ Jesus, who, although He existed in the form of God, did not regard equality with God a thing to be grasped, but emptied Himself, taking the form of a bond-servant, and being made in the likeness of men. Being found in appearance as a man, He humbled Himself by becoming obedient to the point of death, even death on a cross.

There is just something irresistible about the sincere service of a true servant on behalf of others. Whether it's the help offered by a boss to her employees, an officer to his soldiers, a father to his children, a captain to his crew, a coach to her players, and so on, genuine servanthood is utterly compelling. It is a holy improvement on a quote from former New York Yankee baseball manager Casey Stengel: "Management is getting paid to help other people hit home runs."[31]

Jesus issued the new commandment in the context of washing his disciples' feet. He had arisen from supper, laid aside his garments, and girded himself with a towel. "Then He poured water into the basin, and began to wash the disciples' feet and to wipe them with the towel with which He was girded." After he was finished, he drove the lesson home: "You call Me Teacher and Lord; and you are right, for so I am. If I then, the Lord and the Teacher, washed your feet, you also ought to wash one another's feet. For I gave you an example that you also should do as I did to you" (John 13:5, 13-15).

A series of "one another" principles in the New Testament further spell out the nature of the selfless, humble service we are to offer to others in love. They are actually unconditional imperatives — you are commanded to do them no matter what — that tell us what we are to do and not do in our relationships with one another. Positively, we are to be at peace, devoted, like-minded, kind, tender-hearted, forgiving, submissive, and hospitable to one another, without complaint.[32] We are also to accept, admonish, care for, show patience with, speak the truth to, comfort, encourage, build up, seek the good of, stimulate, confess sin to, pray for, serve, and be humble towards one another, and regard others as more important than ourselves.[33] We are also to greet one another by name and with a holy kiss — or with a warm hug or handshake, as we might say today.[34]

Negatively, we are not to lie to, speak about or complain against, be-

---

31. Stengel's original quote is "Managing is getting paid for home runs someone else hits."

32. Mark 9:50; 1 Thessalonians 5:13; Romans 12:10; Romans 12:16; 15:5; Ephesians 4:32; Colossians 3:13; Ephesians 5:21; 1 Peter 4:9.

33. Romans 15:7; Romans 15:14; Colossians 3:16; 1 Corinthians 12:25; Ephesians 4:2; Colossians 3:13; Ephesians 4:25; 1 Thessalonians 4:18; 1 Thessalonians 5:11; Hebrews 3:13; 10:25; 1 Thessalonians 5:15; Hebrews 10:24; James 5:16; 1 Peter 4:10; 1 Peter 5:5; Philippians 2:3.

34. 3 John 14; Romans 16:16; 1 Corinthians 16:20; 2 Corinthians 13:12; 1 Peter 5:14.

come boastful over against, challenge, or envy one another. If we bite and devour one another, we will be consumed by each other.[35]

If to this inventory we add six rather well known responsibilities, we would realize that love for one another also consists in honoring parents, in refraining from murder, in not committing adultery, in not stealing, in not lying, and in not coveting.[36] For these reasons, Paul said that love like this, which embodies the second greatest commandment, is the fulfillment of the entire Old Testament law. Any other specific duty we have is summarized in the general command to "love one another," which is repeated some seventeen times in the New Testament. Peter conveys this all-encompassing obligation:

> Since you have in obedience to the truth purified your souls for a sincere love of the brethren, fervently love one another from the heart, for you have been born again not of seed which is perishable but imperishable, that is, through the living and abiding word of God. (1 Pet. 1:22-23)

No discussion of this kind would be complete without 1 Corinthians 13, since it is the one chapter in the New Testament devoted entirely to Christian love. The first three verses of this chapter demonstrate love's pre-eminence by showing that speech, no matter how eloquent, that prophecy, knowledge, and faith, no matter how sophisticated, and that giving of one's substance or self, no matter how sacrificial, are incomplete without love.

> If I speak with the tongues of men and of angels, but do not have love, I have become a noisy gong or a clanging cymbal. If I have the gift of prophecy, and know all mysteries and all knowledge; and if I have all faith, so as to remove mountains, but do not have love, I am nothing. And if I give all my possessions to feed the poor, and if I surrender my body to be burned, but do not have love, it profits me nothing.

The next four verses list love's properties and actions. Here love is noticeably practical rather than emotional, though the emotions of love won't necessarily be absent from its practice. For the full effect, replace Christ's name and then yours for the word "love" as you read:

---

35. Colossians 3:9; James 4:11; 5:9; Galatians 5:26; 5:15.
36. Romans 13:9-10; see also Exodus 20:12-17; Deuteronomy 5:16-21.

Love is patient, love is kind and is not jealous; love does not brag and is not arrogant, does not act unbecomingly; it does not seek its own, is not provoked, does not take into account a wrong suffered, does not rejoice in unrighteousness, but rejoices with the truth; bears all things, believes all things, hopes all things, endures all things. Love never fails.

The last six verses of 1 Corinthians 13 address the permanence and superiority of love. When prophecy, tongues, and knowledge are fulfilled at the end of time when the perfect comes, love will remain. Should we compare everlasting love to the other great virtues of faith and hope, it would surpass them both. All three are great, but the greatest is love.

But if there are gifts of prophecy, they will be done away; if there are tongues, they will cease; if there is knowledge, it will be done away. For we know in part and we prophesy in part; but when the perfect comes, the partial will be done away. When I was a child, I used to speak like a child, think like a child, reason like a child; when I became a man, I did away with childish things. For now we see in a mirror dimly, but then face to face; now I know in part, but then I will know fully just as I also have been fully known. But now faith, hope, love, abide these three; but the greatest of these is love.

One of the things that makes this kind of love so demanding is that it is to be applied not just to family and friends, but also to enemies. We are naturally inclined to love our loved ones and to hate our adversaries, but this is a trait of people who do not know God. There is no merit to emulating them in their favoritism. On the other hand, love is most God-like when it is generously given away to those who neither deserve nor appreciate it. We are to be imitators of God, who causes sun to shine and rain to fall on the just and the unjust alike. We must give openhandedly to others whether they like us or love God or not, or whether we like or love them or not. Only if we love our enemies and pray for those who persecute us will we be "perfect" as God is perfect (Matt. 5:43-48).

We should certainly understand this kind of generosity toward adversaries, because we have already experienced it. Though we were the enemies of God in our sin, this did not stop God from demonstrating his own love for us in the death of his Son. This unmerited love manifested in Christ has reconciled us to God, making us God's friends and saving us from his wrath (Rom. 5:8-10). God did not withhold his love from us despite our opposition, and we must not withhold it from people who are estranged from us. With God's help, we love them with the love of God in Christ, that they might find their ultimate good in him and become our brothers and sisters in Christ, and also our friends.[37]

Of course, fervent love for others, whether they are friends or enemies, must be expressed not just in words, but also in deeds. It does no good to respond to someone's lack of food and clothing verbally without giving them what they need for their bodies. It merely reveals the sterility of heart from which the empty words flowed, and a need for repentance. If faith without works is dead, as James teaches, then love without deeds is dead as well (James 2:15-17). On the other hand, if faith really lives only with works, so love flourishes only with good deeds.

The above reference to supplying food and clothing reminds us that we must love people as whole persons in both body and soul. Out of the abundance or the scarcity of our resources — with a million or a mite — our goal is to meet the intertwined physical and spiritual needs of people in order to put an end to their suffering or pain. Indigence of any kind is symptomatic of a loss of shalom, and the goal of giving is to restore peace and well-being. Hence, we graciously supply food, clothing, and shelter, or truth, goodness, and beauty, or faith, hope, and love, as needs may dictate. We give to others as we would have others give to us, not in stinginess but generously, not in arrogance but humbly, not begrudgingly but with gladness of heart, knowing that someday in our hardships we will be the recipients of reciprocal giving and gifts.[38]

We also are motivated to love in tangible ways because it will be the basis for our reward on judgment day. When Jesus returns, he will gather the nations of the world before him and separate believers and nonbelievers as a shepherd separates the sheep from the goats. The sheep on his right will be ushered into the eternal kingdom because they honored the presence of Christ in the humblest of human beings by giving them food, drink, and clothing, and by showing them hospitality and comfort in time of need. The goats on his left will be cast into eternal punishment

---

37. Augustine, *Ten Homilies on the First Epistle of John*, trans. H. Browne, rev., notes Joseph H. Myers, *Nicene and Post-Nicene Fathers*, ed. Philip Schaff, First Series, vol. 7 (Peabody, Mass.: Hendrickson Publishers, 1994), p. 524 (§10.7).

38. Stimulated by Augustine, *Ten Homilies on the First Epistle of John*, p. 508 (§8.5).

because they failed to minister to Christ in the needy in such practical ways (Matt. 25:31-46).

The presence or absence of love is the continental divide in the human race. One way or the other, love directs the course of our lives and determines our destiny. Its presence manifests righteousness and salvation. Its absence signals impiety and damnation. Love involves risks, but not to love is the greatest risk of all.

> To love at all is to be vulnerable. Love anything, and your heart will certainly be wrung and possibly broken. If you want to make sure of keeping it intact, you must give your heart to no one, not even to an animal. Wrap it carefully round with hobbies and little luxuries; avoid all entanglements; lock it up safe in the casket or coffin of your selfishness. But in that casket — safe, dark, motionless, airless — it will change. It will not be broken; it will become unbreakable, impenetrable, irredeemable. The alternative to tragedy, or at least to the risk of tragedy, is damnation. The only place outside of Heaven where you can be perfectly safe from all the dangers and perturbations of love is Hell.[39]

## Reordered Love for Creation

> *"The whole world is a theatre for the display of the Divine goodness, wisdom, justice, and power. . . ."*
>
> John Calvin, *Commentary on the Book of Psalms*[40]

The first and second commandments require love for God and people. But why isn't there a third great commandment to love the creation? If God so loved the *world*, then you would think he would demand that we love it, too. Why is the requirement to love the Creator and Redeemer of heaven and earth not accompanied by a requirement to love his masterpiece? We search in vain for a single passage of Scripture that contains such a command. Nowhere in the Bible do we find any indication that God expects us to have some kind of love or affection for nature.

39. Lewis, *The Four Loves*, p. 121.

40. John Calvin, *Commentary on the Book of Psalms*, vol. 5, trans. James Anderson (Grand Rapids: Baker Book House, reprint 2003), p. 178 (Ps. 135:10).

Or does he? Actually, he does. But God's demand that we love what he has made is implicit, not explicit, and it needs some explanation. If we stop and think about it, we are commanded to love the creation as a part of the second greatest commandment because it demands that we love people, who are creatures and are a part of the created order. We know that this is our status, yet we tend to forget it. We are inclined to elevate ourselves above the creaturely realm, perhaps because we are conscious beings and possess self-determination. Be this as it may, that God is our Creator and that he formed us from the dust of the earth itself is clear in Genesis. The first fact about us is that we are *creatures,* and we necessarily love creation insofar as we love other human creatures as we love ourselves.

Furthermore, love for people and the creation are inextricably combined. People can love people only when they lovingly tend to the world God has made. If food, clothing, and shelter are necessary to meet the concrete needs of people in whom Christ is present, then the only way such goods and services are available is through the devoted labor of people who have made these things out of the goods of the earth. No need can be met, no service can be rendered, no gift can be given apart from the resources it provides. Thankfully, somebody along the way formulated antibiotics, created contact lenses, designed jetliners, invented golf, and strung a guitar so people could heal, see, travel, play, and make music (among countless other things). All these things are gifts of love to people, even if love wasn't the conscious motivation for their development. We can't love people without creational engagement, cultivation, and care.

Even the most spiritual of activities require creational resources (and a little technology) for their implementation: bread and wine for communion, water for baptism, oil for anointing, paper and ink for Bibles and books, and a house or at least a shade tree as a sacred space to hold church. Bodies are necessary for worship as well: tongues for preaching, praying, and singing, ears for listening, noses for smelling, eyes for reading and seeing, minds for thinking, hands to lift heavenward and to make the sign of the cross, knees for genuflecting and kneeling, and lips for a holy kiss. There is simply no way to love others or worship God without creation — caring for and cultivating the very good world God has given to us.

We love the creation insofar as it is the source of the resources for our lives, our love, and our worship. It points naturally to God, who created, sustains, redeems, and renews it all. We love the world, not supremely but secondarily, not in a disordered but in a reordered way, not as an idol but as an image or icon of God's presence and glory. Alexander Schmemann explains the sacramental character of creation:

> . . . the world, be it in its totality as cosmos, or in its life and becoming as time and history, is an *epiphany* of God, a means of His revelation, presence, and power. In other words, it not only "posits" the idea of God as a rationally acceptable cause of its existence, but truly "speaks" of Him and is in itself an essential means both of knowledge of God and communion with Him, and to be so is its true nature and its ultimate destiny.[41]

## The Mark of the Christian

> *"They will know we are Christians by our love, by our love,*
> *Yes, they'll know we are Christians by our love."*
>
> Peter Scholtes, "They'll Know
> We Are Christians by Our Love"[42]

The gospel of Jesus Christ reorders our love for God, ourselves, other people, and for the entire creation. In the holy of holies of the first commandment, we must love God in his supremacy with all our heart, soul, mind, and strength. In the holy place of the second commandment, we must love our neighbors as we love ourselves. In the Golden Rule, we should treat other people as we would wish to be treated. In the new commandment and "one-another" principles, we must love each another as Christ has loved us. In 1 Corinthians 13, we are inspired with a grand vision of the preeminence, the properties and actions, and the permanence of love.

One unidentified group of early believers took the responsibilities of love seriously. A second-century Christian apologist named Aristides described the way they loved one another as essential proof of the truth of their faith:

41. Alexander Schmemann, *For the Life of the World: Sacraments and Orthodoxy* (Crestwood, N.Y.: St. Vladimir's Seminary Press, 1973), p. 120 (emphasis original).

42. Peter Scholtes, "They'll Know We Are Christians," © 1966 F.E.L. Assigned 1991 to the Lorenz Corporation. All rights reserved. International copyright secured.

They walk in all humility and kindness, and falsehood is not found among them, and they love one another. They despise not the widow, and grieve not the orphan. He that has distributes liberally to him who has not. If they see a stranger, they bring him under their roof, and rejoice over him, as [if he] were their own brother; for they call themselves brethren, not after the flesh, but after the Spirit and in God; but when one of their poor passes away from the world, and any one of them see him, then he provides for his burial according to his ability; and if they hear that any of their number is imprisoned or oppressed for the name of their Messiah, all of them provide for his needs, and if it is possible that he may be delivered, they deliver him. And if there is among them a man that is poor and needy, and they have not an abundance of necessaries, they fast two or three days that they may supply the needy with their necessary food.[43]

If Christians sported a tattoo, then love would be it. "By this all men will know that you are my disciples," said Jesus, "if you have love for one another" (John 13:35). Love is the distinguishing mark of the Christian and the final apologetic.[44] There is no greater sign of the validity of the gospel in deed and in truth than the reordered loves and the reordered lives of Christians.

43. Quoted in Robin Keeley, ed., *Eerdmans' Handbook to Christian Belief* (Grand Rapids: Eerdmans, 1982), p. 267. For the complete quote, see Aristides, *The Apology of Aristides*, trans. D. M. Kay, *Ante-Nicene Fathers*, ed. Allan Menzies, vol. 9 (Peabody, Mass.: Hendrickson Publishers, 1994), pp. 276-79.

44. Francis A. Schaeffer, *The Mark of the Christian* (Downers Grove, Ill.: InterVarsity Press, 1970).

CHAPTER SIX

# Reordered Lives: All Things New

*"Therefore if anyone is in Christ, he is a new creature; the old things passed away; behold, new things have come."*

2 Corinthians 5:17

## Introduction

Eustace *was* an "unmitigated nuisance." At least that is how some of his family members once *felt* about him. The past tense verb is important, since it signals a change.

His story goes like this.[1] In C. S. Lewis's *Voyage of the "Dawn Treader,"* the progressively educated Eustace Clarence Scrubb was Edmund and Lucy's disagreeable nine-year-old cousin. Together the three of them were whisked unexpectedly into Narnia through the picture of a Viking ship that hung in Lucy's bedroom. They found themselves aboard the *Dawn Treader,* captained by King Caspian. He was on a search-and-rescue mission to find the seven Narnian lords whom the usurper Miraz had sent to explore distant lands beyond Narnia's eastern shore. Also on board was the brave little mouse Reepicheep, who was hoping to find Aslan's own country by this precarious journey into the land of the sunrise. Eustace,

---

1. C. S. Lewis, *The Voyage of the Dawn Treader* (New York: Macmillan, Collier Books, 1952, 1970). This summary of the Eustace story is drawn from the epilogue of my own book, *Worldview: The History of a Concept* (Grand Rapids: Eerdmans, 2002), pp. 346-48.

however, was disgruntled by the whole affair. He bickered constantly with his companions and found the valiant little rodent insufferable.

On a stop at one island, the typically independent Eustace wandered off from his shipmates on a walk. While he was out exploring, he happened upon a fire-breathing dragon who was breathing his last. It was raining unmercifully at the time, so Eustace took refuge in the dragon's empty lair nearby. To his great delight, there he found the cave filled with seemingly limitless crowns, coins, rings, bracelets, ingots, cups, plates, and gems. The sight of such treasure ignited his greed and excited him with the possibility of becoming a wealthy young man in this new world he was just discovering. After slipping a golden bracelet on his upper left arm, he fell asleep out of weariness from his adventure.

Eustace awoke with a start. He was suddenly aroused by an acute pain in his upper arm where the bracelet was. He realized that something shocking had occurred during his nap: his true inner state had manifested itself in his outward appearance. He was once a little boy, but he had become an ugly, scaly monster. His thoughts and desires had so deformed him that he had literally become "endragoned."

His first thought was to employ his newly acquired powers to terrorize his little cousins fiendishly. This was his one chance to get them back for all of their perceived abuse. The more he thought about it, however, the less inclined he was to do so. Unexpected feelings began to swirl in his heart. He sensed a crushing loneliness and began to wonder if he was the nice little boy he thought he was. He realized that Edmund and Lucy really weren't the ogres he thought they were. He wanted to hear their voices and be their friend. How happy he would be even if little Reepicheep would say a nice, squeaky word to him. He desperately wanted to talk, laugh, and share things, like real people do. He was overcome with sadness in realizing he was a monster, cut off from everyone and everything that made his life worthwhile. Eustace wanted desperately to be "undragoned" and become human again. It seemed out of the question, however. "Once a dragon, always a dragon" was the thought that haunted his soul. He pleaded for help, but none seemed available.

Then a lion appeared suddenly and led Eustace to a garden on the top of a mountain where there was a pool of clear water. His dragonish heart began pounding in hope that this magnificent liquid could ease the piercing pain in his upper arm where the bracelet was. According to the lion, he would first have to remove his dragon skin for the waters to work their magic. Eustace tried three times at de-scaling himself, but to no avail. The lion indicated that he would have to do the job himself, using the sharp, pointed nails of his claws to rip it off. Eustace was terrified at the prospect, but submitted to it nonetheless. It was his only hope for recovery and a new life. As he describes the experience, his metamorphosis was not without considerable pain.

> The very first tear he [the lion] made was so deep that I thought it had gone right into my heart. And when he began pulling the skin off, it hurt worse than anything I've ever felt. . . . Well, he peeled the beastly stuff right off — just as I thought I'd done it myself the other three times, only they hadn't hurt — and there it was lying on the grass: only ever so much thicker, and darker, and more knobbly looking than the others had been. And there I was as smooth and soft as a peeled switch and smaller than I had been (90).

As soon as the process was over, the lion threw the svelte Eustace into the pool of water as a baptism of sorts. His arm pain disappeared and the lion dressed him in a new suit of clothes. When he returned to camp, his cousins celebrated his return and rejoiced at his transformation. The "undragoned" Eustace was a boy once again — different, though, than he was before. When Edmund explained what he thought had happened, he said, "I think you have seen Aslan" (p. 91).

Indeed he had. The redemptive swipe of the lion's claws had reordered Eustace's life. He wasn't automatically perfect and could still be quite intractable at times. Nonetheless, his old ways began to fade along with the pain in his arm. "The cure had begun" (p. 93).

Our cure begins, to extend the medical analogy, when God as the Great Physician applies the medicine of the cross to the disease of our sin and nurses us through the love of the Holy Spirit into good health according to the prescriptions of his Word. The application of this divinely therapeutic balm of the gospel transforms our loves and reorders our lives. We become worshippers of God instead of idolaters. We trade in our vices for virtues. God breaks the power of our habits and addictions and undermines any propensities we may have toward violence. Our lives can only be reordered by God in his love:

> But transformation of apostate man
> From fool to wise, from earthly to divine,

Is work for Him that made him. He alone,
And he by means in philosophic eyes
Trivial and worthy of disdain, achieves
The wonder; humanizing what is brute
In the lost kind, extracting from the lips
Of asps their venom, overpow'ring strength
By weakness, and hostility by love.[2]

## Reordered Lives of Worship

*"The dearest idol I have known,*
*Whate'er that idol be,*
*Help me tear it from thy throne,*
*And worship only thee."*

William Cowper, "Walking with God"[3]

We are as we worship, and when we were idolaters, that meant trouble. However, in Jesus Christ — the one who served and worshipped God faithfully in life and death — our primary vocation as worshippers of God has been restored. The English word "worship" means "worth-ship." It denotes the honor and excellence of the object of worship and the act of ascribing the worth it deserves. The biblical words for worship (*saha* and *proskyneo*) refer to acts of bowing down, paying homage, and having adoration. Worshipping God, then, involves acknowledging and declaring God's absolute perfection. Out of gratitude for his mercy in our lives, we offer ourselves totally and unconditionally to him, not conformed to the assumptions and values of the fallen world, but transformed in mind to do his good will in all things (Rom. 12:1-2). Worship is an individual matter. It should mark every realm of our lives. It is also the central purpose of the assembly of the church.

---

2. William Cowper, "The Winter Morning Walk," book 5 in *The Task*, in *Cowper: Poetical Works*, ed. H. S. Milford, 4th edition, with corrections and notes Norma Russell (London: Oxford University Press, 1967), p. 215 (lines 695-703).
3. William Cowper, "Walking with God," in *Cowper: Poetical Works*, p. 433 (lines 17-20).

### Worshipping God Individually

We worship God at a personal level when we are unconditionally committed to him and walk with him intimately and obediently each day of our lives. The Creator and Redeemer of the universe is our sovereign Lord, the ultimate concern with whom we are ultimately concerned. In the worship of personal devotion, we place him first *before* all things, and we put him first *in* all things, we glorify him *through* all things.

As a way of acknowledging God as your top priority, you can begin each day by making the sign of the cross on your forehead, lips, chest, and the palms of your hands, praying respectively:

> May Christ be in my *mind* in what I *think*.
> May Christ be in my *mouth* in what I *speak*.
> May Christ be in my *heart* in what I *love*.
> May Christ be in my *hands* in what I *do*.

You may also want to employ John Calvin's morning prayer of dedication, saying, "My heart I offer to you, O Lord, promptly and sincerely." Or you may choose to recite the Lord's Prayer as a way of acknowledging God's holiness and submitting yourself to God and his purposes for your life and the world.

As committed Christians, we enjoy fellowship, or *koinonia*, with God as we participate in the divine life and love of the Father, Son, and Holy Spirit. We pour out our hearts before him that he may search and examine them. To him we express our joys and sorrows, our praises and laments, our affirmations and doubts, our hopes and fears. As we grow in our knowledge of God, we also grow in knowledge of ourselves, and we understand more about his world and our place in it. Our love for him increases proportionately. We respect his divine majesty and are prompted to faithfulness and obedience to his will. We seek to serve the Lord with gladness, as gratitude and praise come to expression in our lips and lives. As we draw near to him, he draws near to us (James 4:8).

## Worshipping God in All of Life

The personal worship of God should flow naturally to the public areas of our everyday lives. If worship is the condition of our existence, then we will do everything for God and his acclaim in culture and society, thereby making a positive difference in the world around us.

Unfortunately, many Christians limit worship to their personal devotions or the services of a church. Life is part sacred and part secular — that's the way we too often see it. We worship here but not there, now but not then. Religious experience, in other words, is its own distinctive realm of life, separated from the push and pull of daily life.

This is a common perspective, but it's wrong. The Bible repudiates the sacred/secular distinction and instead affirms that God is the Creator and Redeemer of all things, and that the Lordship of Jesus Christ applies to all of life and to all of life equally. We rely on the Holy Spirit to teach us and lead us in the very public areas of our lives. Life is religion, as philosopher Evan Runner liked to say, and we should acknowledge God and worship him in spirit and truth regardless of the setting.

To worship God expansively, we must recognize and repudiate the non-Christian worldviews that govern various social and cultural domains, and contrariwise, understand fundamental biblical perspectives on things and how they apply to our callings and activities in the world. If this is our approach, then students can learn to worship God in their studies, and the same applies to employers and employees in their work, spouses in their marriage, parents in their child-rearing, athletes in their sports, politicians in their politics, journalists in their reporting, ministers in their ministries, bosses in their bossing, and so on. Worshipping God holistically "involves nothing less than offering up our whole lives to God so that *all we do* is in conformity with God's character and standards, rather than with the attitudes and values of the world."[4] The world as a whole is our sanctuary for worship.

This is not nearly as easy as it may sound. Indeed, it shouldn't even sound easy. Integrating faith and life as worshippers takes lots of thought, study, prayer, and skillful living. And the opposition is strong. There is a spiritual battle raging in every realm of life and for every realm of life. It involves considerable conflict and tension, and we need to be prepared

---

4. *The Complete Book of Everyday Christianity*, ed. Robert Banks and Paul Stevens (Downers Grove, Ill.: InterVarsity Press, 1997), s.v. "Worship" (emphasis added).

both to defend the faith and extend the faith tacitly and explicitly in our diverse environments, but not in a defensive or offensive manner. We also need the support of the church to assist us in our efforts to live faithfully amidst the challenges of the social and cultural contexts into which God has called us to serve.

## Worshipping God in Church

Worshipping God personally and publicly is on a continuum with the worship of a local church on a weekly basis. Christians worship God when scattered in their daily lives; they worship God in a prescribed, concentrated way when gathered together in the sanctuary; and the two realms of worship are mutually reinforcing. What we bring to church and what we bring from church should be reciprocally strengthening. That's why it's important to go to a God-honoring, biblical church, not forsaking "our own assembling together, as is the habit of some, but encouraging one another, and all the more, as you see the day drawing near" (Heb. 10:25).

Sunday by Sunday, we worship God in hearing his word read and proclaimed, by sharing in the sacraments of communion and baptism, by singing songs, hymns, and spiritual songs of thanksgiving and praise, by offering thanks, by pouring out our laments, by confessing sin, by saying prayers, and by encouraging one another in the life and service of faith. In worship we remember God's mighty deeds and praise him accordingly. In worship, the Spirit renews us as God's image according to the example we have in Jesus Christ. In worship, we are equipped to use our gifts in service to the body of Christ. In worship, we are motivated to do our work in the world with excellence.

Simultaneously, weekly worship warns us of the lingering power of idols that deform our lives. Even as believers, it is still easy for us to fail to love things properly in God, and to worship and serve some aspect of the creation rather than the Creator. Worship thwarts such hypocrisy and keeps us on the pathway of a reordered life. For this reason, John concludes his first epistle with this simple but sober warning: "Little children, guard yourselves from idols."

## Reordered Lives of Virtue

*"Virtue may be defined as an activity of the whole person in conformity with love of God and love of neighbor."*

Benjamin W. Farley, *In Praise of Virtue*[5]

Reordered love reorders worship, and it also overhauls our character and conduct in virtuous ways. Our mental poverty, deadly vices, and indifference to creation gradually give way to intellectual, moral, and physical virtues that allow us to experience the deep meaning of happiness. Virtues are the signature strengths of an authentically reordered Christian life.[6]

The Bible's vision of the virtues is unique. To know the good isn't necessarily to do the good, as Socrates taught, and the virtues are not formed in us just by habituation, as Aristotle believed, though knowledge and practice are part of the process. In a Christian perspective, the virtues are deeply embedded dispositions of heart and qualities of life based on a redemptive relationship with God. They are the fruit of the Holy Spirit at work in our lives to conform us to the character of Jesus Christ. There is an aesthetic quality to virtue, since it refashions our humanity in persuasive ways.[7] A virtuous life that flows from reordered loves is a sign of God's grace at work in our lives; it changes us and makes us holy. As 1 Peter 1:14-16 commands, "As obedient children, do not be conformed to the former lusts which were yours in your ignorance, but like the Holy One who called you, be holy yourselves also in all your behavior; because it is written, 'You shall be holy for I am holy.'"

---

5. Benjamin W. Farley, *In Praise of Virtue: An Exploration of the Biblical Virtues in a Christian Context* (Grand Rapids: Eerdmans, 1995), p. 160.

6. Researchers outside the Christian community have recognized the significance of virtue or "signature or character strengths" to human flourishing based on evidence that is global in scope. See Christopher Peterson and Martin Seligman in *Character Strengths and Virtues: A Handbook and Classification* (New York: Oxford University Press, 2004).

7. Josef Pieper, *A Brief Reader on the Virtues of the Human Heart*, trans. Paul C. Duggan (San Francisco: Ignatius Press, 1991), p. 9.

## Reordered Lives of Intellectual Virtue

> *"Hence appears the immeasurable felicity of the godly mind."*
>
> John Calvin, *Institutes of the Christian Religion*[8]

A reordered love for God reorders how we think and prompts us to cultivate intellectual virtues, or holy habits of mind, in Christ. A fundamental blessing of redemption is the gift of the mind of Christ (1 Cor. 2:16), and it comes with a commission to develop it. Jesus demands in the greatest commandment that we are to love God intellectually, not only with heart, soul, and strength, but also with our minds (Matt. 22:37). In Philippians 2:5, Paul admonishes believers to "Have this attitude [or mind] in yourselves, which was also in Christ Jesus," especially when it comes to a way of thinking about service and sacrifice on behalf of others. Paul also asserts in 1 Corinthians 14:20 that naiveté in wickedness but sophistication in thought are essential components of Christian discipleship. "Brethren," he says, "do not be children in your thinking; yet in evil be infants, but in your thinking be mature." As a part of this rising chorus, Peter also challenges us with the succinct admonition to "prepare your minds for action" (1 Peter 1:13). If we ignore these injunctions, we could fall prey to what John Stott has called "the misery and menace of mindless Christianity." Rather, we are after, to use Stott's words again, "a warm devotion [to Christ] set on fire by truth."[9]

Our minds and imaginations were subject to futility, darkness, and ignorance when unredeemed. Salvation shifts our mental paradigm and changes our intellectual status considerably. As theologian Bernard Lonergan has pointed out, redemption "dismantles and abolishes the horizon in which our knowing and choosing went on and it sets up a new horizon in which the love of God will transvaluate our values and the eyes of that love will transform our knowing."[10] Or as Paul puts it rather

---

8. John Calvin, *The Institutes of the Christian Religion,* ed. John T. McNeill, trans. and index Ford Lewis Battles, The Library of Christian Classics, gen. eds. John Baillie, John T. McNeill, Henry P. Van Dusen, vol. 20 (Philadelphia: The Westminster Press, 1960), p. 223 (§1.17.10).

9. John Stott, *Your Mind Matters: The Place of the Mind in the Christian Life,* foreword Mark A. Noll, IVP Classics (Downers Grove, IVP Books, InterVarsity Press, 1972; Americanization and foreword, 2006), pp. 17, 18.

10. Bernard Lonergan, *Method in Theology* (New York: Herder and Herder, 1972), p. 106, quoted by Ronald R. Nelson, "Faith-Discipline Integration: Compatibilist, Reconstruction-

simply in 1 Corinthians 1:5, believers in Christ are "enriched in Him, in all speech and all knowledge." For where there is love for God, there is also love for his truth and wisdom, and where there is love for his truth and wisdom, there is also love for God. In short, we now have a longing to know.[11]

We develop the virtues of the mind of Christ by immersion in the overarching stories of creation, fall, and redemption in the biblical narrative that shape our view of the world. A knowledge of the doctrines about God, humanity, sin, salvation, and other important teachings in Scripture also refashions our mental frameworks. New words, symbols, and images derived from the Bible and the tradition of the church enrich our minds and give us new ways of naming and explaining the world. In this rich framework of faith and reason, we seek understanding of all things, and by "all things" I mean the kinds of things studied at, say, the university. Now that we love God, we also love learning.

We are not only herbivores or plant-eaters, and carnivores or meat-eaters, but we are also "verbivores" or the eaters of words. We devour language and are nourished by it, especially if the words we consume concern truth, goodness and beauty. For, indeed, all truth is God's truth, all goodness is God's goodness, and all beauty is God's beauty. Jeremiah the prophet was a "verbivore" *par excellence*.

> Your words were found and I ate them,
> And Your words became for me a joy and the delight of my heart;
> For I have been called by Your name
> O LORD God of hosts. (Jer. 15:16)

To be sure, the call to the intellectual virtue of a Christian mind is not a call to extraordinary brilliance as such, though believers ought to be as smart as they can be. Instead, it's a call to the faithful cultivation and use of our minds in service to God's kingdom in all realms of life. We should strive, then, through vigorous effort to cultivate various habits of mind

---

ist, and Transformation Strategies," in Harold Heie and David L. Wolfe, eds., *The Reality of Christian Learning: Strategies for Faith-Discipline Integration* (Grand Rapids: Christian University Press, a subsidiary of the Christian College Consortium and William B. Eerdmans Publishing Company, 1987), p. 335.

11. Esther Lightcap Meeks, *Longing to Know: The Philosophy of Knowledge for Ordinary People* (Grand Rapids: Brazos Press, 2003).

necessary to think God's thoughts after him. These would include such traits as inquisitiveness, teachableness, persistence, precision, courage, patience, integrity, fairness, honesty, clarity, orderliness, and especially humility.[12] With virtues like these in place, we will taste a morsel of that perfection of intellect so well described in these words from John Henry Newman in his classic work *The Idea of a University:*

> That perfection of the Intellect . . . is the clear, calm, accurate vision and comprehension of all things, as far as the finite mind can embrace them, each in its place, and with its own characteristics upon it. It is almost prophetic from its knowledge of history; it is almost heart-searching from its knowledge of human nature; it has almost supernatural charity from its freedom from littleness and prejudice; it has almost the repose of faith, because nothing can startle it; it has almost the beauty and harmony of heavenly contemplation, so intimate is it with the eternal order of things and the music of the spheres.[13]

Therefore, let us love God with our minds, and with our minds let us love God, praying with Thomas Aquinas that God will grant us grace in the cultivation of the virtues of a mind like Christ's.

> Creator of all things, true source of light and wisdom, lofty origin of all being, graciously let a ray of your light penetrate the darkness of my understanding.
>
> Take from me the double darkness in which I have been born — an obscurity of sin and ignorance.
>
> Give me a sharp sense of understanding, a retentive memory, and the ability to grasp things correctly and fundamentally.
>
> Grant me the talent of being exact in my explanations and the ability to express myself with thoroughness and charm. Point out the beginning. Direct my progress, and help in the completion. I ask this through Christ our Lord, Amen.[14]

---

12. James W. Sire, *Habits of the Mind: Intellectual Life as a Christian Calling* (Downers Grove: InterVarsity Press, 2000), p. 110.

13. John Henry Newman, *The Idea of a University*, in *Rethinking the Western Tradition*, ed. Frank M. Turner (New Haven: Yale University Press, 1996), p. 101.

14. A version of this prayer is found at http://www.catholic-forum.com/churches/luxver/Aquinas/todays.htm (accessed July 13, 2007).

### Reordered Lives of Moral Virtue

> "A purely mental life may be destructive if it leads us to substitute
> thought for life and ideas for action."
>
> Thomas Merton, *Thoughts in Solitude*[15]

Which would you choose if a crook with gun in hand confronted you and
said: "Your riches or your reputation?" If you had to choose between
goodness or gold, which would you go for? Silver or your standing in the
community? This is a test of what you love in your life. Proverbs 22:1 presents a countercultural vision in these words:

> A good name is to be more desired than great wealth,
> Favor is better than silver and gold.

A "good name" refers to exemplary character and "favor" denotes
positive social standing, and both are more important than money. If an-
ecdotal evidence is any indication, however, the value of actual capital
seems to "trump" the value of moral and social capital in our culture most
of the time.

This is why the reordering of our loves and lives is so important. The
gospel so alters our fundamental structure of desire that we actually learn
to love moral virtue over affluence, believe it or not. This reversal doesn't
mean the repudiation of wealth *per se,* but it does domesticate it in a redemptive context.

Proverbs 22:1 doesn't explain *why* a good name is better than riches.
It just assumes we know that it is. It's not very smart to jeopardize your
reputation, or perhaps even jail time, just for a few bucks. It's not wise to
forfeit your own soul now and forever, even if you do gain the whole
transient world, and some fame, in the process. There are just some
things *we know and cannot not know,* and the importance of reputation over
riches is one of them.[16] What the New Testament teaches about virtue
confirms this.

---

15. Thomas Merton, *Thoughts in Solitude* (New York: Farrar, Straus and Giroux, 1999), p.
16.

16. J. Budziszewski, *What We Can't Not Know: A Guide* (Dallas: Spence Publishing Company, 2004).

**Virtues in the New Testament**   Jesus, along with Paul and Peter, taught that a virtuous life, born of God's Spirit, was central to Christian identity and experience. The purpose of cultivating virtue according to the Scriptures is to conform us to the character of Jesus Christ. Paul taught that if we walk in dependence upon the Holy Spirit as our essential spiritual resource, we won't carry out the sinful desires of the "flesh" ("flesh" understood here in an ethical rather than in a physical way). The Spirit and the "flesh" are at war, and we are helpless to win that battle on our own. The victory is ours if the Spirit leads us and makes us spiritually productive. "But the fruit of the Spirit," Paul notes, "is love, joy, peace, patience, kindness, goodness, faithfulness, gentleness, self-control; against such things there is no law" (Gal. 5:22-23).

Peter was just as enthusiastic about the power of faith to foster virtues in our lives. By God's grace, on the basis of God's promises, we have escaped from cultural corruptions and are being transformed into the image of God as partakers of the divine nature. In sharing in the life of God in Christ through the Spirit, we grow in the faithful practice of a variety of virtues that spell out significant personal renovation. Peter writes,

> Now for this very reason also, applying all diligence, in your faith supply moral excellence, and in your moral excellence, knowledge, and in your knowledge, self-control, and in your self-control, perseverance, and in your perseverance, godliness, and in your godliness, brotherly kindness, and in your brotherly kindness, love. (2 Pet. 1:5-7)

Peter knew how the possession and ongoing cultivation of these intertwined qualities would prevent us from wasting our lives. If we fail to realize this, it means that we have overlooked our salvation somehow, and are blind to its benefits.

> For if these qualities are yours and are increasing, they render you neither useless nor unfruitful in the true knowledge of our Lord Jesus Christ. For he who lacks these qualities is blind or short-sighted, having forgotten his purification from his former sins (vv. 8-9).

Peter wanted us to confirm our callings in Christ by cultivating these traits with vigor. This will keep us from making a disaster area out of our lives, and will pave the way for a warm welcome into God's everlasting kingdom.

Therefore, brethren, be all the more diligent to make certain about His
calling and choosing you; for as long as you practice these things, you
will never stumble; for in this way the entrance into the eternal kingdom of our Lord and Savior Jesus Christ will be abundantly supplied to
you (vv. 10-11).

The beatitudes in the Sermon on the Mount are attitudes and attributes that ought to be. But I may be jumping to conclusions. These famous words of blessing have been interpreted in different ways over the
years. Some understand them as statements of the difficult circumstances
of life in which God's kingdom comes to us and relieves us of our misery.
Blessed if you are spiritually destitute (i.e., humble or poor in spirit), for
God's kingdom can be yours.[17]

On the other hand, the beatitudes have been interpreted in a classic
way as the virtues that distinguish disciples of Christ in the kingdom of
God. As kingdom virtues, they are the polar opposites of the seven
deadly sins — and their antidotes, if you will. They are like the "seven
contrary virtues" derived from an ancient epic poem called *Psychomachia*
*(Battle of the Soul)* written by Prudentius in the fifth century. This Roman
Christian poet depicted the vices and virtues in mortal combat, pitting
humility against pride, kindness against envy, abstinence against gluttony, chastity against lust, patience against anger, liberality against
greed, and diligence against sloth. The virtues, illustrated through various biblical figures, were victorious in this customary battle of the
soul.[18]

If the seven deadly sins reflect disordered loves and lives, then the beatitudes are examples of loves and lives that have been reordered in
Christ. A comparative list (on p. 159) and a little explanation will show the
difference.[19]

Poverty of spirit or genuine humility is the answer to the self-
absorption and self-assertion of overweening pride (Matt. 5:3). To mourn

17. Dallas Willard, *The Divine Conspiracy: Rediscovering Our Hidden Life in God* (San Francisco: HarperSanFrancisco, 1998), chapter 4. Willard cites Alfred Edersheim's noted work
*The Life and Times of Jesus the Messiah* (1953) in support of this perspective, p. 102.

18. See Rosemary Burton, *Prudentius Psychomachia*, Bryn Mawr Latin Commentary Series (Bryn Mawr, Penn.: Bryn Mawr Commentaries, 1989).

19. Peter Kreeft, *Back to Virtue: Traditional Moral Wisdom for Modern Moral Confusion*, foreword Russell Kirk (San Francisco: Ignatius, 1992), p. 93.

| Seven Deadly Sins or Vices | Seven Virtues of the Beatitudes |
| --- | --- |
| Pride | Humility |
| Envy | Mournfulness |
| Anger | Meekness and Peacemaking |
| Sloth | Hunger and Thirst for Righteousness |
| Avarice or Greed | Mercy |
| Gluttony | Perseverance under Persecution |
| Lust | Purity of Heart |

and show empathy at another's loss is contrary to the pernicious envy we often feel at the success or happiness of others (Matt. 5:4). Meekness and peacemaking, which require courage and strength, are the antonyms of an anger that seeks to harm or destroy other people whom we believe have wronged us (Matt. 5:5, 9). To hunger and thirst for righteousness in pursuit of God stands out in bold relief to commonplace spiritual and moral slothfulness (Matt. 5:6). If you are merciful and generous in giving to others, you will distinguish yourself from the greedy or avaricious person who gains and holds tightly onto the gold and goods of the world (Matt. 5:7). There is also a contrast in character between those who have the moral fiber to withstand unjust persecution for the cause of Christ and the softness of the glutton whose gorging or fussiness over food discloses an entirely different mindset and lifestyle (Matt. 5:10-12). Finally, the man or woman of a pure heart and wholesome character stands out in a crowd of those whose inordinate lusts for food and sex dominate their lives (Matt. 5:8). On the one hand, there are self-absorbed, jealous, embittered, and apathetic people who are consumed with appetites that are never fully satisfied. On the other hand, happy are those who are unassuming, empathetic, gentle, holy, gracious, steadfast, and pure. Vices block beatitude. Virtues promote it.

**The Seven Cardinal Virtues** The ancient philosophers and the early church fathers also recognized the significance of the virtues and their integral connection to well-lived lives. Plato, for example, emphasized the importance of courage, justice, temperance, and prudence for each part of a well-developed human soul. Aristotle promoted the cultivation of intellectual and moral virtues for the sake of human flourishing. Early Christian thinkers focused on the three theological virtues of faith, hope, and love, based on 1 Corinthians 13:13. Eventually, the three theological and four philosophical virtues were combined to form the classic list of the seven "cardinal" virtues — faith, hope, love, courage, justice, temperance, and prudence.

They are called the cardinal virtues because they are the virtues upon which all other virtues "hinge" (from the Latin *cardo*, a "hinge"). Faith breeds loyalty. Hope induces cheerfulness. Love prompts devotion. Courage requires strength. Justice fosters impartiality. Temperance begets sobriety. Prudence precipitates discretion. And so on.

Just as the seven deadly sins are manifestations of disordered loves and disordered lives, so the seven cardinal virtues are manifestations of reordered loves and reordered lives. Whether it's the seven vices or the seven virtues, they show what we care about most deeply in our hearts, and they incline us to one way of life or another — either to a life of wisdom or foolishness, of blessing or cursing, of life or death, of shalom or sadness.

*Faith*   To borrow a biblical phrase, this virtue and reordered way of life consists of "the assurance of things hoped for, the conviction of things not seen" (Heb. 11:1). So defined, faith involves trusting in God, whom we have not seen, and having assurance on the basis of God's character that what he has promised in his word is true and will come to pass. Without this kind of faith, "it is impossible to please Him, for he who comes to God must believe that He is and that He is a rewarder of those who seek Him" (Heb. 11:6).

Faith begins with confidence in what the Bible says about God and the world. It tells us about God's excellent greatness and the mighty deeds he has done in history. Scripture tells it like it is, and we trust in its truth to guide us in our lives in time and for eternity. Jude 3 calls this revealed biblical body of knowledge in which we believe "the faith," and says we are to defend it earnestly against its detractors (see also 1 Peter 3:15).

Faith as a virtue also means cleaving to the Lord with confidence in all the ups and downs of life. On a day-to-day basis, we trust in him who loved us and gave himself up for us (Gal. 2:20). If he died for us, he will provide for us in whatever we need (Rom. 8:32). We walk by faith, not by sight, believing that he is working all things together for good according to his purposes (2 Cor. 5:7; Rom. 8:28). Self-reliance is foolish, but God will guide if we rely on him.

Trust in the LORD with all your heart
And do not lean on your own understanding.
In all your ways acknowledge Him,
And He will make your paths straight. (Prov. 3:5-6)

Faith also means having confidence in God to do what he says and serve him as we should. If the Old Testament saints are any example, however, faithful obedience is no cakewalk. It involves trusting God to empower us to perform heroic acts, undergo hardships, persevere in persecution, and endure intense suffering even to the point of death (Heb. 11:32-40). New Testament saints fared little better, especially John the Baptist, who lost his head, and Jesus himself, who was crucified (not to mention Stephen's stoning, Peter's inverted crucifixion, and Paul's beheading, all out of obedience to God and the gospel). Whether we will face extraordinary tests of our commitment to Christ or not, the Scriptures affirm that the righteous man or woman lives by faith in God, whose lovingkindness never ceases, whose compassion never fails, and whose faithfulness is great (Lam. 3:22-24). Therefore, we also have hope.

*Hope* This virtue and reordered way of living is based on the victory of God's kingdom and the rule of God's providence in the world. In hope we are confident that God in his goodness will care for us as his children and bless our lives with favor both now and forever.

Purely human hope is but wishful thinking for uncertain goods. Maybe I'll get that job. Maybe she'll say "Yes." Maybe I'll win the lottery. God's triumph in Christ, on the other hand, "has caused us to be born again to a living hope through the resurrection of Jesus Christ from the dead" (1 Pet. 1:3). Sin has been expiated, and we are forgiven. Death has been conquered, and we fear it no more. Satan has been defeated, and we have escaped his power. We have received the gift of the Holy Spirit. We are members of the body of Christ. God is directing our daily lives and will accomplish what concerns us. We will spend eternity with God. The gospel is full of divine assurances as we set our hope on "God who richly supplies us with all things to enjoy" (1 Tim. 6:17).

Despite the tests we inevitably face — some mild and some severe — we refuse to lose heart. We have an obstinate hope. God is good, and so is life in Jesus Christ, even in the midst of suffering and pain. We persevere because we believe that what God has promised, he will also perform. We hope because we stand on the solid rock of Jesus Christ.

His oath, his covenant, his blood
Support me in the whelming flood;
When all around my soul gives way,
*He then is all my hope and stay.*
On Christ the solid rock I stand;
All other ground is sinking sand,
All other ground is sinking sand.[20]

This hope of the kingdom of God is not only personal, but also historical. In the midst of the growing complexities of the global scene, we are assured that God will sort all things out in the end and bring justice to the earth. This is the certain goal, even if we aren't exactly sure how, when, or where God will do it. We know that since he faithfully fulfilled the Old Testament promises of redemption in the first coming of Christ, God will also complete his redemptive work in the future when Christ returns. Christ has died. Christ has risen. Christ is coming again. In this time between the times, we wait, we work, and we pray as Christ taught us to pray:

Your kingdom come,
Your will be done,
On earth as it is in heaven. (Matt. 6:10)

*Love*   If we have the virtues of faith and hope, it is because we are confident in God's love for us. We don't trust people if we don't think they love us. We don't place our expectations in people unless we are convinced that they care. Likewise, we wouldn't trust God or anticipate good things from God if we didn't believe he was kindly disposed toward us and benevolent in every way.

The same is true with the virtue of love. We love because God loved us first. He loved us first by sending Christ to be the propitiation for our sins and the source of our life. If God so loved us in this way, we ought to love him back. If God so loved us in this way, we ought to love one another (1 John 4:7-21). We love God and our neighbors now, whereas before we didn't care that much about anyone beyond ourselves. If we love, however, it's a sign we know God and have been born of him. If we don't love, it in-

---

20. "The Solid Rock," words Edward Mote, 1832, tune William B. Bradbury, 1863. *Baptist Hymnal* (Nashville: Convention Press, 1975), p. 337 (emphasis added).

dicates the reverse. If we live in love, we live in God, and if we live in God, we live in love, for all who live in love belong to God.

*Courage* This virtue and reordered way of life means loving God and others and serving them in tangible ways, despite the risks or costs involved. It denotes our resolve to do what is right regardless of the obstacles or consequences. Courage does not mean fearlessness, much less pride. It does mean we are moved by love to promote God's glory, to assist others in faith and life, and to make the world a better place in which to live, regardless. God's word to Joshua in facing the Canaanites is symbolic for us: "Be strong and courageous! Do not tremble or be dismayed, For the Lord your God is with you wherever you go" (Josh. 1:9).

Shadrach, Meshach, and Abednego were profiles in courage (Dan. 3). On pain of the fiery furnace, they refused to bow down to Nebuchadnezzar's golden image. When faced with the punishment for their civil disobedience, they expressed their commitment to do what was right, whether God saved them or not. "If it be so," they said, "our God whom we serve is able to deliver us from the furnace of blazing fire; and He will deliver us out of your hand, O king. But even if He does not, let it be known to you, O king, that we are not going to serve your gods or worship the golden image that you have set up" (vv. 17-18). These men showed the "courage of their convictions" in their refusal to compromise, and that refusal was based on their faith and hope in God and his love.

*Justice* This virtue and reordered way of life certainly takes courage, since it involves treating God, people, and all creatures with due regard and fairness, whatever the relationship, situation, or context. Justice is multifaceted in character, and there are several aspects to its application. In its distributive form, justice means the fair allocation of goods, services, and respect. In its retributive form, justice means responding properly to wrongdoing — making the punishment fit the crime. In its compensatory form, justice has to do with fair compensation for an injury or hardship suffered. Whatever its form, we should treat others justly, as we would wish to be justly treated.

Some say that justice is a basic natural law. Others argue that it's a human invention and a social contract. In a Christian perspective, justice originates in the very character of God, which Deuteronomy 32:4 describes in these words:

The Rock! His work is perfect,
For all His ways are just;
A God of faithfulness and without injustice,
Righteous and upright is He.

Theologians have explained that God in his "rectoral" justice imposes his righteous laws upon us impartially, and depending upon our response he punishes or rewards us in perfect fairness as an expression of his "distributive" justice. In any case, the Scriptures teach that God is a God who takes delight in exercising lovingkindness, justice, and righteousness on the earth (Jer. 9:24). He is a righteous judge who must do right, and he justly judges the world (Pss. 7:11; 96:13; Gen. 18:25).

In fact, God has already judged the world in his justice in the person and work of Jesus Christ. Jesus was the epitome of divine justice in his life and death. Horizontally, he treated all people — young or old, male or female, friend or foe — with the respect and fairness they deserved. Vertically, he satisfied the demands of God's justice by offering himself sacrificially on the cross as a propitiation for our sins through his blood. In averting God's wrath in this way, he reconciled the world to God and made it possible for us to be justified in God's sight. Having been justified by faith, we have peace with God through him (Rom. 3:21-26; 5:1; 2 Cor. 5:18-19).

Since the world's judgment has already taken place in Christ, Christians are now agents of his justice in the world. To do righteousness and justice, to plead the cause of the afflicted and needy, "'Is not that what it means to know Me?' declares the Lord" (Jer. 22:15-16). The work of Nobel laureate and retired archbishop Desmond Tutu is a case in point. He embodied the virtue of justice in his sacrificial efforts in confronting the sin of apartheid in South Africa and by working diligently as the head of its Truth and Reconciliation Commission to bring healing to his country. The manner in which he fulfilled his calling is a poignant example of God's vision of a good life set forth by Micah the prophet:

He has told you, O man, what is good;
And what does the LORD require of you
But to do justice, to love kindness,
And to walk humbly with your God? (Mic. 6:8)

*Temperance*  This virtue and reordered way of life refers to the Spirit-induced capacity of self-control in a culture and society that seems to have gone haywire. Temperance literally means to be moderate, and it denotes the capacity to subordinate our appetites and desires to clear thinking and biblical standards, an aptitude to restrain our passions that we might be free to cultivate healthy habits of mind and body that are good for ourselves and others.

In relation to avarice or greed, temperance curtails love of money and possessions and fosters economic frugality and thriftiness. In relation to gluttony, temperance limits the intake of food and drink and may entail abstinence from both. In relation to lust, temperance is modesty and chastity with reference to dress and sexual activity. In relation to pride, temperance means not thinking more highly of ourselves than we ought to think, but to think so as to have sound judgment (Rom. 12:3). Intemperance is unbecoming of a woman or man made in the image and likeness of God. A temperate life decorously fits our dignity as children of God.

For Plato, temperance or self-control was an essential virtue. He illustrates it in an analogy of two horses and a charioteer in one of his writings called the *Phaedrus*. One horse is well bred and behaved, runs without a whip, and represents reasonable behavior. The other is poorly bred and behaved, requires a whip, and represents the soul's irrational passions and desires. The charioteer is the intellect and rational part of the soul that must keep the two horses in line so that the soul as a whole can be directed to ultimate truth and enlightenment.[21]

Paul's example is more down-to-earth. He compares himself to an athlete who must exercise self-control if he wishes to win the prize in a race or a boxing match. For the sake of an eternal reward rather than a perishable wreath, Paul says, "I run in such a way, as not without aim; I box in such a way, as not beating the air; but I discipline my body and make it my slave, so that, after I have preached to others, I myself will not be disqualified" (1 Cor. 9:26-27). Paul didn't want a profligate life to jeopardize his reputation as a minister of the gospel and cause him to lose his reward. He knew he couldn't muster up self-control on his own, and that's why he listed it as a fruit of the Holy Spirit. For Paul, temperance was essential to a

---

21. Plato, *Phaedrus*, trans. Benjamin Jowett, *Great Books of the Western World*, ed. Robert Maynard Hutchins, vol. 7 (Chicago: William Benton, Publisher, Encyclopedia Britannica, Inc., 1952), pp. 124-28 (§246a-254e).

well-lived Christian life, a prerequisite for ministry, and a requirement for church leaders. It was particularly becoming, he said, of older men and women (1 Tim. 3:2, 11; Titus 1:8; 2:2).

To discipline our desires is not only a personal imperative but also a political requirement, especially in democracies where the government is presumably "of the people, by the people and for the people." If the people lack self-control, however, then woe be to that democracy — it could become anarchy. As we note in singing "America the Beautiful," self-control is essential to the well-being of America and a key to its survival as a nation:

> America! America!
> God mend thine ev'ry flaw,
> Confirm thy soul in *self-control*,
> Thy liberty in law.[22]

*Prudence*   The meaning of this virtue and reordered way of life is indicated in its root words that denote "anticipation" and "foreseeing" (Latin, *prudens* and *providens*). Like God's "providence" in history, we are prudent if we can look ahead and see how to order our lives and relationships wisely toward their proper goals. Classical philosophers connected prudence "to shrewdness, exceptionally good judgment, and the gift of *coup d'oeil* — the 'coup of the eye' — which could take in the whole of a situation at once and know almost automatically how to proceed. Aristotle called it *phronēsis* or 'practical wisdom' in the *Nicomachean Ethics*."[23]

Prudence has an influential relationship on all the other virtues.[24] It enables us to know which of them to apply as the wisest course of behavior in any situation. It also guides us in their exercise to prevent their distortion and preserve their true form. Prudence prevents courage from succumbing to cowardice or foolhardiness. It keeps justice from slipping into laxity or severity. It protects temperance from libertarianism or legal-

---

22. Second stanza of "America the Beautiful" by Katharine Lee Bates, the final version of which was written in 1913 (emphasis added). On the issue of American temperance or self-control, see Peter N. Steams, *Battleground of Desire: The Struggle for Self-Control in Modern America* (New York: New York University Press, 1999).

23. Aristotle, *Nicomachean Ethics*, trans. Terence Irwin (Indianapolis/Cambridge: Hackett Publishing Company, 1985), pp. 158-61 (§1141b8-1142a30). See p. 411 in this volume for additional references to *phronēsis* as practical wisdom in this work.

24. *The Catholic Encyclopedia*, s.v. "Prudence." Available at: http://www.newadvent.org/cathen/12517b.htm (accessed July 17, 2007).

ism. Prudence helps us discern the golden mean in our behaviors. Each virtue is, indeed, a form of prudence.[25] For where there is prudence, there is also virtue, and where there is virtue, there also is prudence.

One purpose of the book of Proverbs is to give prudence to naïve, simpleminded people (1:4). It frequently connects prudence with knowledge and understanding (13:16; 18:15). Prudent people understand their way, carefully consider their course in life, and heed correction, especially from parents (14:8, 15; 15:5). They know when to remain silent, and they hide themselves from evil and avoid its consequences (17:28; 22:3; 27:12). Imprudent or "foolish" people neglect this advice wholesale.

There is a general form of prudence that touches the whole of life, like the good sense required of church overseers (1 Tim. 3:2). Otherwise, prudence is specific to specific realms of life: "jurisprudence" in law, "linguistic prudence" in speech, "epistemic prudence" in knowledge, "moral prudence" in behavior, "aesthetic prudence" in the arts, "conjugal prudence" in marriage, "familial prudence" in the home, "ecclesiastical prudence" in the church, and so on. Indeed, the realms requiring prudence are virtually endless. In the parable of the ten virgins, it was the prudent who "took oil in flasks along with their lamps" in waiting for the return of the bridegroom (Matt. 25:4).

Abraham Lincoln demonstrated exceptional political prudence in the way he handled slavery and the issue of emancipation. In grasping the big picture, with several goals in mind, he used federal legislation, a military order (the Emancipation Proclamation), and trust in divine providence to skillfully navigate one of the most tumultuous periods in U.S. history. He wedded the faith and morality of the Puritans to the secularism and rationality of the Enlightenment throughout the entire ordeal with exemplary skillfulness. As Allen Guelzo asserts, "Lincoln's procedure was at every step a model of prudence."[26]

---

25. This is according to Thomas Aquinas as quoted in *The Great Ideas: A Syntopicon, The Great Books of the Western World*, vol. 2, s.v. "Temperance."

26. Allen C. Guelzo, "The Prudence of Abraham Lincoln," *First Things*, January 2006, p. 12.

## *Reordered Lives of Physical Virtue*

> *"O LORD, how many are Your works!*
> *In wisdom You have made them all;*
> *The earth is full of Your possessions."*

Psalm 104:24

A reordered life born of reordered loves generates new attitudes and actions in regard to all things physical. Some Christians unfortunately denigrate creation as insignificant, as did the second-century Gnostics, who elevated the spiritual realm to supremacy and counseled escape from the alleged evil of the material world. In Scripture, however, matter matters.

**Body Care**  Physical embodiment is essential to our humanity and has been from the beginning. Our bodies are the means by which God manifests his image and presence in the world. Though sin disrupted this abiding purpose, it is being renewed in Christ through the bodies of believers individually and the body of Christ corporately, since both are the temples of the Holy Spirit. "Or do you not know," Paul asks rhetorically, "that your body is a temple of the Holy Spirit who is in you, whom you have from God, and that you are not your own? For you have been bought with a price: therefore glorify God in your body" (1 Cor. 6:19-20; cf. 3:16-17). This teaching is fraught with theological significance and is the basis for a revolution in how we think about ourselves as physical beings.

We tend to think of ourselves as free, independent beings, and we have been led to believe that we can do whatever we want with ourselves and our bodies as long as we don't hurt others. This autonomous and privatized mentality is quite contrary to the biblical vision. In the Bible we read that we should shift our perspective from ownership, rights, and individualism to stewardship, responsibilities, and communal concern.

God made us, has redeemed us, and now dwells in us as the Lord of our lives and bodies. We don't belong to ourselves, but to God. We have no rights to do with our bodies as we please, but we must care for them as good stewards of the property that is ultimately God's. We must treat ourselves in ways that please God and reflect his image in us. We must not burden others with the results of our foolish behaviors, but live responsibly to build up the communities of which we are a part.

Am I free to get tattooed? What about body piercing? Am I eating and drinking too much? Do I exercise regularly and get enough rest? Have drinking and drugs become a way life? Do I dress in a modest manner? Am I obsessed with my weight or appearance? Is my hairstyle a neurotic concern? These are all important questions to ask in cultivating the virtue of body care.[27]

**Creation Care** "How can Christianity call itself catholic," asked philosopher Simone Weil, "if the universe is left out?"[28] It can't, and we must remember that "the earth is the Lord's, and all it contains/The world, and those who dwell in it" (Psa. 24:1). We have indeed forgotten that the world belongs to God, however, just as we have forgotten that our bodies are God's as well. According to Philip Sherrard, having "desanctified" ourselves, we then proceeded to "desanctify" the creation as well. We have "invented a worldview in which nature is seen as an impersonal commodity, a soulless source of food, raw materials, wealth, power, and so on, which we think we are quite entitled to experiment with, exploit, remodel and generally abuse."[29] This perspective explains the reasons for a whole host of earthly problems, including land degradation, deforestation, species extinction, water pollution, global toxification, atmospheric alteration, and other sins against God's very good world.[30]

Any hope of reversing these catastrophes, whether locally or globally, depends on a shift in underlying assumptions — not in the direction of pantheism, but on the basis of a robust Christian theism with all of its implications for creation care. One group articulates the vision like this:

> Because we worship and honor the Creator, we seek to cherish and care for the creation.
>
> Because we have sinned, we have failed in our stewardship of cre-

27. For practical suggestions about how to care for our bodies, see Don Colbert, M.D., *The Seven Pillars of Health* (Lake Mary, Fla.: Siloam Press, 2007); Rex Russell, *What the Bible Says about Healthy Living*, foreword Joe S. McIlhaney (Ventura, Calif.: Gospel Light Publications, 1997); Kenneth H. Cooper, *Faith-Based Fitness* (Nashville: Thomas Nelson, 1997).

28. Simone Weil, *Waiting for God* (London: Fontana, 1959), p. 116.

29. Philip Sherrard, *Human Image: World Image: The Death and Resurrection of Sacred Cosmology* (Ipswich: Golgonooza Press, 1992), p. 3.

30. "An Evangelical Declaration on the Care of Creation," published by the Evangelical Environmental Network, cited at http://www.creationcare.org/resources/declaration.php (accessed July 17, 2007).

ation. Therefore we repent of the way we have polluted, distorted, or destroyed so much of the Creator's work.

Because in Christ God has healed our alienation from God and extended to us the first fruits of the reconciliation of all things, we commit ourselves to working in the power of the Holy Spirit to share the Good News of Christ in word and deed, to work for the reconciliation of all people in Christ, and to extend Christ's healing to suffering creation.[31]

At the heart of this outlook is making the wonderful rediscovery of the world as God's very good creation and his ownership of it. We should reflect more deeply on the biblical teachings about creation itself and investigate the wonders of its divine design and the marvelous laws by which it operates. We ought to cultivate a sacramental perspective on reality that detects the glory of God in all things. We must repent of attitudes that debunk the value of God's creation and our failure to be its responsible stewards. We must confess how we are morally implicated in the world's wanton desecration. We should interpret our mandate to have dominion over the earth in terms of a stewardship from God in which we cultivate and manage the earth's inhabitants and resources responsibly before him. We ought to imitate God's creativity and imagination in cultivating an aesthetic vision that includes a concern for beauty in all our cultural endeavors. We must understand the cosmic scope of Christ's redemption that includes the renewal and completion of God's original purposes for creation. We must examine our ways of life and take on more of a "green" lifestyle that moves us from wastefulness and overconsumption to frugality and self-control. We must contribute diligently to the healing of creation and to the formulation of just and responsible economic systems from a Christian perspective that will enable all people to flourish in God's world.

**Animal Care**   As God's noble creatures, animals in their incredible diversity and fabulous traits reflect God's infinite wisdom and vast imagination, whether in fish, birds, the great sea monsters, cattle, creeping things, and the beasts of the earth.[32] Unfortunately, the fall of humanity into sin

31. This statement and the following reflections are from "On the Care of Creation: An Evangelical Declaration of the Care of Creation" (see previous note).

32. *Dictionary of Biblical Theology*, ed. Xavier Léon-Dufour, 2nd ed. (New York: Seabury Press, 1973), s.v. "Animals." This paragraph is drawn from this source.

destroyed the original harmony of creation, and it resulted not only in man's inhumanity to man but also in man's inhumanity to animals as well. "Hence date the persecution and the pain/That man inflicts on all inferior kinds,/Regardless of their plaints," writes the poet William Cowper.[33]

The question is how redemption should affect our mind-set toward and life together with animals in this world. There is indeed a "defensible theological vision of animals and their place in the moral universe,"[34] for at least two reasons. First, since God created the animals and cares for them, we must also treat them with the integrity, justice, and compassion they deserve. Animals and people share a variety of biological characteristics, and the first man gave the animals their original names (Gen. 2:19-20). God instructed the righteous Noah to save them from destruction in the flood, and they are partners with us in God's covenant never to destroy the world with water again (Gen. 6–9). The Law grants animals rest on the Sabbath (Exod. 20:8-11), and it demands that they should be fed properly for their labor (Deut. 25:4). Their perfections as expressions of God's glory even prompted a recalcitrant Job to repentance (Job 38–42). Indeed, God's wisdom and mercy are embodied in all his creatures, animals included, and not a sparrow falls to the ground without his awareness (Pss. 104:24; 145:9; 147:9; Matt. 10:29). On these grounds, John Calvin said "it must be remembered that [we] . . . are required to practice justice even in dealing with animals."[35]

Therefore, we emulate God as their Creator when we treat animals ethically. Such treatment is even a sign of rectitude. As Proverbs 12:10 states, "A righteous man has regard for the life of his animal, but even the compassion of the wicked is cruel." As Francis Schaeffer concludes, "Christians of all people, should not be the destroyers. We should treat nature with an overwhelming respect."[36]

Second, animals are our inferiors, and God has placed them under

33. William Cowper, "The Winter Walk at Noon," in *Cowper: Poetical Works*, p. 228 (lines 384-86).

34. Robert N. Wennberg, *God, Humans, and Animals: An Invitation to Enlarge Our Moral Universe* (Grand Rapids: Eerdmans, 2003), p. 308.

35. John Calvin, *Calvin: Commentaries*, trans. and ed. Joseph Haroutunian, The Library of Christian Classics, vol. 23 (Philadelphia: Westminster Press, 1958), p. 329.

36. Francis A. Schaeffer, *Pollution and the Death of Man: The Christian View of Ecology* (Wheaton: Tyndale House, 1970), p. 74.

our dominion for our service and use. They are our companions in their domestication and even serve as sources of therapy and entertainment. They have supplied us with food and clothing. They have assisted us in agricultural pursuits, as means of transportation, and in biomedical research. They have been of use in warfare and in disaster missions of search, rescue, and recovery. In some cases they provide biological controls (birds that devour mosquitoes, for example). After the fall and flood, the flesh of animals became a divinely sanctioned source of food, though we must remember we are "carnivorous, through sin."[37] Animals were also essential to Israel's sacrificial system of worship, and as such they prefigured the death of the Lamb of God who takes away the sin of the world (John 1:29).

Putting these two points together, we can affirm with Basil the Great (A.D. 329-379) "that animals live not for us alone, but for themselves and for God." He offers this thoughtful prayer on their behalf:

> For those, O Lord, the humble beasts, that bear with us the burden and heat of the day and offer their guileless lives for the well-being of humankind; and for the wild creatures whom Thou hast made wise, strong, and beautiful we supplicate for them Thy great tenderness of heart for Thou has promised to save both man and beast and great is Thy loving kindness, O Master, Saviour of the world.[38]

When the peaceable kingdom returns with Christ, harmony in creation will be restored at last. In a Christian ethic of reverence for life, we can prefigure a sliver of this coming reign of shalom by treating animals with proper regard and by refusing to show unnecessary cruelty to any living thing.

> And the wolf will dwell with the lamb,
> And the leopard will lie down with the young goat,
> And the calf and the young lion and the fatling together;
> And a little boy will lead them. . . .
> They will not hurt or destroy in all My holy mountain,
> For the earth will be full of the knowledge of the LORD
> As the waters cover the sea. (Isa. 11:6, 9)

37. Cowper, "The Winter Walk at Noon," p. 229 (line 457).
38. Quoted in Wennberg, *God, Humans, and Animals*, p. 303.

**A Reordered Life of Virtue**   In chapter three, I offered a short description of a disordered life resulting from the disordered loves of the seven deadly sins. To balance this account, how, then, might we describe a reordered life of virtue rooted in reordered loves? What might a virtuous person in Christ look like? Here's a possible portrait:

> Thanks to the grace of the gospel, my loves and my life have been transformed. I have turned from the worship of idols to the worship of the one, true, living God, and that has made all the difference in the world. I wasn't much interested in learning before, but now I have a virtually insatiable desire to grow in my faith intellectually, to seek a faithful understanding in all things, and to develop the virtues of a Christian mind. Now that I have a personal relationship with the Creator and Redeemer of the universe, I believe in the truth of his word, and I am learning how to trust God and walk by faith in every situation in life. Formerly I lived in hopelessness and despair, but my confidence in the goodness of God and his faithfulness to his promises has given me hope for the present and future, for myself and for the world. My previous selfishness has given way to a growing love for God and a genuine care and concern for other people, just as I have learned to love myself. With the help of the Holy Spirit, I am cultivating the courage to obey God, serve others, and do what is right regardless of the risks or costs involved. I am outraged at evil and seek to treat other people and all things justly, fairly, and with the regard they deserve as creations of God. I realize that my cravings for various things must be controlled, and I seek with God's help to live a life of temperance and moderation. Because there is much foolishness in the world, I realize the importance of cultivating prudence, that I might conduct all of my affairs skillfully in accordance with God's truth and wisdom. I am learning how to care for my body as the temple of the Holy Spirit. I am discovering what it means to be a good steward of and to care for God's creation. I am recognizing the role that animals play in life and the world, and I am attempting to develop a biblically based ethic of animal care.

Compare this word picture of a reordered life of virtue with the one of a disordered life of vice on page 78. The differences are striking, and so are their respective personal and social consequences. Any preferences? As

Augustine noted, "For every man's life is good or bad according as his heart is engaged."[39]

## Undermining Habits and Addictions, Crime and Warfare

*". . . having been freed from sin, you became slaves of righteousness."*

Romans 6:18

Let's do the math. Worshipping God plus the cultivation of the intellectual, moral, and physical virtues add up to a reordered life. On this foundation, we find strength to overcome bad habits and addictions and to thwart propensities toward violence, crime, and warfare.

Occasionally, some people are freed rather miraculously from their compulsive behaviors. For most, however, the weaning process is incremental as the despotic rule of those behaviors is slowly broken. The journey to freedom is a complex physiological and spiritual process, and we don't want to oversimplify it. Fundamentally, however, it is a work of the Holy Spirit, who uses various natural and human means to secure our fulfillment in God, reorder our loves for people, places, and things, and bring us to blossom through a process of rehabilitation, however arduous it may be. God's grace is sufficient, and God's power is perfected in weakness (2 Cor. 12:9). Overcoming habits and addictions requires considerable patience and perseverance. There will be an inevitable series of setbacks and victories along the way. We must develop a variety of Christian disciplines to keep us on the road to victory (see the next chapter). Thankfully, God never gives up on us, nor should we on him. God is at work for his pleasure and our good. Having begun this work in us, he will complete it until the day Christ returns (Phil. 2:13; 1:6).

The best way to reduce crime is through a significant overhaul of our loves and lives through the gospel. It's the best crime-stopper of all. Knowing God, building self-esteem, fostering personal responsibility, growing in virtue, and cultivating genuine love can't help but curtail deviant behaviors over time. More prisons, more police, and tougher policies

---

39. Augustine, "Reply to Faustus the Manichean," trans. Richard Stothert, in *The Nicene and Post-Nicene Fathers*, ed. Philip Schaff, New Series, vol. 4 (Peabody, Mass.: Hendrickson Publishers, Inc., 1994), p. 167 (§6.11).

and penalties may be needed, but they won't ultimately lower the crime statistics. We must treat the causes of the problems, not just their symptoms. Thoreau once said that for every thousand hacking away at the branches of evil, there is only one striking at the roots. By his sacrifice, Christ struck at the roots of crime in dealing with sin, death, and the devil. A gospel renewal of consciousness and conscience, a reordering of the mind in its thoughts and the heart in its desires, is the secret of changing people and creating a better world. Not incidentally, creating a better world, in turn, creates better people because of the improvement in the environments in which people are raised. The process is reciprocal.

Of course, criminals must be held accountable for their deeds and appropriately punished. Nonetheless, whether they are incarcerated for minor violations or capital crimes, they are candidates for lifelong change in Jesus Christ. Charles Colson refers to the process as "restorative justice."[40] The success rate of Prison Fellowship has been impressive in reducing the recidivism of lawbreakers and in transforming prisoners into productive, law-abiding citizens. "The solution to crime," Colson says, "is no different from — indeed, it is a subset of — the solution to the human predicament as a whole. We are at odds with God; we cannot repair this situation ourselves; God has repaired it for us and offers us a part of that great eternal solution" in the gospel. Drawing on the thought of C. S. Lewis, Colson adds, "Only when the will [that is, what we love, want, and desire] is converted do we have the capacity to do what is right and just; only the transformation of the will can deal with the problem of crime at its roots."[41] A healing of this magnitude — one that strikes at the roots — is the presupposition upon which Paul makes his appeal for an exchange of robbery for industry and generosity: "He who steals must steal no longer; but rather he must labor, performing with his own hands what is good, so that he will have something to share with one who has need" (Eph. 4:28).

The same spiritual calculus is also the secret weapon in the ongoing human struggle to end all wars. War is hell, and without a radical alteration of the sum and substance of the human heart, warfare, like crime, will be a perpetual part of the human condition. Large, disordered loves such as pride, envy, anger, greed, gluttony, and lust in the large, disordered lives of nefarious political leaders are the causes of wars large and small,

---

40. Charles Colson, *Justice That Restores* (Wheaton: Tyndale House Publishers, 2001).
41. Colson, *Justice That Restores*, pp. 90, 96.

wherever they are in the world. "The loves of a few men move the lives of many. History itself seems to turn in one direction rather than another with the turning of an emperor's heart."[42]

Gospel transformation is the only hope we have of thwarting the combative nature of fallen humanity to pave a way for peace. It is equally fundamental for a just military response to unjust aggression or for the possible exercise of a just preemptive war to thwart an unjust invasion or impending attack. This kind of orientation prompted by faith also distinguishes the callings of Christian statesmanship and soldiering from its non-Christian counterparts. It holds the key to the possible prevention of war or to its fair administration once it becomes inevitable.

As long as history endures, the goal of war justly waged is always that of peace. There is a time for a war and a time for peace (Eccles. 3:8). Thankfully, a day will come when Christ returns in judgment, fights the final battle against his enemies, and restores the kingdom of God to his world. At long last, warrior nations "will hammer their swords into plowshares and their spears into pruning hooks. Nation will not lift up sword against nation, and never again will they learn war" (Isa. 2:4b). Then and only then will the peace of the New Jerusalem envelop the earth and reintroduce us fully to the happiness of paradise.[43]

---

42. *The Great Ideas: A Syntopican*, vol. 1 in *The Great Books of the Western World*, s.v. "Love."
43. *Dictionary of Biblical Theology*, s.v. "War."

CHAPTER SEVEN

# A Mended Heart and the
# Deep Meaning of Happiness

*"Now God designed the human . . . to run on Himself. . . . God
cannot give us a happiness and peace apart from Himself, because
it is not there. There is no such thing."*

C. S. Lewis, *Mere Christianity*[1]

## Introduction

Happiness? Come on, really? Perhaps in heaven, but not now. Many of us are
serious skeptics when it comes to felicity. Happiness is rare and fleeting at
best. As the character Mac Sledge played by Robert Duval in the film *Tender
Mercies* uttered on one occasion, "I don't trust happiness. Never did, never
will."[2] Similarly, humorist Garrison Keillor of Lake Wogebon fame, nurtured
in a religiously conservative midwestern fatalism, also said in an interview,
"We come from people who brought us up to believe that life is a struggle.
And if you should ever feel really happy, be patient. This will pass."[3]

Life is very difficult, an extraordinary struggle. As the author of the

---

1. C. S. Lewis, *Mere Christianity* (New York: The Macmillan Company, 1958), p. 39.

2. Mac Sledge in *Tender Mercies* (1983), cited at http://www.imdb.com/title/tt0086423/
quotes (accessed January 2, 2007).

3. Quoted in Sam Anderson, "Not in Lake Wobegon Anymore," *The Dallas Morning
News*, Sunday, June 25, 2006.

book of Job proclaims, "For man is born for trouble, as sparks fly upward" (Job 5:7). We wonder if a happy life is possible, even if our loves and lives are rightly ordered.

In response to our despair or our fatalism about happiness, we need to reflect on the extent of the deep meaning of happiness that is possible now and what awaits us in the future. We must understand that service, sacrifice, and suffering are essential parts of God's redemptive plan at this point in history. We must also look at various disciplines that help create and maintain the proper dispositions of our hearts to keep us on the pathway of reordered love and life. The virtues tell us what we are supposed to be as persons, and the disciplines help us turn them into actions. A part of my own story fits in well here. Then we will conclude with something rather surprising that Jesus may have hidden from us while he was on earth because he knew we couldn't handle it now. These are our topics for this final chapter.

## "Already" but "Not Yet"

*"Peace I leave with you; My peace I give to you."*

John 14:27

As we have noted, *shalom* is one of the great words in the Bible. Its fortunes ebb and flow as the plot of Scripture unfolds in the narratives of creation, fall, and redemption. This is what I was trying to communicate in my modest poetic efforts on pages 125-27, where I used the form of the word *shalom* in code. In the section on creation, it appears with a capital letter and the whole word is italicized, indicating the vigorous condition of soundness, wholeness, and well-being that God intended for humanity and the earth in the very beginning — the edenistic happiness of Genesis 1–2. In the second part of the poem on the fall, it has a strike through it to indicate that the original form of flourishing God had in mind was significantly marred by sin. In the third stanza on redemption, the first part of the word is italicized and without a capital letter, symbolizing the partial, though adequate, nature of our renewed state of blessing in Christ right now. In the last stanza, it appears in all capital letters, fully italicized and followed with an exclamation point. The peace of God will envelop the new heavens and earth in its entirety when God sums up all things with an administration suitable to the fullness of the times in Jesus Christ (Eph. 1:10). We can understand the nature of our present and future experiences of happiness as Christians in this framework. Let's elaborate on this just a bit.

We live at the "hyphen" or "dash" between the "already" but "not yet" in terms of our Lord's redemptive work.[4] The New Testament announces that the kingdom-rule of God has "already" broken into the world in the person and work of Jesus Christ with an opening victory over sin, death, and Satan. The new age of forgiveness is now available to those of us who believe. We are presently justified by faith alone and are being renewed by the Holy Spirit.

Though Jesus has inaugurated this new era of redemption, it remains to be finished or consummated. The kingdom in Christ slipped into the midst of the old age without obliterating it. We are still living under the residual influence of sin, death, and Satan, even though Christ has defeated these enemies and broken their powers. There is an overlapping of the ages — this age and the age to come — and that's why we are to be "in the world, but not of it." This is the reason we are currently living as "aliens and strangers," not in relation to creation, but in regard to its lingering sin. The righteous "wheat" and the wicked "tares" live side by side until the "final harvest." Then the "wheat" will be gathered into Christ's barn and the "tares" will be burned (Matt. 13:30).

This arrangement has been compared often to D-Day and VE-Day in World War II. On D-Day (June 6, 1944), Western Allies launched the Battle of Normandy that promised the liberation of Western Europe from Nazi occupation. *"The decisive battle... may already have occurred in a relatively early stage of the war, and yet the war still continues,"* as one author put it.[5] Eleven months later, on VE-Day (May 8, 1945), the Allied forces finally achieved their ultimate victory over Germany and Hitler's Third Reich and set Europe free.

Analogously, Christ's D-Day was his first coming, in which he launched his opening assault on the spiritual "Nazism," if you will, that had wrecked God's creation. In particular, *"that event on the cross, together with the resurrection which followed, was the already concluded decisive battle."*[6] His

4. Appropriated for a different purpose from Justo L. Gonzalez, ¡Alabadle! Hispanic Christian Worship (Nashville: Abingdon, 1996), p. 16, quoted in Cornelius Plantinga Jr. and Sue A. Rozeboom, Discerning the Spirits: A Guide to Thinking About Christian Worship Today (Grand Rapids: Eerdmans, 2003), p. 164.

5. Oscar Cullmann, Christ and Time: The Primitive Christian Conception of Time and History, rev. ed., trans. Floyd V. Filson (Philadelphia: Westminster Press, 1964), p. 84 (emphasis original).

6. Cullmann, Christ and Time, p. 84 (emphasis original).

VE-Day will coincide with his second coming when he completes his redemptive work and celebrates his final triumph over his enemies. George E. Ladd explains the present and future aspects of Christ's kingdom:

> Our central thesis is that the Kingdom of God is the redemptive reign of God dynamically active to establish His rule among human beings, and that this Kingdom which will appear as an apocalyptic act *at the end* of the age, has *already come* into human history in the person and mission of Jesus to overcome evil, to deliver people from its power, and to bring them into the blessings of God's reign. The Kingdom of God involves two great moments: fulfillment within history [already], and consummation at the end of history [not yet].[7]

Right now we are between these two great moments of fulfillment and consummation, living at the "hyphen," as I mentioned, between what is already but not yet. Therefore, we should avoid the error of an overblown *optimism* or an unjustified *pessimism* in favor of a biblically based *realism* as a golden mean between two extremes. We can be hopeful despite challenging conditions. Along the way, we need to prepare ourselves to endure the smiles and sunshine of the excessively happy-clappy or the grimaces and gloom of the unnecessarily cheerless and depressed. We should strive for a perspective that combines the positive and negative realities of our present circumstances in redemptive history.

The kingdom of God as both present and future can be compared profitably to spring break (my students like this one). Spring break is a taste of summer right in the middle of the semester. Yet the semester continues, with its many tasks and tests. The hope of the coming of a full-fledged summer encourages students to keep at their studies until school is out and they are finally free. Similarly, we are experiencing the substantial blessings of the "spring break" of God's kingdom in Christ right now in the midst of the semester of history, and we have a lot to look forward to.

What we have to look forward to is Christ's final victory, when things will change substantially. In this final estate, death will be abolished and there won't be any more crying or mourning or pain or tears. God will make all things new (Rev. 21:4-5). Until then, the "semester" continues, and

---

7. George E. Ladd, *A Theology of the New Testament*, rev. ed., ed. Donald A. Hagner (Grand Rapids: Eerdmans, 1974, 1993), pp. 89-90 (emphasis added).

during this time we seek to abound in the work and service of the Lord. We suffer and sacrifice with patience and perseverance as we are called to do. We strive to be more than conquerors through him who loved us (1 Cor. 15:58; Rom. 8:31-39).

## Service, Suffering, and Sacrifice

*"Only he who believes is obedient, and only he who is obedient believes."*

Dietrich Bonhoeffer, *The Cost of Discipleship*[8]

Salvation has its privileges and responsibilities. If we are called to Christ, we are also called to serve him in all aspects of life. We have good work to do in the church and the world. The biblical notion of calling is the key to understanding how we are to occupy ourselves until Christ returns.

Service   Despite rhetoric to the contrary, we can't do anything we want to do, or be anything we want to be, but we can do and be the things for which we have been gifted and to which we have been summoned by God. We all have strengths and weaknesses according to the way God has designed us. Our daily tasks fall into place as we discover what we are to do to fulfill God's specific purposes for our lives. He has given each of us a part to play, one for which we are ideally casted. We take our places on the stage of life, make our entrances and exits, and fulfill the roles God has given to us, however illustrious or lackluster, lucrative or unprofitable, they may be.[9] In short, we have callings to fulfill. How should we define the notion of "calling"? According to Os Guinness, it is the idea that *"God calls us to himself so decisively that everything we are, everything we do, and everything we have is invested with a special devotion, dynamism, and direction lived out as a response to his summons and service."*[10]

Puritan writer William Perkins has noted that everyone has a distinctive *vocatio* or calling from God, and that this calling constitutes the central

8. Dietrich Bonhoeffer, *The Cost of Discipleship*, rev. ed. (New York: Macmillan Publishing Company, Inc., 1963), p. 69.

9. My allusion here, of course, is to Shakespeare, *As You Like It* (Act II, Scene VII).

10. Os Guinness, *The Call: Finding and Fulfilling the Central Purpose of Your Life* (Nashville: Word Publishing, 1998), p. 29 (emphasis his).

purpose of our lives that we must find and fulfill. Simultaneously, we serve both God and human beings in the work God summons us to do. "Every person," Perkins states, "of every degree, state, sex, or condition without exception must have some personal and particular calling to walk in. The main end of our lives . . . is to serve God in the serving of men in the works of our callings."

We don't choose a calling (or a career), but are given a calling ordained for us by God. That sphere of service is not just for our success, but for the good of all. In Perkins's words, it is "a certain kind of life, ordained and imposed on men by God, *for the common good*." Though our daily tasks differ significantly in kind, they have the same value in the sight of God and are equally pleasing to him. "The action of a shepherd in keeping sheep . . . ," Perkins affirms, "is as good a work before God as is the action of a judge in giving a sentence, or of a magistrate in ruling, or a minister in preaching."[11] Butchers, bakers, candlestick makers, missionaries, preachers, and teachers are on the same level of vocational ground at the foot of the cross. All callings and virtuous work, whether religious or non-religious, are significant and give God glory, as Gerard Manley Hopkins explains:

> It is not only prayer that gives God glory but work. Smiting on an anvil, sawing a beam, whitewashing a wall, driving horses, sweeping, scouring, everything gives God some glory if being in His grace you do it as your duty. To go to communion worthily gives God great glory, but to take food in thankfulness and temperance gives Him glory too. To lift up the hands in prayer gives God glory, but a man with a dungfork in his hand, a woman with a slop pail, give Him glory too. God is so great that all things give Him glory if you mean that they should. So then, my brethren, live.[12]

Our callings are vocational, but they also go beyond work. They concern all our God-given roles and responsibilities. God leads us to marry a particular person or remain single, raise our natural, adopted, or stepchildren, honor and obey our parents or guardians, love our blood or blended brothers and sisters, care for our extended families, minister in

11. Quoted in Leland Ryken, *Work and Leisure in Christian Perspective* (Portland: Multnomah Press, 1987), pp. 95, 97.

12. Gerard Manley Hopkins, "On St. Ignatius's Spiritual Exercises: The Principle or Foundation," in *A Hopkins Reader*, revised and enlarged, ed. and intro. John Pick (Garden City, N.Y.: Image Books/Doubleday & Company, Inc., 1966), pp. 395-96.

our churches, feed the hungry, clothe the naked, heal the sick, teach the ignorant, protect the vulnerable, administer justice, save the lost, sanctify the saved, serve in the community, and so on. As Luther pointed out rather colorfully, God milks the cows through the dairymen called to that specific task. As we pray "Give us this day our daily bread," bakers have long been at their stoves working before dawn that our prayers might be answered. Through our callings, in other words, we share in God's providence and provision in meeting the needs of the world.[13]

In these various spheres of life in which we serve, we are agents of the healing power of the kingdom of God. "We need Christian people," says N. T. Wright, "to work as healers: as healing judges and prison staff, as healing teachers and administrators, as healing shop keepers and bankers, as healing musicians and artists, as healing writers and scientists, as healing diplomats and politicians. We need people who will hold on to Christ with one hand and reach out the other, with wit and skill and cheerfulness, with compassion and sorrow and tenderness, to the places where our world is in pain."[14]

In serving as healers, we must remember that we, too, are wounded and in need of healing. We are not just healers, but "wounded healers," as Henri Nouwen has reminded us.[15] We are all damaged goods, undergoing our own remedial process and in need of the gifts and services of others, just as others need our services and gifts. This mentality keeps pride at bay as we seek to mend others in a spirit of gentleness, looking to ourselves, lest we too be tempted (Gal. 6:1). In the lyrics to "The Servant Song,"

> Sister, let me be your servant,
> Let me be as Christ to you;
> Pray that I may have the grace to
> Let you be my servant too.[16]

**Suffering and Sacrifice**   We do not need to abandon our regular work in the world and retreat to a religious institution in order to suffer and sacri-

---

13. Lee Hardy, *The Fabric of This World: Inquiries into Calling, Career Choice, and the Design of Human Work* (Grand Rapids: Eerdmans, 1990), pp. 47-48.

14. N. T. Wright, *For All God's Worth: True Worship and the Calling of the Church* (Grand Rapids: Eerdmans, 1997), p. 101.

15. Henri J. M. Nouwen, *The Wounded Healer* (New York: Doubleday, 1972).

16. Richard Gillard, "The Servant Song," © 1977 Scripture in Song / Maranatha Music / ASCAP. All rights reserved. Used by permission.

fice for Christ's sake. Opportunities to bear our crosses will find us out right where we are. Cross-bearing is a natural part of Christian living and service in the regular workaday world. The fears, anxieties, hazards, frustrations, disappointments, failures, injustices, incompetencies, jealousies, superficialities, politics, stupidities, foolishness, depressions, illnesses, persecutions, or whatever else may bedevil us day to day afford many a splendid opportunity to follow Christ faithfully with patience and fortitude. Christian living is automatically cruciform in character. "For you have been called for this purpose," writes the apostle Peter, "since Christ also suffered for you, leaving you an example for you to follow in His steps" (1 Pet. 2:21).

There is a providential oversight in the inevitable struggles we will encounter in the course of our daily lives. John Calvin recognized that every God-ordained role would bring a multitude of difficulties with it. Their sovereign orchestration, however, should bring us comfort and generate perseverance, as the great Reformer has noted.

> Again, it will be no slight relief from cares, labors, troubles, and other burdens for a man to know that God is his guide in all these things. The magistrate will discharge his functions more willingly; the head of the household will confine himself to his duty; each man will bear and swallow the discomforts, vexations, weariness, and anxieties in his way of life, when he has been persuaded that the burden was laid upon him by God. From this will arise also a singular consolation: that no task will be so sordid and base, provided you obey your calling in it, that it will not shine and be reckoned very precious in God's sight.[17]

If we are convinced of God's oversight of our callings, in difficult circumstances we will cast our anxieties upon him, because he cares for us (1 Pet. 5:7). John Milton's situation is a case in point. In the closing lines of his sonnet "When I Consider How My Light Is Spent," he wondered, in some agitation, if God still expected him to be as productive in his blindness as he was when he could see. In answering his own question, the poet asserts that we also serve God when we bear our burdens well and simply wait on him.

---

17. John Calvin, *The Institutes of the Christian Religion*, ed. John T. McNeill, trans. and index Ford Lewis Battles, The Library of Christian Classics, gen. eds. John Baillie, John T. McNeill, Henry P. Van Dusen, vol. 20 (Philadelphia: The Westminster Press, 1960), p. 725 (§3.10.6).

"Doth God exact day-labor, light denied?"
I fondly ask. But Patience, to prevent
That murmur, soon replies: "God doth not need
    Either man's work or his own gifts; who best
    Bear his mild yoke, they serve him best. His state
Is kingly: thousands at his bidding speed,
    And post o'er land and ocean without rest;
    They also serve who only stand and wait."[18]

To endure patiently the limitations and losses in this life, whatever
they may be, is not easy, especially when others seem to move ahead in
their pursuits unencumbered. What should be our focus when our time of
testing comes? "Our task," says N. T. Wright, "is to be faithful to the calling
of the cross: to live in God's new world as the agents of his love, and to
pray that the cross we carry today will become part of the healing and reconciliation of the world."[19]

While carrying our crosses and bearing our burdens in the contexts
of our callings in his kingdom, our confidence in God's purposes for our
lives will sustain us in hope and prevent us from adopting the "whatever"
of nihilistic resignation. The last two lines of the final stanza of the Irish
hymn "Be Thou My Vision" express this alternative perspective:[20]

Heart of my own heart, *whatever befall,*
Still be my vision, O ruler of all.[21]

Ken Gire in his book *Life as We Would Want It . . . Life as We Are Given It*
has compared our stressful times of testing to the interesting geological
history of the great state of Colorado.[22] The flat terrain of the eastern part

18. John Milton, "When I Consider How My Light Is Spent," in *The Norton Anthology of
English Literature*, gen. ed. M. H. Abrams, vol. 1 (New York: W. W. Norton & Company, 1968),
p. 1015 (lines 7-14).

19. Wright, *For All God's Worth*, p. 59.

20. A point taken from a lecture by Dr. Steven Garber, Dallas Baptist University, Febru-
ary 24, 2007.

21. "Be Thou My Vision," trans. Mary Byrne, versified Eleanor Hull, harmonized David
Evans, in *Rejoice in the Lord: A Hymn Companion to the Scriptures*, ed. Erik Routley (Grand
Rapids: Eerdmans 1985), p. 67 (emphasis added).

22. Ken Gire, *Life as We Would Want It . . . Life as We Are Given It: The Beauty God Brings from
Life's Upheavals* (Nashville: W Publishing Group/Thomas Nelson, 2007).

of the state, which has seen little seismic activity and rarely draws a tourist, is comparable to our desire for an easy, placid life as we wish it would be. However, the results of such a comfortable existence, as in the land, are noticeably bland and ordinary.

On the other hand, the breathtaking beauty of the Rockies in the western part of the state is the result of stupendous tectonic shifts, violent geological upheavals, cataclysmic tremors, and massive earthquakes. As a result, people flock from all over the world to witness their grandeur and enjoy a Rocky Mountain high. Likewise, the oftentimes surprising shifts, upheavals, tremors, and earthquakes in our lives are frequently means by which God molds us into the people he wants us to be through the work of the Holy Spirit. God's goal, Gire asserts, is to make everything beautiful in its time. This may not be life as we want, but it is life as we get it. In faith, we are obstinate in our conviction that God is working all things together for good to conform us to the beauty of his Son (Rom. 8:28-29).

Helpful as Gire's analogy is — it's a form of what is called a "soul-making theodicy" — the things we go through still mystify us and leave us with many unanswered questions. Why me? Why now? Why this? O Lord, how long? In the midst of the mysteries, we trust in the providence of God, even if his purposes are hidden from us, learning how to worship, obey, and give thanks *in* all things. As Thomas Traherne has said, a Christian is an "oak flourishing in winter."[23]

## The Education of the Heart

*"I pray that the eyes of your heart may be enlightened."*

Ephesians 1:18

A life of service, suffering, and sacrifice is challenging. We need to be prepared for tests and temptations that will come our way. We also need to advance in faith, hope, and love even while we are tested and tempted. We must do everything we can to stand firm (Eph. 6:13) and to press on toward the goal of the upward call of God in Christ Jesus (Phil 3:14). Other-

---

23. Quoted in Richard H. Schmidt, *Glorious Companions: Five Centuries of Anglican Spirituality* (Grand Rapids: Eerdmans, 2002), p. 86.

wise, we may capitulate or stagnate, and forfeit what we have gained. To keep us on the road of reordered loves and lives, we must enroll as lifelong learners in the school of Christ to be trained in the spiritual disciplines for the education of our hearts.

What is a spiritual discipline? Simply put, it is an activity we choose to practice on a regular basis to generate, maintain, and increase godly dispositions of mind and heart and to foster holy conduct according to the teachings and example of Jesus Christ. The spiritual disciplines are the means to the end of the virtuous Christian life. If such a life is our goal, we will have to discipline ourselves for the purpose of godliness (1 Tim. 4:7b).

The practice of the disciplines is essential, *since we learn by doing and become what we do.* Any athlete will tell you that it's practice, practice, practice, and a little more practice that makes for progress in one's sport. The things we do over and over again shape our minds and train our muscles, sharpen our skills and perfect our behaviors, especially if we submit our development as apprentices to a mentor whom we can watch and follow and from whom we can receive constructive feedback. Aristotle called the disciplinary process "habituation" because he believed that a deliberate, repetitive process would form the moral and intellectual virtues within us. Even if we don't enjoy the experience initially, we can learn to love it if we keep at it over time. Our rites, routines, and rituals shape us as persons, even if we are unconscious of how or when this happens. So it is with the spiritual disciplines.

The name "spiritual disciplines," however, is somewhat misleading. It suggests they pertain exclusively to the spiritual or non-physical side of life. But what about our bodies? Aren't our souls connected to them? Aren't our bodies also in need of discipline? If we are whole persons of body and soul — ensouled bodies or embodied souls — then the spiritual disciplines are physical disciplines too, and physical disciplines are spiritual disciplines as well. Think of fasting or temperance or hospitality or Sabbath-keeping, for example. We must "do justice," says Dallas Willard, "to the nature of human personality, as embodied, incarnate."[24] Perhaps then we should call them the "disciplines" or the "Christian disciplines," since they pertain to the whole person. Regardless of the name, they are

24. Willard, *The Spirit of the Disciplines: Understanding How God Changes Lives* (San Francisco: HarperSanFrancisco, 1988, 1991), p. 18.

the primary curriculum in the school of Christ, and God uses them to conform us to the image of his Son as his student-disciples.

## Disciplines for the Purpose of Godliness

*"It is a paradox of human life that in worship, as in human love, it is in the routine and the everyday that we find the possibilities for the greatest transformation."*

Kathleen Norris, *The Quotidian Mysteries*[25]

We need not reinvent the wheel in terms of the Christian disciplines. They have been around for several thousand years, having been practiced by the Old Testament saints and sages, by believers in the New Testament church, by the earlier Christian mothers and fathers, and most importantly, by ordinary, devoted disciples of Jesus throughout the ages.

Many writers have brought these significant rituals of formation to our attention recently, and I recommend their fine books and resources.[26] I'd like to review what a couple of leading authorities have had to say on this topic, and then offer a few comments about some habits and practices that have served me well in my own Christian journey for nearly forty years.

Richard Foster appears to be the grandfather of the disciplines movement in recent times. His book, *Celebration of Discipline: The Path to Spiritual Growth* was originally published in 1978, and it begins with these sobering sentences: "Superficiality is the curse of our age. The doctrine of instant satisfaction is a primary spiritual problem. The desperate need today is

25. Kathleen Norris, *The Quotidian Mysteries: Laundry, Liturgy and "Women's Work,"* 1998 Madeleva Lecture in Spirituality (New York: Paulist Press, 1998), p. 82.

26. See Adele Ahlberg Calhoun, *Spiritual Disciplines Handbook: Practices That Transform Us* (Downers Grove: InterVarsity Press, 2005) for a comprehensive summary of the disciplines and bibliography of recent works on this topic. See also the resources available at the Valparaiso Project on the Education and Formation of People in Faith. The mission of this group is "to develop resources that speak to the spiritual hunger of our contemporaries with the substantive wisdom of the Christian faith, especially as this wisdom takes shape in Christian practices." Information is available at http://www.practicingourfaith.org/index.cfm (accessed July 26, 2007).

not for a great number of intelligent people, or gifted people, but for deep people."[27]

To move us from the baby pool to the deep end of the Christian life, he explains and illustrates twelve classic disciplines under three major categories. First, he describes the "Inward Disciplines" of meditation, prayer, fasting, and study (pp. 13-76). Second, he takes a look at the "Outward Disciplines" of simplicity, solitude, submission, and service (pp. 77-140). Third, he reflects on the "Corporate Disciplines" of confession, worship, guidance, and celebration (pp. 141-201). Here are Foster's succinct definitions of each discipline.

- Meditation: The ability to hear God's voice and obey His word.
- Prayer: The interactive conversation with God about what we are doing together.
- Fasting: The voluntary denial of an otherwise normal function [of eating] for the sake of intense spiritual activity.
- Study: The process whereby the mind takes on an order conforming to the order of whatever we concentrate upon.
- Simplicity: An inward reality that results in an outward lifestyle.
- Solitude: The creation of an open, empty space in which we can be found by God and by which we are freed from competing loyalties.
- Submission: The discipline which frees us to let go of the everlasting burden of always needing to get our own way.
- Service: Experiencing the many little deaths of going beyond ourselves which produces in us the virtue of humility.

27. Richard J. Foster, *Celebration of Discipline: The Path to Spiritual Growth*, 25th Anniversary edition (New York: HarperCollins, 2002). Subsequent page numbers in parentheses are found in this volume. See also Richard J. Foster's *Study Guide for Celebration of Discipline* (New York: HarperCollins, 1983). Though himself a Quaker, Foster recognizes the remarkable contributions that a diversity of Christian traditions make to our understanding and practice of the Christian faith. In his later work *Streams of Living Water: Celebrating the Great Traditions of the Christian Faith* (New York: HarperCollins, 2001), Foster introduces us to the ways six major Christian communities have fulfilled the divine paradigm of the imitation of God, namely through (1) the Contemplative Tradition of the prayer-filled life, (2) the Holiness Tradition of the virtuous life, (3) the Charismatic Tradition of the Spirit-empowered life, (4) the Social Justice Tradition of the compassionate life, (5) the Evangelical Tradition of the Word-centered life, and (6) the Incarnational Tradition of the sacramental life. Each of these traditions offers an indispensable contribution of faith and practice to the cultivation of an educated heart that leads to Christ-like loves and Christ-like lives.

- Confession: Entering the grace and mercy of God in such a way that we experience healing of the sins and sorrows of the past.
- Worship: Entering into the supra-natural experience of the *Shekanyah*, or glory of God.
- Guidance: Knowing an interactive friendship with God in daily life.
- Celebration: A life of "walking and leaping and praising" God (Acts 3:8).[28]

Foster continues his introductory comment about the reigning super-ficiality of our age: "The classical Disciplines of the spiritual life call us to move beyond surface living into the depths" (p. 1). The goal of their prac-tice, he says, is "the total transformation of the person" (p. 62). In the terms of this book, this must include a transformation of the loves and disposi-tions of the heart, from which all things flow.

Dallas Willard has followed in Foster's wake in a work titled *The Spirit of the Disciplines: Understanding How God Changes Lives*.[29] His main point in this book is that "we can become like Christ by doing one thing — by fol-lowing him in the overall style of life he chose for himself. . . . We can, through faith and grace, become like Christ by practicing the types of ac-tivities he engaged in, by arranging our whole lives around the activities he himself practiced in order to remain constantly at home in the fellow-ship of his Father" (p. ix).

For Willard, there are two large categories of fifteen total disciplines that make this possible. The spiritual disciplines, he says, generate a "transforma-tive friendship" with Jesus Christ, that is, "the opportunity of a vivid com-panionship with him, in which [we] . . . will learn to be like him and live as he lived" (p. xi). First, then, since we are "to abstain from fleshly lusts which wage war against the soul" (1 Pet. 2:11), Willard believes that the "Disciplines of Ab-stinence," comprised of solitude, silence, fasting, frugality, chastity, secrecy,

---

28. Foster's definitions were provided in an email correspondence with Lynda L. Graybeal, Foster's personal assistant (July 24, 2007), and are based on the successive chap-ters in his book *Celebration of Discipline*.

29. Willard, *The Spirit of the Disciplines*. Subsequent page numbers in parentheses are found in this volume. See other related books by Willard, including *The Divine Conspiracy: Re-discovering Our Hidden Life in God*, foreword Richard J. Foster (New York: HarperCollins, 1998); *Renovation of the Heart: Putting on the Character of Christ* (Colorado Springs: NavPress Publishing Group, 2002); and *The Great Omission: Reclaiming Jesus' Essential Teachings on Disci-pleship* (New York: HarperCollins, 2006).

and sacrifice, will help us to "exhale" typical sins of commission that undermine Christ-like character and living (pp. 159-75). On the other hand, such self-restraint creates space in our lives for things that need to be there, "inhaling" as it were, the "Disciplines of Engagement," such as study, worship, celebration, service, prayer fellowship, confession, and submission, which otherwise might be missing in our lives — that is, the proverbial sins of omission (pp. 175-90). Whether of abstinence or engagement, "The spirit of the disciplines . . . is this love of Jesus, with its steadfast longing and resolute will to be like him" (p. 251). To be sure, if these disciplines make us like him, then our loves and our lives will be significantly reordered, resulting in our growing discipleship for the glory of God and the good of all.

In addition to thinking of the disciplines as inward, outward, or corporate practices as Foster does, or as disciplines of abstinence or engagement as does Willard, it is also possible to think of them in a third way as either *mandated or prudential*.[30] Practices that are *mandated* in the Bible must be part of every Christian's life. These include worship, prayer, fasting, attention to God's word, communion, fellowship, forgiveness, thanksgiving, confession of sin, giving, hospitality, resting, and so on. At the same time, there are also *prudential* disciplines that are not commanded in Scripture, but we would probably be wise to pursue them — keeping a journal, for example, or spiritual jogging or walking, going on a retreat, fasting from technology, participating in small groups, having a quiet time, and other, similar pursuits.

Apart from what is required for worship in the church, the Bible does not demand that we pursue the disciplines in any particular systematic or organized way. While all things should be done decently and in order, the manner in which we practice the disciplines can be somewhat unique to our personalities and the demands of our daily lives.

Despite the biblical freedom to practice the disciplines in personalized ways, some have advocated rather unbending approaches to their implementation. In the past, a rigorous formula for their application has characterized some monastic and ascetic traditions. In the present, some communities seem to take a quasi-scientific approach to the disciplines as a guaranteed technology of the spiritual life. Pharisaical attitudes toward

---

30. This and the next several paragraphs are taken from *The Complete Book of Everyday Christianity*, ed. Robert Banks and R. Paul Stevens (Downers Grove, Ill.: InterVarsity Press, 1977), s.v. "Spiritual Disciplines."

the disciplines, however, could spell trouble — they could lead to legalism or idolatry. Shouldn't we exercise the disciplines as much as possible out of love and joy, rather than duty or fear? Shouldn't we worship the God of the disciplines rather than making gods out of the disciplines? In either case, we might confuse doing the disciplines with genuine spirituality and intimacy with God, and any consistency we may have in their practice in this context could become a source of pride.

We must also remember that the exercise of the Christian disciplines does not have to take place in a special religious realm separated from regular life. Rather, these good habits of mind, heart, and body must be forged on the anvil of lived experience and in the laboratory of life. True spirituality is worked out in the midst of the everyday and for its sake. Biblical personalities were shaped as the people of God in the realms of work, marriage, homemaking, family life, friendship, travel, and politics; in the responsibilities of showing hospitality, working, parenting, and leading; in the conditions of grief, celebration, success, failure, frustration, suffering, and exile; in the experiences of barrenness, childbearing, health, disease, wealth, disability, and slavery.

Likewise, our everyday circumstances provide us with plenty of opportunities to put the disciplines into practice and transform us at the root of our beings and in the fruit of our lives. Most importantly, they usher us into the presence of God. "And because we are human," Kathleen Norris writes, "it is in the realm of the daily and the mundane that we must find our way to God."[31] Oftentimes it's the little things that really count, as John Calvin recognized:

> The devil has so blinded men that he has persuaded them to believe that in little things they do not have to worry whether God is honored or served: and this he accomplished on the pretext that such things are of the world. When a man works in his labor to earn his living, when a woman does her housework, and when a servant does his duty, one thinks that God does not pay attention to such things, and one says that they are secular affairs. Yes, it is true that such work is proper to this present and fleeting life; however, that does not mean that we must separate it from the service of God.[32]

31. Norris, *The Quotidian Mysteries*, p. 78.
32. Quoted in Hardy, *The Fabric of This World*, p. 59n.32.

## The Disciplines and Me

*"O thou lord of life, send my roots rain."*

Gerard Manley Hopkins, "Thou Art Indeed Just"[33]

I became a Christian at the age of seventeen by watching a televised Billy Graham crusade in August 1970 (now you know how old I am!). I didn't realize it at the time, but that very night — about the twentieth of the month — I was enrolled in the school of Christ to be trained as one of his disciples for the education of my heart. In a biblical sense, I believe the word "heart" refers to me as a whole person — mind, emotions, will, and body.[34] Within a few short weeks of my conversion, I got involved with my Young Life club during my senior year of high school. I grew so much in my faith over the next year that I changed my college plans to work as a student volunteer with this organization that seeks to introduce kids to Jesus Christ and help them grow in their faith.[35] That association lasted for well over six years. Retrospectively, I am convinced that God was at work in our leadership group there in my hometown of Fort Worth, Texas, in ways few of us recognized at the time. In this dynamic community of faith, I learned about and began to pursue some foundational Christian disciplines that have stuck with me to this day. By the grace of God, I have experienced some successes, and because of my own weaknesses, I have known my share of failures when it comes to the practice of the disciplines. To the extent that I have kept at them, even if unevenly, they have shaped the contours of my mind, reordered my basic loves and desires, and kept me on the narrow path for the most part over the years. Let me tell you just a bit about how several practices and habits have been great graces in my life, with the hope that something from my story might be profitable for you.

**The Bible and Books**     From early on, I was taught and have believed that the Bible is the infallible Word of God and the foundation and final authority for Christian faith and practice. Because living authentically as a

---

33. Gerard Manley Hopkins, "Thou Art Indeed Just," in *A Hopkins Reader*, p. 82.

34. Karl Barth, for example, says "the heart is not merely *a* but *the* reality of man, both wholly of soul and wholly of body." See his *Church Dogmatics*, III/2, trans. Harold Knight, J. K. S. Reid, and R. H. Fuller (Edinburgh: T&T Clark, 1960), p. 436 (emphasis original).

35. For more information on this outstanding organization to which I owe so much, see http://www.younglife.org/.

Christian is impossible apart from a steady exposure to and intake of truth, I have prayed over the years that God would give me a hunger and thirst to know the truth of the Scriptures as a means to knowing God in all of his works.

In Ezra 7:10, I discovered a three-part pattern that shaped my own approach to the Bible: "For Ezra had set his heart *to study* the law of the LORD and *to practice* it, and *to teach* His statutes and ordinances in Israel." As a result, I have asked God for desire, diligence, and discipline to read and study the Bible regularly, to apply it to my life, and to teach the Scriptures to others (there's nothing like a teaching assignment to get your nose in the Word).

I have read and studied the Bible over the years in both academic and devotional ways. In our Young Life group, we were taught an inductive Bible study method that consisted of observation, interpretation, application, and correlation (that is, how a passage fits in with the rest of Scripture). With a Bible dictionary, a concordance, and a copy of the Scriptures in hand (for me, it's always been the New American Standard), this training inspired me as a college student to do many independent Bible studies and even to write some amateur commentaries of considerable length on a variety of Old and New Testament books (the Song of Solomon was particularly interesting). Through these efforts I gained considerable insight into the Scriptures, and much of what I learned remains with me to this day.

Currently, my Bible reading is more devotionally oriented and akin to what is known as *lectio divina*. I "crawl" through a book these days, reading shorter portions of Scripture more intensively and meditating on specific words, images, phrases, and passages. I read, reread, and then reflect upon what I read, listening for the voice of God as I pray through his Word.

There have been lots of times when I have felt little if any motivation or desire to spend time in Scripture. The initial impulse simply wasn't there. When I have chosen to do it anyway, the desire has often followed the performance of the duty, and I have found myself captivated by what I was reading or studying. I was glad I made the decision to delve into the Word even if I didn't feel like it at the time. Once I was there, I rejoiced in God's Word as one who found great spoil (Ps. 119:162).

Unsurprisingly, I have discovered that I cannot live by bread alone. I need the words that proceed from the mouth of God to nourish and sustain me in life and to shape my thoughts, order my loves, and direct my actions in accordance with what Scripture teaches. I am a philologist in that I love words and language. I am a "verbivore" in that I devour words and feed upon them that I may live. Relishing Scripture and feeding upon it is an indispensable part of a disciplined Christian life. Where would I be without Scripture? What would I be without God's Word in my heart?

Reading books about the Book, and many other kinds of books as well, has also been an indispensable part of my regimen as a believer. As a bibliophile or lover of books, I am rarely without a book wherever I go (this always helps when people ask: "What are you reading these days?"). I can also trace this literary habit back to my early Christian training in Young Life. When I graduated from high school my club leader, Ted Kitchens, took me to a Christian bookstore, where I spent about seventy dollars on about twenty books that I read over the course of that summer (books were a lot cheaper back then). Our mentors constantly encouraged us to read one C. S. Lewis book or another, or the latest work by Francis Schaeffer. So I did, and as I did, my love for reading grew, and more and more authors and titles were recommended and channeled my way. Not only did I read these books, but I also talked about them with my friends who were reading the same works along with me. We learned from one another.

I read new books. I read old books. (C. S. Lewis recommends that for every three new books we read, we read at least one old one).[36] I read classics. I read clunkers. I read books by Christians. I read books by non-Christians. I read books on biblical studies, theology, and the spiritual life. I read books on the sciences, the humanities, the arts, and more. In short, I have sought and still seek to be a person of the Book and of books, that I might know God and more and more about his world in the context of faith.

Klaus Bockmuehl has argued that books are "God's tools in the history of salvation," and that *"Literature is the second leg of Christian proclamation."*[37] He quotes James Clarke, who offers these words in praise of books:

> Let us thank God for books. When I consider what some books have done for the world, and what they are doing, how they keep up our

---

36. C. S. Lewis, "On the Reading of Old Books," in *God in the Dock: Essays on Theology and Ethics,* ed. Walter Hooper (Grand Rapids: Eerdmans, 1970).

37. Klaus Bockmuehl, *Books: God's Tools in the History of Salvation* (Vancouver, B.C.: Regent College and Helmers & Howard, 1986), p. 26.

hope, awaken new courage and faith, soothe pain, give an ideal life to those whose homes are hard and cold, bind together distant ages and foreign lands, create new worlds of beauty, bring down truths from heaven — I give eternal blessings for this gift, and pray that we may use it aright, and abuse it not.[38]

The expression of praise about books and reading reminds me of one of my favorite lines from Emily Dickinson:

There is no Frigate like a Book
To take us lands away[39]

In any case, never before have more books been available to the people of God than right now. If we fail to take advantage of these great gifts because we are so busy amusing ourselves to death, then one day we will have to explain to God why we failed to be disciplined readers of Scripture and also the remarkable literary resources he has provided for us.

Therefore, let's read books and give them away to others. "If he shall not lose his reward who gives a cup of cold water to this thirsty neighbor," said Thomas à Kempis, "what will not be the reward of those who by putting good books into the hands of those neighbours, open to them the fountain of eternal life?"[40] I think it is interesting that at the very end of his life, right before he was executed, Paul asked Timothy to bring two things to him in Rome. The first was his coat. The second was books (2 Tim. 4:13). Apparently, this great apostle was still reading right up to the end.

**Church and Community**  The primary purpose of the church is the worship of God. It is the place where God's gospel is preached, God's Word is taught, and the sacraments are administered. It is the meeting place for the fellowship of believers and the communion of the saints. It is the location from which Christians are launched into the world to serve and represent God and the gospel through a diversity of callings. The church is at once a theological, liturgical, educational, social, and missional institution. On the basis of the Nicene Creed, Christians for cen-

---

38. Quoted in Bockmuehl, *Books: God's Tools in the History of Salvation*, p. 34.

39. Emily Dickinson, "There is no Frigate Like a Book," in *The Complete Poems of Emily Dickinson*, ed. Thomas H. Johnson (Boston: Little, Brown and Company, 1960), p. 553.

40. Quoted in Bockmuehl, *Books: God's Tools in the History of Salvation*, p. 34.

turies have believed in the one, holy, catholic, and apostolic church as its four distinctive notes or marks. Its unity, its purity, its universality, and its authority distinguish the church as the body of Christ from all other institutions on the face of the earth. In biblical terms, the church devotes itself "to the apostles' teaching and to fellowship, to the breaking of bread and to prayer" (Acts 2:42). It takes a church to grow a Christian.

I have attended services and ministered in churches in just about every denomination. I have held membership in Methodist, Bible, and Baptist churches. I have also been involved in other denominations, several parachurch organizations, various campus ministries, and in academic and student communities in the world of Christian higher education. My experiences in these groups have been rich and rewarding, but not romantic, profitable and yet sometimes painful. Such is the nature of participating in any institution comprised of people and their politics — even if it is a church.

My involvement in the church on both the giving and receiving ends has been essential to my spiritual formation as a Christian. In church I was baptized as a public expression of my faith and commitment to the Lordship of Christ. In church I have learned God's Word. In church I have been nourished in the sacrament of communion by receiving the body and blood of Christ. In church I have been equipped for the work of service to the building up of the body of Christ. In church I have been encouraged to faithfulness in my various callings in life. In church I have learned to give thanks, sing, and pray. In church I have enjoyed fellowship and made friends with other believers. In church I have been challenged to bear witness to the gospel in word and deed before a watching world.

Church attendance and ministry is not an option, but a godly habit. Serving in the church according to giftedness is mandatory. Preserving the unity of the Spirit in the bond of peace is a virtue that requires wisdom, godliness, and discipline. If we miss, we are amiss. If we miss, we will miss. If we miss, we will be missed.[41] How can we fulfill our vocation as believers and be shaped as disciples of Christ in mind, heart, and body without the gracious presence and effective ministry of the church in our lives? As the lyrics to one lovely song put it,

41. I owe thought to Dr. George Mason, pastor of Wilshire Baptist Church, Dallas, Texas.

How beautiful,
How beautiful,
How beautiful is the body of Christ.[42]

**Prayer**   Prayer is talking with God — silently and aloud. Jesus, of course, is the model for prayer. As devotional writer Andrew Murray has said, "Christ's life and work, his suffering and death — it was all prayer, all dependence upon God, trust in God, receiving from God, surrender to God. Your redemption, O believer, is a redemption worked out by prayer and intercession. *Your Christ is a praying Christ.*" Christ "did not say prayers some of the time. He *was* prayer all of the time."[43] Like the disciples, we need to ask the Lord to "teach us to pray" (Luke 11:1). In responding to my prayer about prayer, the Lord has guided me to utilize two basic models.

The first is the A.C.T.S. pattern of prayer as an all-inclusive guide consisting of **A**doration, **C**onfession, **T**hanksgiving, and **S**upplication. It prompts me to begin my prayers with an expression of worship to God for his mighty deeds and excellent greatness. I praise him for all the things he has done and for the kind of God that he is. I also express my complete love and devotion to him as the Creator-Redeemer God of my life.

Having been ushered into his presence, I feel the weight of my transgressions bearing down upon me, and I am compelled to confess my sins and seek God's forgiveness. I learned 1 John 1:9 early in my Christian experience, and it contains the promise of pardon upon which I have regularly relied: "If we confess our sins," John writes, "He is faithful and righteous to forgive us our sins and to cleanse us from all unrighteousness."

Knowing that God has been merciful to me, a sinner, and sensing that the obstacles between us have been removed, I move forward to convey my gratitude for his comprehensive blessings in my life and in the lives of others. I have also sought to be grateful in the midst of difficulty, learning to rejoice always, to pray without ceasing, and in everything to give thanks, since giving thanks is God's will for us in Christ Jesus (1 Thess. 5:16-18).

42. Twila Paris, "How Beautiful," © 1990 Ariose Music / Mountain Spring Music (both admin. by EMI Music Publishing c/o Music Services). All rights reserved. Used by permission.

43. Both quotes are in Margaret Magdalen, *Jesus: Man of Prayer — Expanding Your Horizons in Prayer,* foreword Michael Green (Guildford, Surrey, England: Eagle of Inter Publishing Service, 1987), p. 17. The language in the Murray quote has been updated from the original.

Finally, I offer prayers of supplication on behalf of others and the various circumstances in their lives. If we ask anything according to God's will, God hears us. If we pray in Christ's name and in faith, he will answer. We are assured that the effective prayer of a righteous Christian can accomplish much. Therefore, I ask, seek, and knock (1 John 5:14-15; Matt. 21:22; John 14:13-14; James 5:16; Matt 7:7). Prayers of supplication also remind me that I might be the means by which God answers the very prayers I am praying. I then conclude this fourfold way of praying with the prayer that our Lord taught us to pray, saying:

Our Father which art in heaven,
Hallowed be thy name.
Thy kingdom come,
Thy will be done in earth, as it is in heaven.
Give us this day our daily bread.
And forgive us our debts, as we forgive our debtors.
And lead us not into temptation, but deliver us from evil:
For thine is the Kingdom, and the power, and the glory, forever.
Amen. (Matthew 6:9-13, KJV)

Second, God has led me to develop a specific way to pray for myself. This may sound very selfish, at least at first. The fact of the matter is, however, we aren't much good for others if we are not in very good shape ourselves. One of my favorite sayings goes like this: "We can't impart to others what we don't possess." So I need to pray for myself for my own sake and also for the sake of others. My prayers for myself consist of the following components.

**Purpose, Profession, Partner**   I realized early on in my Christian life that the three most important decisions I would ever make would concern (1) my *purpose,* or what I would live my life for, (2) my *profession,* or what I would spend my life doing, and (3) my *partner,* or who I would spend my life with. I call these prayers the "Three P's" — prayers for my purpose, profession, and partner. (Some have opted for the "Three M's" of master, mission, and mate.)

Regarding prayer for my "purpose," I have prayed that God would reveal to me life's greatest good and source of the happy life, and God has shown me that this is to be found in loving union and communion with God. Consequently, I have asked him daily to draw me into a closer relationship with himself. I have asked him to conform me to the image of his Son Jesus Christ by any road, no matter what the cost. My request has been that God would restore me as his image and likeness, that I might be truly and fully human under God, for his glory and my good, that I might be of service to others and an instrument of God's kingdom in the world.

In praying for my "profession," I have asked that God would lead me into the vocational calling of his choice. It wasn't something I wanted to choose, but rather to discover. Before I knew what it was, I asked God to help me discover my gifts, to confirm my suspicions of a calling through successful experiences and the affirmations of those I served. There were lots of trials and lots of errors along the way. I also asked God to lead and guide me to opportunities, to open and close doors, to generate and fulfill my desires. I placed my calling in his hands.

Having discovered that I was designed by God to help believers develop a comprehensive, holistic Christian worldview based on the Bible and drawing on other resources available in the Christian, Western, and global intellectual and spiritual traditions, I was led to fulfill this mission in life as a Christian professor and scholar in a university setting. For many years, I have asked God by his grace and strength to enable me to be faithful and fruitful in this calling as a teacher, mentor, writer, and speaker. I also committed myself before God to excellence and professionalism in my work, to do my very best, for God's glory and the benefit of others.

When I have prayed for my "partner," I did my best to place this area of my life in God's hands. First of all, I asked God whether I was to marry at all — and that wasn't the easiest prayer to pray. Hoping that I was to marry, I used words like "whoever, whenever, and however" — whoever she was, whenever it was supposed to be, and however it was supposed to happen. Having met and married a particular woman at a particular time and in a particular way — my wife Deemie Naugle — I have asked him to help me love her as Christ loved the church and as I love my own body. It's a prayer with dividends, for as Paul points out, he who loves his own wife loves himself, because the husband and wife become one in the covenant of marriage (Eph. 5:28-31). I know I have a long way to go in this area.

In any case, I am grateful that early on in my Christian experience I realized that the biggest decisions I would ever make would concern the three "P's" — purpose, profession, and partner. On the basis of my own experience, I recommend that you wholeheartedly offer these areas of your life to God and pray like crazy for his guidance. In answering these prayers, God fulfills the desires of our hearts, and we find ourselves at the center of his plan for our lives.

**The Devil, Flesh, and World**   By committing my purpose, profession, and partner to God, I knew I would encounter opposition from various forces that would attempt to thwart the fulfillment of these commitments in my life. In general, I knew that I was engaged in spiritual warfare, and that my enemies would try to distract, devour, and destroy me — and that's not overstated. They wish to render us null, void, and valueless in the kingdom of God. I knew I needed protection from and victory over these adversaries, that God might fulfill his goals for my life.

What are these foes that seek to work us woe? They are the devil, the flesh, and the world — D. F. W. Since I live in the **D**allas–**F**ort **W**orth area, these opponents have been easy for me to remember. The devil prowls about like a roaring and hungry lion seeking to eat me alive. The flesh, as the principle of sin within, wars against the Holy Spirit to keep me from doing the things that I should. The fallen world seeks to conform me to its basic assumptions and corrupted ways of life (1 Pet. 5:8; Gal. 5:17; Rom. 12:2). In combination, the devil works through the temptations of the world to stimulate my flesh, that I might succumb to sin, betray my commitment to Christ, be a bona fide hypocrite, and dishonor the gospel in the world. I know that in my weakness, I have given in to the persuasions of my enemies on many occasions.

Day by day, therefore, I claim the victory of the kingdom of God over these enemies by the power of the Holy Spirit working in my life. In Christ, the devil has been judged and disarmed (Col. 2:15). In Christ, the flesh with its disordered passions and desires has been put to death (Gal. 5:24). In Christ, I have been crucified to the fallen world, and the fallen world has been crucified to me (Gal. 6:14).

In response to my prayers for protection over these defeated foes, God in his grace has freed me to grow in faith, hope, and love, to experience his blessings in my life, and to serve him in my callings with a measure of effectiveness and joy. Thus along with the apostle Paul I say, "But thanks be to God, who always leads us in triumph in Christ, and manifests through us the sweet aroma of the knowledge of Him in every place" (2 Cor. 2:14).

**Virtue and Vice**   In addition to praying to God to experience his best in the areas of my purpose, profession, and partner, and in asking him for victory over my adversaries, I have also appealed to God to help me cultivate virtue and to shun vice. I try to evaluate where I stand morally in terms of the seven deadly sins and the seven cardinal virtues in the context of my prayers for myself. These two lists serve as useful grids to help me detect strengths and weaknesses in my character and conduct. The seven deadly sins are seven disordered loves, so I ask God to show me where I am out of bounds and pray that he would correct me. The seven cardinal virtues are seven reordered loves, so I ask God to fortify these Spirit-produced dispositions, that I might grow and excel in these qualities still more. Just when I think I am doing well in one area, another area demands my attention. These vices and virtues help me to know exactly where I stand in terms of what I really love and how I am really doing. I am thankful for the analysis, correction, and guidance they provide.

**Thinker, Lover, Doer**   I don't know where I heard it first or who said it originally, but one of my favorite quotes goes like this:
     There are three marks of a great person:

• One who is a great thinker;
• One who is a great lover;
• One who is a great doer.

I like this quote because it highlights the faculties of the whole person — the intellect or mind in thinking, the feelings or emotions in loving, and the will or volition in doing. Lots of people tend to promote one of these capacities at the expense of the others. Romantics as the great lovers among us say the emotions or feelings of the heart are most important, and they diminish the importance of the mind and the will. Pragmatists as the great doers assert that the activities and achievements of the will are the most important, and they lessen the value of the mind and heart. Intellectuals as the great thinkers argue that the theories and ideas in our minds are most important, and they reduce the significance of the heart and the will.

So which of these faculties is, in fact, the most important? Is it the mind? Is it the heart? Is it the will? Is thinking, or loving, or doing supreme? As the quote suggests (and this is why I like it), all are equally important for human greatness. There are three marks — not one, not two, but three marks of a great person, and all three of these faculties must be integrated into a coherent personality.

My longing and desire has been to be a better thinker, lover, and doer: to be more knowledgeable of God, his word, and his world, to grow in my love for God and for my neighbors as for myself, and to be more obedient to God's word and more active and effective in his service. I have asked God to help me develop all of these capacities to the best of my ability and to blend them together in a unified way to make me a better person under God and for his glory.

These three capacities functioning together in unity are an inkling of the Trinity in our makeup as the image of God. There is one God in three persons, three persons in the one God. Likewise these three faculties make up the single self, and the single self consists of these three faculties. In asking God to help us be better thinkers, lovers, and doers, we are in effect asking God to make us more like himself in the unity and well developed capacities of mind, heart, and will.

**Concluding Requests**   I round out these prayers for myself by asking God to give me the desire, diligence, and discipline to pray and seek God in his Word, and that I would also be fervent and faithful in the practice of other spiritual disciplines as well.

I also ask God to teach me how to love, serve, and give, and I request he would give me courage, boldness, wisdom, and humility. These requests have grown out of special needs in my own life for confidence, competence, and a humble heart. I conclude by praying that I give myself to God in the style of Romans 12:1-2 — to be a living sacrifice, to live in nonconformity to this age, and to be transformed in every area by the renewing of my mind.

For me, these prayers and God's answers have been the secret to keeping my loves and life rightly ordered. Perhaps a version of these prayers can do the same for you. It's a good way to pray for others as well. It's not so selfish after all.

## Conclusion

*"Omnia vincit Amor."*

Virgil, Eclogue 10

"Love conquers all things," said the Roman poet Virgil, and he added, "yield we too to love!"[44] Love does conquer all, and we do yield to it because love comes from God, who is all-loving just as he is all-knowing and all-powerful. We yield to its conquering power since we are Love's finite human imitators. We love because God is love, and we sense that our love and its objects are the way to learning the deep meaning of happiness.

The problem, as we have seen, is that in our insurgency against God, we have abused our loves in search of an enduring happiness, but with miserable results. Disordered loves equal disordered lives. The grace of the gospel has quelled our revolt against God and ended our alienation from him. In our redemption, we have redirected our loves in search of happiness in him, with satisfying results. Reordered loves equal reordered lives. Now we know something of shalom. We have discovered the happy life in Christ — a mere "foretaste of glory divine." There is no reason to be skeptical about it.

"Joy . . . is the gigantic secret of the Christian," wrote G. K. Chesterton at the end of his book *Orthodoxy*.[45] This jovial Catholic apologist says that joy is the distinctively human trait:

> Man is more himself, man is more manlike, when joy is the fundamental thing about him, and grief the superficial. Melancholy should be an innocent interlude, a tender and fugitive frame of mind; praise should be the permanent pulsation of the soul. Pessimism is at best an emotional half-holiday; joy is the uproarious labour by which all things live (p. 364).

Agnostics, cynics, and skeptics render joy small and even futile. They make pessimism and grief likely and very large. But these are the attitudes

---

44. Virgil, *The Eclogues*, trans. James Rhoades, *The Great Books of the Western World*, ed. Robert M. Hutchins, vol. 13 (Chicago: William Benton, Publisher, Encyclopedia Britannica, Inc., 1952), p. 34 (Eclogue 10, line 69).

45. G. K. Chesterton, *Orthodoxy*, in *G. K. Chesterton: Collected Works*, ed., intro., and notes David Dooley, vol. 1 (San Francisco: Ignatius Press, 1986), p. 366. Subsequent page numbers in parentheses are from this work.

and experiences of a world stood on its head. Christianity turns people and things right-side up, such "that by its creed joy becomes something gigantic and sadness something special and small" (p. 365).

This joyfulness doesn't seem to be a trait of Jesus, however. The God-man we meet on the pages of the Gospels seems to be anything but a smiling Savior, or a cheerful Christ, or joyful Jesus. We know him in somberness and sobriety. He was a man of sorrows and acquainted with grief. We observe him in his righteous anger. We witness his sweat, his tears, his blood.

But if joy is a distinctively human trait, and one that is also divine, then perhaps there was something that Jesus restrained. Maybe he had to conceal aspects of his inner life from us. Could it be that he lived in a state that was so profound and overwhelming that he had to hide the better part of it simply because it would have been too much for us to bear? We wouldn't understand it. We couldn't endure it. Maybe there was a dimension of Jesus' life he could only share with his Father in heaven. Perhaps this powerful sensation was the reason why he would occasionally fall silent or leave abruptly for another place. Jesus was a patient and compassionate man, so it couldn't have been his love or kindness that caused his occasional quirky behavior.

What was it, then, that Jesus was reluctant to reveal to others? What was it that he chose to keep close to his chest? What might have caused him to act in unusual ways on occasion? Chesterton answers these questions with succinct but stirring words: "There was some one thing that was too great for God to show us when He walked upon our earth; and I have sometimes fancied that it was His mirth" (p. 366).

> The Lord bless you, and keep you;
> The Lord make His face shine on you,
> And be gracious to you;
> The Lord lift up His countenance on you,
> And give you *Shalom*. (Num. 6:24-26)

# Questions for Discussion

## Chapter One

1. Privately or with a group (if appropriate), describe the ways in which your own heart has been broken. Have these experiences in your story inclined you to despair or caused you to hope for happier life? Do you think that the desire for happiness is an essential, even God-given, component of human nature?

2. Are Americans *uniquely* obsessed with happiness? If so, why? What current moral, cultural, or social factors might be especially responsible for the intense interest in happiness and the success of the so-called happiness business?

3. Why do you think Bob Dylan (and Switchfoot) considered happiness and unhappiness "yuppie" words? Listen to Switchfoot's song "Happy Is a Yuppie Word" from the CD *Nothing Is Sound* and discuss its lyrics. Is happiness a legitimate Christian concept and concern? Is God concerned about your holiness or happiness, or both? Might these notions be related somehow?

4. Do your own experiences validate or invalidate the six ingredients of God's recipe for human happiness based on Genesis 1–2? What is the difference between hedonistic and edenistic happiness? How does Job's response to his sufferings illustrate God's original intentions for human flourishing?

5. How does the biblical notion of *shalom* connect to happiness? How is *shalom* illustrated in Celtic Christianity and in the thought of John Cal-

vin and the poet William Cowper? Discuss and evaluate the definition of the happiness offered on pages 21-23.

6. How has sin affected human happiness? Discuss Augustine's point that by sinning we lost happiness, but not our love for it. Describe your own experiences of *Sehnsucht* or longing, as delineated by C. S. Lewis. What meaning have you attributed to these experiences?

## Chapter Two

1. Augustine probably wrote the *Confessions* because he believed his story was typical of everyone's—especially concerning his ignorance and disordered love in searching for happiness. Do you recognize any significant parallels between this account of his life and your own?

2. Describe the conditions of the four candidates for happiness according to St. Augustine, and explain which one/s you identify with the most and why. What key question does Augustine say must be answered in pursuing genuine happiness?

3. How does theology account for our ignorance and wrong desires? What are the chief cultural influences that affect our thinking about happiness, especially the roles of worldviews and popular culture?

4. What is the precise nature of disordered love, especially in terms of the *nature* of the objects we love, the *manner* in which we love them, and the *expectations* we have regarding the outcome of our love? Do you identify with the blunder associated with disordered love that C. S. Lewis called "The Fool's Way"?

5. How does ignorance and disordered love not only affect our personal lives, but also govern the course of history itself? (Hint: the two cities) How are these errors manifested in the church as well? (Hint: scornfulness)

6. Do you agree that the human mind and heart are battlefields of ideas and affections when it comes to learning the deep meaning of happiness? What has been your experience in this area?

## Chapter Three

1. How might the things you regard as excessively precious "gollumize" you in character and conduct? Have these disorders in your loves and life affected your physical being—even in the way you look?
2. Define idolatry in terms of disordered love and explain its impact on the way you live your life.
3. Identify the seven deadly sins and explain how each is an expression of disordered love. How might you use this list of chief sins in a practical way to evaluate the inclinations of your heart and the tendencies in your behavior?
4. Imagine what your life would be like if it was dominated by the seven deadly sins. What kind of impact would you (or such a person) have on others and the world as a whole?
5. How do the seven deadly sins proceed to become deadly habits and addictions as well? Explain the integral connection between idolatry, the seven deadly sins, habits and addictions, and crime and warfare? Is it really possible to trace habits and addictions and even crime and warfare back to disordered love?
6. What major lesson should the Old Testament book of Ecclesiastes help you learn about your hope for a happy life? How might humor be of assistance, especially when it comes to recognizing your continuous *inability* to discover the deep meaning of happiness? How might your struggles point you to Jesus Christ and his gospel?

## Chapter Four

1. What theological significance should we attach to the raising of Lazarus from the dead in John 11? How does this event illustrate the meaning of the Christian gospel as a whole?
2. Relate Augustine's famous quote about the heart's ongoing restlessness and the lyrics of Switchfoot's song "The Beautiful Letdown." How can "letdowns" be beautiful and potentially lead your restless heart to finding its rest in God?
3. Who is Jesus Christ? How is he portrayed in the Gospel of John? How is Jesus viewed in popular and academic culture, and also in the church? How might a fresh rereading of the Gospels correct distorted

views of Jesus? What does it mean to say that Jesus is God incarnate? Of the three options regarding the identity of Jesus—Liar, Lunatic, or Lord—which one makes the most sense and why?

4. What is the kingdom of God and its redemptive nature? In what way is the kingdom of God a mystery? How is it connected to the death of Christ on the cross?

5. What is the definition of and biblical support for propitiation, redemption, reconciliation, and justification as these terms convey the meaning of Christ's sacrifice and the victory of the kingdom of God? How does Christ's work on the cross make it possible for you to have peace with God and to learn the deep meaning of happiness in him?

6. What must you do to be saved? What role do repentance and faith play in this process? What are the costs and benefits of salvation? What are the three signs of a sincere commitment to Christ, and how do they signal a reordering of your deepest loves and desires?

## Chapter Five

1. How were Johnny Cash's loves reordered by his return to Christ and the gospel? Do you detect any parallels between his story and St. Augustine's; between their stories and yours?

2. According to Thomas Chalmers, what is the only effective way disordered loves can be replaced with reordered loves through the gospel? Does your own experience validate Chalmers' insights? How might Chalmers' ideas need to be modified?

3. How has the gospel reordered your love for God? How should you love God? Why should you love God in the way the first greatest commandment requires?

4. How has the gospel reordered your love for yourself? Why is self-love assumed rather than commanded in the second greatest commandment? How does reordered love for self help explain Jesus' "hard sayings" in the Gospels that command us to deny or hate ourselves? How should you rightly love yourself?

5. How has the gospel reordered your love for your neighbors? How do the Golden Rule, Christ's New Commandment, the "one another" principles, and 1 Corinthians 13 teach you to love your neighbor as you love yourself? What about loving your enemies?

6. How has the gospel reordered your love for creation and all creatures? How are love for people and love for creation inextricably combined in practical ways? Why and how should love be the mark or "tattoo" of the Christian?

## Chapter Six

1. Discuss the theological symbolism of Eustace's transformation from his "endragoned" state back into a boy again. Note any personal parallels you might be able to draw from this story about how the gospel reorders your loves and life.
2. Why would a reordered life begin with the renewal of the worship of God? How is God to be worshipped personally and in every area of life? How is worship of God in daily life reciprocally connected with weekly worship in church? What role should the church at worship play in guarding you from idols and helping you to keep your loves and life rightly ordered?
3. How is a reordered life of intellectual, moral, and physical virtue an expression of reordered love flowing out of the gospel? Describe the intellectual virtues of the Christian mind. What moral virtues, embodied in the life of Jesus Christ himself, do Jesus, Peter, and Paul recommend in the New Testament for the cultivation of your character? What roles does the Holy Spirit play in the formation of a virtuous life?
4. Discuss the meanings of the three theological virtues (faith, hope, love) and the four philosophical virtues (courage, justice, temperance, prudence). How do these virtues challenge you at a personal level to become a more Christ-like person? What specific traits should characterize care for your body and for the creation?
5. Compare the description of a reordered life of virtue in this chapter with the description of a disordered life of vice in chapter three. What are the personal and public implications of these two radically alternative ways of life?
6. Is a reordered life of the worship of God combined with the vigorous cultivation of intellectual, moral, and physical virtue really capable of breaking the chains of bad habits and addictions? Could this same

spiritual calculus curtail crime and even thwart the pursuit of violence and war? Why or why not?

## Chapter Seven

1. Do you sometimes wonder if happiness is possible in this life, even in its deep meaning of reordered loves and lives?

2. How might the coded meanings of the word *shalom* in the poem on pages 125-27 help you understand the manner in which the deep meaning of happiness is to be experienced at this point in God's narrative plan for history? How does the New Testament view of the kingdom of God as both "already" but "not yet" also provide the proper context for understanding the proximate form of happiness available today?

3. How is service, as part of the deep meaning of happiness at this point in redemptive history, connected to an all-encompassing view of vocational calling? How can you serve and be served, heal and be healed through them? Why is it unnecessary to seek opportunities outside your daily traffic patterns in life to suffer and sacrifice for Christ and the kingdom's sake?

4. What is a spiritual discipline? How are the spiritual disciplines developed? Why might "spiritual disciplines" be a misleading name? Discuss and evaluate Richard Foster's and Dallas Willard's categories, meanings, and purposes of the disciplines. What dangers can accompany the practice of the disciplines? In what contexts or life-settings are the disciplines best cultivated?

5. Are there any insights or practices in the author's story of his experience with the spiritual disciplines with which you resonate or find helpful, whether related to the Bible and books, to the church and community, or to prayer in general and for oneself?

6. In what way, as G. K. Chesterton has claimed, is joy the gigantic secret of the Christian? What was it Jesus may have hidden from us while he was on earth? Why would he have kept it hidden?

# Index